Secrets of Chef Walter

Walter N. Lambert
with a special contribution by Anne Wayland Lambert

Published by Pullman Press for
Taste Matters and Volunteer Television
© 2007 Taste Matters
Cover Design: Davis Newman Payne
Marketing Communications

ISBN (10-digit) 0-9660904-6-2
ISBN (13-digit) 978-0-9660904-6-8

Introduction

One can find many nice things about getting to visit with folks and talk about food. You are constantly learning new things from the people you meet. You are constantly being reminded that there are folks like you who derive great pleasure from cooking, eating, and talking about food. All these are good things.

In addition, you get to work with lots of good people. In the almost 18 years I have been at WVLT, I have never worked with a better group of folks. And this applies throughout the organization. Chris Baker, General Manager at Volunteer TV has been a constant source of support, and I appreciate him. But the good things have not stopped there. I have worked with a number of folks you never get to meet who care about what we do. Some cynics say that is because we feed them. Of course not! They are just devoted to their craft and they only eat because it would hurt me if they did not. You know Bob and Jessa and Scott who we spend time with most days and you know we enjoy each other's company. It makes working nice. I must admit that I miss having Kelly Parker on the noon show. It is such fun to pick on Kelly knowing that she is going to pick right back.

However, it is important to note that I would not have had the pleasure of coming to visit with all you good folks for all these years if someone had not been willing to pay the bills. What a lucky day it was for me when the sponsor became Food City. Once again from the top down, this is a group of people who are superb. Someone asked me recently why I liked Food City so much. I observed that all the stores had to offer was superior groceries at outstanding prices with dedicated service. But I have to tell you the truth; all that is absolutely true. But what warms my heart as I work with this company is the quality of people I get to work with all the time. This starts in my home store where Pam Moore and her folks look after me with tender care. If I need something they get it. And this same spirit goes right up the corporate ladder to the very top.

I, of course, appreciate "Ms Anne" for putting up with me all these years. After 45 years of marriage, we have much to be happy about. She still proofs, and checks and keeps me in line. And I still love her for it. I particularly want to thank Heather Castellaw for her invaluable help. In addition, Frances Graves and Betty Castellaw both read very well. Finally, I am deeply indebted to the good people who watch the show and write me nice letters and go to the web site and get the recipes. Your kindness keeps me going. Now let's stop talking and start cooking.

Chapter 1
Appetizers

Cheesy Black-Eyed Pea Dip

    2 or 3 slices hog jowl bacon
    ½ medium onion, chopped
    ½ lb Cheezy Does It (or Velveeta)
    8 ounces sharp cheddar, shredded
    2 15-oz cans black-eyed peas, drained
    1 jalapeno pepper, seeds & ribs removed, diced
    1 4-oz can chopped green chilies (or 2 small fresh)
    ½ teaspoon garlic salt

Cut the hog jowl bacon into a fine dice. In a medium saucepan, fry the bacon until brown. With a slotted spoon, remove the bacon. Add the onion to the rendered fat and saute until golden brown. Turn heat to low, add the cheese, and stir until melted. Add the black-eyed peas, jalapeno, green chilies, and garlic salt. Cook for 5 minutes, stirring constantly. Serve hot with tortilla chips.

Bonefish Grill Warm Mango Salsa

    1 cup red onion, charred and chopped into quarter inch pieces
    1 quart small diced mango (drain & chopped in quarter inch pieces)
    1/4 cup diced red pepper (eighth of an inch pieces)
    ½ cup mango puree
    1/4 cup scallions (chopped on bias)
    1/4 cup chopped cilantro

Peel and slice red onion in 2 to 3 large pieces lay on hot grill and char. Chop the red onion into quarter inch pieces. Dice the mango and red pepper. Mix all ingredients together. When ready to serve heat in microwave or on stove top for three minutes. Add scallions and cilantro and serve over grilled fillet. Makes eight servings.

Better than Buffalo Chicken Bites

    1/4 cup butter, melted
    1/4 cup chili sauce
    1/4 cup hot pepper sauce (or to taste)
    1 to 1 ½ lb boneless, skinless chicken breasts cut into 1" cubes
    celery sticks
    blue cheese dressing

Mix butter, chili, and hot pepper sauces. Pour half that mixture over chicken and toss to mix. Heat a non stick skillet and add chicken. Cook, stirring about 8 to 10 minutes over medium heat. Chicken should be well browned and white in center. Stir in remaining hot sauce and serve with celery sticks and blue cheese dressing.

This makes a fine tailgating item. Just prepare chicken, place in a thermal bag, and put it out at the site with dressing and celery. It's better than Buffalo wings because there are no bones.

Creamy Salsa Dip
        1 8 oz pkg cream cheese, softened
        2 TBSP chopped fresh cilantro
        1 cup salsa, drained (You may use mild, medium or hot depending on taste)
        Tortilla chips or vegetables

Place cream cheese in mixing bowl and stir until smooth. Stir in cilantro and salsa. Serve with tortilla chips or vegetables.

Spinach Balls
        2 10 oz pkgs frozen chopped spinach
        2 cups herb-seasoned stuffing mix
        1 cup shredded Parmesan cheese
        6 eggs, beaten
        3/4 cup butter, softened
        salt and pepper to taste (be careful, don't get too much)

Thaw spinach and drain well. Combine spinach with all remaining ingredients in a bowl and mix well. Roll into about 1" balls and place on baking sheet. Freeze and then store in an airtight bag. To serve, place frozen balls on a lightly greased baking sheet and bake at 350 deg for about 10 to 15 minutes or until browned. Serve hot or warm.

Crab 'N Shrimp Dip
        8 ounces cream cheese, softened
        1 TBSP mayonnaise
        1 green onion, chopped
        1 (6 ounce) can crab meat, drained
        1 (4.5 ounce) can small shrimp, drained

Blend together the cream cheese and mayonnaise. Add the green onion, crab, and shrimp. Place in a covered container and chill overnight. Serve with chips or with celery and carrot sticks.

Clam Dip
        1 clove garlic, cut in half

1 can (8 ounces) minced clams
1 pkg (8 ounces) cream cheese, softened
2 tsp lemon juice
11/2 tsp Worcestershire sauce
½ tsp salt
Dash pepper

Rub a mixing bowl with the cut halves of garlic. Drain clams, reserving 1/4 of the liquid. Combine clams and liquid, the cream cheese, lemon juice, Worcestershire sauce, and seasonings, mixing until well-blended. Chill. Serve with chips, crackers, or raw vegetables.

Pretzel Dip
1 pkg Hidden Valley dip mix (original flavor)
2 8 oz pkgs cream cheese
6 oz beer
2 cups shredded cheddar cheese
Pretzels

Beat the cream cheese until soft. Stir in dip mix and beer. Stir in cheese. Place in a covered bowl and chill before serving. Use pretzels to dip.

Crunchy Cheese Crackers
1 stick butter at room temperature
1 cup cheddar cheese, finely shredded
1 cup flour
1 tsp Tabasco Sauce
2 cups crisp rice cereal

Cream the butter, cheese, and Tabasco sauce until well blended. Beat in the flour. Stir in rice cereal. Shape into small balls (about 3/4 inch across) and flatten onto an ungreased cookie sheet. Bake in a preheated 350 deg oven about 12 to 15 minutes or until lightly browned. Cool on a wire rack and store in an air-tight container. Will keep for a couple of weeks if you can leave them alone that long.

Sharp Cheese Ball
1 lb sharp cheese, grated fine
½ lb blue cheese, crumbled
½ lb cream cheese at room temperature
1 small onion, grated as finely as possible
1 tsp Tabasco sauce
1 TBSP Worcestershire sauce
chopped pecans

Blend all ingredients thoroughly. Shape into three balls and roll each in chopped pecans. Wrap tightly, and refrigerate for at least a couple of days before serving. Serve at room temperature with small crackers.

We sometimes roll this cheese mixture in paprika or in dry parsley instead of the nuts. One of each on a cheese tray makes an attractive arrangement.

Big Orange Meatballs
>1 lb mild pork sausage
>1 lb lean ground beef
>½ cup seasoned breadcrumbs
>2 eggs, lightly beaten
>¼ cup milk
>½ cup finely diced onion
>½ teaspoon each - salt and pepper

Combine all ingredients and shape into 1 ½ inch balls. Place on a lightly greased jelly roll pan or cookie sheet (Be sure it has an edge or you will have grease in the oven). Bake at 375° for 30 minutes, turning after 15 minutes.

Sauce:
>3/4 cup orange marmalade
>¼ cup spicy brown mustard
>1 tsp each- Worcestershire sauce and Tabasco sauce

Combine sauce ingredients in a large skillet or wok over medium heat. Cook for one minute, then add meatballs and cook for 5 more minutes, stirring to make sure they all get coated.

Bacon Ranch Cheese Ball & Crackers
Hidden Valley Family Friendly Food Contest
Nancy Orrick of Knoxville, 1st Place
Won $175 + chance to win $1000 grand prize.
Crackers:
>1 3/4 cups flour
>½ cup cornmeal
>½ tsp baking soda
>½ tsp sugar
>½ tsp salt
>2 TBSP Hidden Valley Original Ranch Dressing & Seasoning Mix
>½ cup cold butter
>1 ½ cups shredded sharp cheddar cheese
>½ cup plus 2 Tbsp cold water
>4 Tbsp. real bacon bits

Combine first 6 ingredients. Cut in butter until crumbly. Stir in cheese. Sprinkle with cold water (½ cup and 2 Tbsp) and toss with a fork until a ball forms. Wrap in plastic wrap and chill until firm. Remove from wrap; divide into six equal parts. On a lightly floured surface, roll each portion into 8" circle. Cut into 8 wedges, sprinkle with bacon bits, press lightly and place on greased baking sheets. Bake at 375 degrees for 14 minutes or until golden brown and crisp. Cool on wire racks. Store airtight. Makes 48 crackers/wedges.

Cheese Ball:
>   2 (8 oz) cream cheese
>   3 cups sharp cheddar cheese
>   ½ cup mayonnaise
>   1 (1 oz) pkg Hidden Valley Original Ranch Dressing & Seasoning Mix
>   1/4 cup minced green onions
>   8 slices bacon, fried, drained and crumbled
>   1 cup chopped pecans

Mix together mayonnaise and Hidden Valley mix. Mix together cream cheese, cheese, mayo mixture, and onion. Mix in bacon and work into ball. Chill for an hour and then roll in pecans. Chill again. Serve with crackers. Yield: 15-20 servings

Dried Fruit Cheese Ball
>   1 (8 ounce) package cream cheese, softened
>   2 TBSP honey
>   1 cup Cheddar cheese, shredded
>   1 (6 ounce) package dried mixed fruit, chopped
>   1 cup chopped pecans

In a medium bowl combine cream cheese and honey; beat until smooth. Stir in cheese and chopped fruit; mix well.   Form into a ball and roll in chopped nuts. Chill for at least 3 hours or overnight.

Crab Bites
>   8 to 10 English muffins
>   1 6 oz can crab meat, drained
>   1 TBSP mayonnaise
>   1 stick butter, softened
>   1/4 tsp garlic salt
>   1 6 oz jar Old English Cheese Spread

Cream softened cheese and butter. Add crab, mayonnaise, and garlic salt. Split muffins and spread with mixture. Cut each into 6 pieces. Place on a cookie sheet and freeze. Place in a recloseable plastic bag and store in freezer. When ready to serve, bake at 375 to 400 deg until hot and browned.

Easy, Spicy Bean Dip

> 1 lb lean ground beef
> 2 cans refried beans (w/ green chilies if you like)
> 1 8 oz pkg cream cheese
> 2 to 3 TBSP sour cream
> pickled Jalapeno peppers, chopped to taste
> 1 Jar of salsa
> 1 Sweet Onion, chopped fine
> Olive Oil

Sauté the onion in a skillet or a pan along with the meat. Add salt and pepper to taste. You may add a TBSP of chili powder if you wish. Combine the beans, salsa, cream cheese, sour cream, and jalapenos in a mixing bowl. Use the flat blade of a mixer to mix these ingredients together while the meat and the onions are cooking. When the meat has cooked, mix in with the bean mix. Mix together completely. Let it stand for 30 minutes to cool down. Serve with tortilla chips or Fritos. This dip keeps to a nice consistency if you place it in a crock pot set on low.

Salsa Fresca

> 2 medium size ripe tomatoes (quartered)
> 1/4 medium size onion
> 4 sprigs cilantro (or parsley)
> 2 cloves garlic
> 1 tsp garlic salt
> 2 TBSP lemon juice
> 1 jalapeno (1/3 for mild, 2/3 for medium, all for hot)

Put all ingredients in your food processor and mix to consistency desired. More spins make finer cuts.

White Queso Dip

Janet Reynolds   Knoxville, Tn.

> 8 oz. cream cheese
> 10 oz can Rotel tomatoes with green chiles, drain but save 1/4 cup for later
> ½ of an onion, chopped
> 1-2 jalapenos, diced
> 1 cup heavy whipping cream, or half and half

In a saucepan begin to heat Rotel and reserved liquid, cream cheese, onion, and jalapenos. Once the cream cheese is melted, stir in whipping cream. Reduce heat to low, and simmer without lid for 20 minutes. Stir frequently, do not let burn. Remove from heat and bring to room temp before refrigerating. Serve chilled with crunchy tortilla chips. This makes about 10 servings, double ingredients for more!!

Hot Country Ham Dip
   2 8 oz package cream cheese, softened
   1 cup sour cream
   ½ - 1 cup Clifty Farm Country Ham, cooked and chopped
   1/4 cup finely minced onion
   ½ tsp garlic powder
   1 TBSP butter
   1 cup chopped pecans
   ½ tsp Worcestershire sauce

Preheat oven to 350 degrees. Combine cream cheese, sour cream, country ham, onion, and garlic powder in a small bowl and place in a baking dish. Then saute butter, pecans, and Worcestershire sauce, and sprinkle over baking dish. Refrigerate until serving time. Bake for 20 minutes. Serve hot with crackers. This fine dip is also very good cold with either crackers or raw vegetables.

Pumpkin Dip
   2 cups pumpkin puree- canned or fresh (that is one 15 oz can)
   1 cup brown sugar
   1 tsp ground cinnamon
   1 tsp ginger
   ½ tsp nutmeg
   ½ tsp cinnamon
   1 8 oz pkg cream cheese, softened

Place cream cheese and brown sugar into a large mixer bowl and mix together. Blend in pumpkin. Add spices. Mix together until smooth and creamy. Refrigerate at least four hours or overnight. Serve with crackers, gingerbread, celery, carrots, etc.
Tips: To make a lighter dip, stir in sour cream until you reach the consistency you like.

Cool Summer Dip
   1 cup sour cream
   1 (8 ounce) package Neufchatel cheese, softened
   ½ cup white sugar
   1 TBSP vanilla extract

In a medium bowl, place the sour cream, Neufchatel cheese, white sugar, and extract. With an electric mixer, blend until smooth. Chill in the refrigerator approximately 30 minutes. Garnish with fresh fruit to serve.

We like this served with slices of fruit, strawberries, or plain cookies. If you wish, you may use orange, lemon, or coconut extract instead of vanilla. If you can find it, raspberry extract will make this dip pink and with some raspberries sprinkled on top, it looks pretty. If you cannot find this, some food color can make it a pretty color.

Pimiento Spread
>1 8 oz pkg cream cheese, softened
>1/4 cup mayonnaise
>1 2 oz jar diced pimientos, drained
>3 TBSP sliced green onions
>1/4 tsp hot pepper sauce (optional)
> Wheat Crackers

Beat cream cheese and mayo in small bowl with electric mixer on medium speed until well blended. Stir in pimientos, green onions, and hot pepper sauce; cover. Refrigerate several hours or until chilled. Serve as a spread with crackers.

Slam Dunk Dip
Cabot Cheese Company   Visit them at www.cabotcheese.com
>1 TBSP Cabot salted butter
>1 TBSP all purpose flour
>3/4 cup mild, medium or hot tomato salsa
>1/4 cup Cabot sour cream
>8 oz Cabot Sharp Cheddar Cheese, grated (about 3 cups)
>tortilla chips
>carrot or celery sticks

In a saucepan over medium heat, melt butter. Add flour and stir for about 30 seconds to cook flour. Stir in the salsa and cook, stirring, until mixture is simmering. Stir in sour cream. Add cheese and continue stirring until cheese is completely melted and mixture returns to simmer. Transfer to a bowl and serve hot surrounded by chips and veggies.

Oyster Cracker Snack
Jean Millis   (Actually Jean's mom, but Jean takes credit)
>3/4 cup salad oil (I use Canola)
>1/4 tsp garlic powder
>1 pkg of Original Ranch dressing mix
>2 tsp dill weed
>12 oz pkg oyster crackers

Mix the first four ingredients in a large bowl. Put in the crackers and carefully stir. Stir the crackers every 20 minutes for 2 hours. Put into air tight containers.

Shrimp Dip
Lana Davis   Maynardville, TN.
>1 can shrimp, drained and mashed
>1 TBSP Worcestershire Sauce
>2 heaping TBSP mayonnaise (may use light)

2 heaping TBSP sour cream
½ bottle of cocktail sauce
2 TBSP horseradish (use from a jar, not fresh)
2 TBSP catsup

Mix well and refrigerate.

Watermelon Salsa
1/4 cup orange marmalade
1/4 cup fresh cilantro, chopped
1/4 cup jalapeno peppers, finely chopped
2 tablespoons white vinegar
1 garlic clove, minced
1/ 2 teaspoon salt
2 cups seeded watermelon, coarsely chopped
1 cup sweet onion, chopped
1 cup orange sections, chopped

Stir together first 6 ingredients. Add watermelon, onion, and orange section, tossing gently. Chill at least 1 hour before serving with Tostidos chips.

Capanota
1 tablespoon plus 1 teaspoon olive oil
1 pound eggplant, diced
1 cup minced green onions
1 cup minced celery
1 medium sweet red pepper, minced
2 cloves garlic, minced
1 (8-ounce) can tomato sauce
1/4 heaping cup black olives, coarsely chopped
3 tablespoons tomato paste
2 tablespoons red wine vinegar
1 tablespoon sugar
1/4 teaspoon pepper
1 teaspoon fresh oregano, chopped
Sprigs of fresh basil and parsley

Heat oil in a large skillet over medium heat. Add eggplant, onions, celery, pepper, and garlic. Cook 10 minutes, stirring frequently. Add sauce and next 6 ingredients, stirring well. Cook over low heat, stirring frequently for 25 minutes or until vegetables are tender. Transfer to a medium bowl, cover, and chill 8 hours. Garnish with basil and parsley sprigs and serve with pita triangles.

Wait Until Next Year Chicken Wings
   2 to 3 lbs chicken wings, cut into sections with tips discarded
   cooking oil spray
   1 tsp salt
   ½ tsp pepper
   1 cup barbeque sauce
   1 tsp (or to taste) hot pepper sauce
   ranch dressing
   celery sticks

Place wings on a large baking sheet with sides and spray with cooking oil spray. Sprinkle evenly with salt and pepper. Bake in a 425 deg oven about 25 to 30 minutes or until browned and liquid runs clear when pierced. Heat barbeque sauce to boiling in a large pan and add hot pepper sauce to taste. Pour hot wings into sauce and toss to mix. Serve with ranch dressing and celery sticks.

Fresh Vegetable Tart
Hidden Valley "Family Friendly Food" Contest   Patricia Wells   1st place
   1 1/4 cup all purpose flour
   1/4 tsp salt
   7 TBSP butter or shortening into pieces
   3 TBSP ice water

Filling:
   12 oz cream cheese
   1 pkg (1 oz) Hidden Valley Ranch salad dressing mix
   1/4 cup mayonnaise
   1/3 cup sour cream
   ½ cup chopped fresh cauliflower
   ½ cup chopped or grated carrots
   1/4 cup chopped green onions
   2 cups broccoli florets
   1 cup grated sharp cheddar cheese
   1/4 cup chopped green peppers
   1/4 cup chopped red peppers

Preheat oven to 450 deg. For crust, sift flour and salt into a small mixing bowl. Using a pastry blender, cut butter into flour until mixture resembles coarse meal. Sprinkle ice water over dough, and mix quickly just until dough forms a soft ball. On a lightly floured surface, with a floured rolling pin roll out dough into a 12 to 13 inch circle. Press dough into an 11 inch part pan. Prick bottom of crust with a fork. Trim the edges, and bake 10 for 12 minutes or until golden brown. Cool completely.

For filling, beat cream cheese in a large bowl until smooth. Add Ranch dressing mix, mayonnaise, and sour cream, beating until smooth. Stir in next 3 ingredients. Spread cream cheese mixture into shell. Refrigerate 8 hours or overnight. Place broccoli florets along edge of crust. Sprinkle peppers and cheese over filling. Slice into wedges and serve chilled. Fruit can be used instead of vegetables. Serves 8.

Cream Cheese Dip
Mary Marsh
    2 8 oz pkg cream cheese, softened
    ½ cup sweet onion and pepper relish
    chopped chipolte peppers to taste

Mix all ingredients, and place in a covered dish. Chill overnight to blend flavors. Serve with chips or veggies.

Big Orange Crunch.
Alice Conner of Nashville.
    2 8 oz pkg cream cheese, softened
    ½ cup each white and brown sugar
    8 oz pkg toffee bits

Stir together. Place in a covered dish. Allow to chill and flavors to blend. Serve at room temperature.

Chapter 2
Salads and Dressings

Green Pea Salad
Evelyn Ray   Oak Ridge, TN
       1 cup celery, chopped
       !/4 cup onion, chopped
       ½ cup pecans, chopped
       2 sweet pickles, chopped
       1 cup sharp cheese, grated
       ½ cup green pepper, chopped
       3 TBSP mayonnaise
       Salt and pepper to taste
       1 15 oz can of LeSueur peas (a must)

Mix all together, adding peas last. Can be prepared ahead of time. Cannot be frozen.

Spinach Salad-Hot Bacon Dressing
       1 bag fresh baby spinach
       1/4 cup chopped onion
       4 slices bacon
       2 hard boiled eggs, chopped
       1/4 cup vinegar
       1 pkg Splenda
       salt and pepper to taste

Cook bacon. Remove and drain on paper towel. Reserve bacon grease. Tear spinach into smaller pieces. Add chopped egg, onion, and crumbled bacon. Slowly add vinegar, pepper, and Splenda to bacon grease in pan. Stir and heat til boiling. Pour on hot dressing, and toss lightly. Add salt to taste. Serve immediately.

Layered Cornbread Salad
       1 9" pan cornbread
       2 cans whole kernel corn, drained
       2 cans pinto beans, drained
       2 cups cheddar cheese, shredded
       ½ cup green pepper, chopped

½ cup green onions, chopped
3 large tomatoes, chopped
10 slices bacon, cooked and crumbled

<u>Dressing:</u>
1 pkg Hidden Valley Ranch Dressing Mix
1 cup sour cream
1 cup mayonnaise

Allow cornbread to cool and crumble. Reserve a small amount of tomato and bacon to garnish the top. Layer half of the cornbread in the bottom of bowl. Sprinkle over it half of the corn, beans, cheese, bacon, green pepper, green onions, and tomatoes. Mix dressing ingredients and spread over. Repeat.   Sprinkle reserved tomato and bacon on top. Cover tightly and allow to chill a couple of hours before serving.

Cornbread Salad
1 (8 ½ oz) pkg, Southeastern Mills Cornbread Mix
1 cup shredded cheddar cheese
1 lb ham
1/3 cup (approx) sweet bread and butter pickles
2 large or medium tomatoes
½ large or medium onion
1/3 large or medium green pepper
½ cup (heaping) mayonnaise
2 TBSP pickle juice
sugar to taste
salt and pepper to taste

Mix and bake cornbread according to directions on the package. Remove from oven, allow to cool, and then crumble the cornbread. Dice the ham. Chop pickles, tomatoes, onion, and pepper. Mix together. Add mayonnaise, pickle juice, and cheddar cheese. Mix well. Add salt, pepper, and sugar to taste. Serve cold.

Walter note: Any good cornbread mix will work. I personally like the Martha White Buttermilk Cornbread Mix.

Black Eyed Pea Salad
3 16 oz cans black eyed peas drained, rinsed, and drained again
1 2 oz jar chopped pimento, drained
1/4 cup sweet pickle relish
½ cup red onion, chopped
1/3 cup each, cider vinegar, balsamic vinegar, sugar, and cooking oil
½ tsp ground cayenne pepper (or to taste)
1/4 tsp salt

Combine the peas, pimento, relish, and onion. Toss gently. Mix all remaining ingredients to form a dressing and pour over pea mixture. Toss to coat. Place in a covered dish and chill several hours before serving.

Grilled Orange Caesar Salad
>48 orange slices, ½ inch thick, seeded, and grilled
>1 ½ lbs romaine lettuce, chopped
>4 oz mushrooms, sliced
>2 oz croutons, ½ inch cubes, prepared
>1/4 cup almond slices, toasted
>1/4 cup Parmesan cheese, grated
>½ tsp cracked black pepper
>1 cup orange caesar dressing (recipe follows)

For one serving: Toss 4 grilled orange slices with 6 oz romaine, 1 oz sliced mushrooms, and ½ oz croutons with 1/4 cup orange Caesar dressing. Mound dressed salad on the center of a large chilled salad plate. Place 8 grilled orange slices around the edge of plate, leaning on salad. Garnish salad with 1 TBSP toasted almond slices, 1 TBSP grated Parmesan, and sprinkle 1/8 tsp cracked black pepper over salad and around plate. Serve immediately.   Whisk fresh-squeezed orange juice and orange zest to taste into prepared Caesar dressing to create an Orange Caesar Dressing.

Three Bean Salad
Sandi Jordan   Dandridge, Tennessee
>2 16 oz cans French style green beans, drained
>1 small can party peas, drained
>1 16 oz can kidney beans, rinsed, and drained
>1 cup carrots, grated
>1 cup celery, chopped
>1 medium onion (red is pretty), chopped
>½ cup vegetable oil
>1 cup sugar
>½ cup apple cider vinegar
>salt and pepper to taste

Combine all the beans. Mix other ingredients together. Pour over beans and stir. Refrigerate for 24 hrs before serving. When ready to serve drain liquid.

Fresh Green Bean Salad
>1 ½ lbs green beans
>1 small red onion, chopped
>2 tomatoes, chopped
>2 oz feta cheese, crumbled
>½ cup olive oil
>1/3 cup lemon juice

1 TBSP Dijon mustard
1 tsp sugar
salt and pepper to taste

String beans and break each bean about once. Cook in boiling water about 8 to 10 minutes or until tender/crisp. Drain and rinse with cold water. Drain completely. Chill. When ready to serve, toss beans with tomatoes. Beat together the oil, lemon juice, mustard, sugar, salt, and pepper. Pour over bean and tomato mixture and toss to coat. Place in a serving dish, and sprinkle with feta cheese before serving. If you like, you may also sprinkle the dish with about ½ cup toasted walnuts.

Green Bean Salad
> 1 16 oz pkg frozen French style green beans
> 3/4 to 1 cup chopped onions
> 3/4 to 1 cup chopped celery
> 3/4 to 1 cup mild salsa
> ½ cup olive oil
> ½ cup red wine vinegar
> 1/4 cup sugar
> 1 tsp dry oregano
> 1 tsp dry basil
> 1 tsp salt
> ½ tsp black pepper

Cook green beans according to package directions. Drain. While still hot, toss in onions, celery, and salsa. In a jar with a tight fitting lid, add remaining ingredients. Cover, and shake to blend. Sugar should be dissolved. Pour over bean mixture and toss to mix. Place in a covered container and chill before serving.

Green Bean Salad 2
> 2 lbs fresh green beans
> 1 cup green onions, sliced
> 1/4 cup white wine vinegar
> ½ cup olive oil
> 1 tsp each salt and black pepper
> 2 TBSP fresh parsley, minced fine
> 2 TBSP sugar

Remove the ends from the beans, and string them if they need it. Break into pieces about 3" long. Place in a large pot with lightly salted water. Cook about 10 to 12 minutes or until just tender-crisp. Drain thoroughly, and allow to cool about 10 minutes. In a bowl with a tight fitting lid, mix the vinegar, oil, salt, pepper, parsley, and sugar. Stir in the beans, and toss to coat completely. Cover and allow to chill for several hours or overnight before tossing again just before serving cold.

Five Bean Salad
>   1 14.5 oz can cut green beans
>   1 14.5 oz can yellow wax beans
>   1 can dark red kidney beans
>   1 can cannellini (or white kidney beans)
>   1 can black beans
>   1 cup sugar (or Splenda)
>   ½ cup vinegar
>   2/3 cup vegetable oil
>   1 tsp salt
>   1 tsp coarse ground pepper

Drain all beans well. Rinse and drain black beans. Place in large bowl. Mix all remaining ingredients, and pour over. Toss to mix. Place in a covered dish, and refrigerate overnight before serving. If you wish, you may add about ½ cup each of chopped onion and chopped celery.

Mandarin Orange Salad
Myrtle Rorex   Louisville, Tn. 37777
>   60 Ritz crackers, crushed
>   1/4 cup sugar
>   1 stick melted butter
>   6 oz. can frozen orange juice concentrate
>   1 can sweetened condensed milk
>   8 oz cool whip
>   2 cans drained mandarin oranges

Mix the cracker crumbs with sugar and butter. Press into the bottom of a 9x13" dish. Mix orange juice with the sweetened condensed milk. Fold in whipped topping and mandarin oranges. Spread over cracker crust. Refrigerate for a few hours before serving.

Circus Peanut Salad
>   2 small boxes orange gelatin
>   2 cups hot water
>   30 Circus Peanuts® candy
>   1 large can crushed pineapple, drained (save juice)
>   1 8 oz carton whipped topping

Mix gelatin and Circus Peanuts® with 2 cups hot water. Stir until dissolved. Add pineapple juice to which water has been added to make 2 cups. Refrigerate until partially set. Fold in pineapple and whipped topping. Chill.

Lemon Mousse Salad
    1 3/4 cups boiling water
    1 (6 ounce) package lemon gelatin mix
    3/4 cup cold water
    1 (12 fluid ounce) can frozen lemonade concentrate, thawed
    1 (12 ounce) container frozen whipped topping, thawed

Dissolve gelatin in boiling water, then stir in cold water and lemonade. Chill in refrigerator until thick but not set (about 30 minutes but watch it). In large bowl beat together chilled lemonade mixture and whipped topping until completely incorporated, smooth, and pale yellow. Pour into a large mold or individual dishes and chill until set.

Jellied Waldorf Salad
    1 pkg lemon gelatin
    1 cup boiling water
    1 cup cold water
    3/4 cup mayonnaise
    2 red skinned apples, cored and chopped (about 2 cups)
    1 cup celery, chopped
    ½ cup chopped walnuts

Dissolve gelatin in boiling water. Stir in cold water. Gently beat mayonnaise into the gelatin. Refrigerate until the mixture is slightly thickened. Fold in remaining ingredients and turn into an attractive gelatin mold. Allow to set. Turn out onto lettuce to serve.

Buttermilk Salad
    1 large can crushed pineapple
    1 large pkg strawberry gelatin (sugar free will work)
    2 cups buttermilk
    1 12 oz pkg whipped topping
    1 cup strawberries, chopped
    1 cup nuts, chopped

Heat the pineapple to boiling. Stir in gelatin until it is dissolved. Cool completely, Add buttermilk, whipped topping, strawberries, and nuts. Turn into a 9x13" pan (or a 2 quart mold) and chill until set.

Hot Ham Salad
    4 cups fully cooked ham, cubed
    1 can (8 oz) pineapple tidbits, drained
    ½ cup bell pepper, chopped (half red and half green is nice)
    1 cup mayonnaise
    ½ cup shredded mozzarella cheese (cheddar will work)
    1 can (11 oz) mandarin oranges, drained

½ cup slivered almonds

Mix ham with pineapple, pepper, cheese, and mayonnaise. Carefully fold in oranges breaking them as little as possible. Turn into a 1 ½ quart baking dish and sprinkle the top with almonds. Bake at 350 deg for about 30 minutes or until heated through. Serve warm.

Curried Shrimp Salad
    1 lb Food Club frozen, peeled and cooked shrimp
    1 8 oz can sliced water chestnuts, drained
    2 celery ribs, sliced very thin
    2 green onions, sliced thin
    3/4 cup mayonnaise
    2 TBSP soy sauce
    1 tsp curry powder
    1/4 cup toasted slivered almonds (optional)

Defrost shrimp according to package directions. Drain thoroughly and remove tails. Toss shrimp, water chestnuts, celery, and onions. Mix mayonnaise, soy sauce, and curry powder, and pour over shrimp mixture and toss to coat. Cover and refrigerate at least 2 hours. Serve on fresh, crisp lettuce, and sprinkle with almonds.

Mandy's Pasta Salad
    1 lb pasta of your choice, macaroni works fine
    2 stalks celery, diced
    1 green bell pepper, diced
    2 apples, peeled, cored and diced
    ½ lb cheddar cheese, diced
    1 TBSP fresh chives, chopped
    1 TBSP fresh parsley, chopped
    3/4 cup mayonnaise
    2 TBSP cider vinegar
    2 TBSP sugar
    salt and pepper to taste

Cook pasta according to package directions. Rinse and allow to cool. Mix mayonnaise, vinegar, sugar, chives, and parsley. Combine pasta with the remaining ingredients and pour dressing over. Add salt and pepper and toss to mix. Adjust seasonings if necessary. Chill before serving.

Antipasto Pasta Salad
    1 pound seashell pasta
    1/4 pound Genoa salami, chopped
    1/4 pound pepperoni sausage, sliced
    ½ pound cheese (of your choice), diced

1 (6 ounce) can black olives, drained, and chopped
1 bell pepper, diced
3 tomatoes, chopped
1 (.7 ounce) package dry Italian-style salad dressing mix
3/4 cup extra virgin olive oil
1/4 cup balsamic vinegar
1/4 cup grated Parmesan cheese
salt and ground black pepper to taste

Cook the pasta in a large pot of salted boiling water until al dente. Drain, and cool under cold water. In a large bowl, combine the pasta, salami, pepperoni, cheese, black olives, bell pepper, and tomatoes. Stir in the envelope of dressing mix. Cover, and refrigerate for at least one hour. Whisk together the olive oil, balsamic vinegar, Parmesan cheese, salt, and pepper. Just before serving, pour dressing over the salad, and mix well.

Amazing Brown Rice Salad
2 cups water
1 cup brown rice
1/4 cup diced red onion
½ cup diced celery
1/4 cup dried cranberries (Craisins)
1/4 cup olive oil
1/4 cup balsamic vinegar
1 tsp salt
½ tsp pepper
1 TBSP sugar

In a saucepan, bring water to a boil. Stir in rice, cover, and reduce heat to low. Simmer for 45 to 60 minutes, or until done. Stir in onion, celery, and cranberries. Mix together remaining ingredients to make a dressing. Pour over salad and toss to mix. Place into a serving bowl. Cover and refrigerate until chilled. Serve cold.

Chinese Chicken Salad
3 TBSP soy sauce
3 TBSP peanut butter
2 tsp brown sugar
3/4 tsp hot chile paste (or Tabasco sauce)
3 TBSP rice wine vinegar
1 TBSP sesame oil
1 pound skinless, boneless chicken breast halves, cooked and cubed
4 cups lettuce -torn, washed and dried
2 cups shredded carrots
1 bunch green onions, chopped
1/4 cup chopped fresh cilantro

To prepare the dressing, whisk together the soy sauce, peanut butter, brown sugar, chili paste, vinegar, and sesame oil.   In a large bowl, combine the chicken, lettuce, carrots, green onions, and cilantro. Toss with dressing and serve.

Simple Tomato Herb Salad
  2 large tomatoes, cored and cut into bite-sized pieces
  2 cups peeled, seeded, and diced cucumbers
  4 TBSP chopped chives
  2 TBSP chopped parsley
  2 TBSP chopped mint
  4 TBSP olive oil
  2 TBSP balsamic vinegar
  1 TBSP lemon juice
  salt & freshly ground black pepper to taste

Mix all ingredients together and chill for an hour.   Adjust salt and pepper to taste just before serving. If you like, some crumbled feta cheese is a nice addition to this salad.

Red Cabbage Slaw
  1 onion, finely chopped
  4 to 5 cups red cabbage, finely sliced
  1 TBSP salt
  2 TBSP lemon juice
  ½ cup mayonnaise
  1 tsp mustard
  1 ½ tsp cumin
  ½ cup toasted walnuts, chopped

Combine cabbage and onion in a large bowl. Sprinkle with salt, and allow to stand at room temperature at least ½ hour. Drain and squeeze out excess water. In another bowl whisk together lemon juice, mayonnaise, mustard, and cumin. Pour over cabbage mixture. Allow to chill a minimum of 1 hours before serving. Place in a serving bowl, and garnish with chopped walnuts.

German Marinated Tomatoes
  4 large Grainger County Tomatoes, peeled and sliced
  1 bell pepper, core removed and sliced
  1 medium onion, peeled and sliced
  2 TBSP fresh basil, chopped
  2 sprigs fresh thyme, chopped
  1 TBSP green onions, chopped
  1 cup vegetable oil
  1/4 cup wine vinegar
  1/4 tsp dry mustard

1 tsp salt
½ tsp pepper

Place tomato slices along with peppers and onions in a large serving bowl. Arrange in attractive layers. Combine remaining ingredients and pour over vegetables. Mix lightly to be sure that marinade reaches all parts of all vegetables. Cover and chill for 1 hour before serving.

Easy Ham and Egg Salad
    6 eggs, boiled, peeled and sliced
    8 oz ham, cubed small
    6 green onions, sliced thin
    1 cup celery, sliced thin
    ½ cup mayonnaise
    2 TBSP yellow mustard
    1 TBSP sweet pickle vinegar
    1 tsp salt
    ½ tsp black pepper

Toss eggs, ham, onion, and celery together carefully. Mix all remaining ingredients and pour over egg mixture. Toss to mix. Cover and allow to chill at least an hour before serving.

Asian Chicken Salad
    4 green onions, thinly sliced
    1 large carrot, shredded
    1 small can water chestnuts, chopped
    1/2 pound sugar snap peas, halved (optional)
    2 cups chopped and cooked chicken breast meat
    1/2 cup fresh cilantro leaves, chopped
    1/2 cup blanched slivered almonds, toasted
    2 TBSP white sugar
    2 TBSP rice wine vinegar
    1 1/2 TBSP sesame oil
    1 TBSP soy sauce

In a large bowl, mix together the onions, carrot, celery, peas, chicken, cilantro, and almonds. Set aside. In a small bowl, whisk together the sugar, vinegar, sesame oil, and soy sauce until smooth. Pour over salad mixture and toss until coated. Chill before serving.

Curried Rice Salad
    3 cups of cold cooked rice
    ½ cup celery, chopped

1/4 cup raisins
3 green onions, thinly sliced
1 6 to 7 oz can shrimp, drained
1 cup mayonnaise
1/4-1/2 cup Major Greys chutney
1 TBSP milk
2 tsp (or to taste) curry powder

Toss the rice, celery, raisins, onions, and shrimp. Mix together the remaining
ingredients and pour over the rice mixture. Toss to mix. Cover and chill before serving.

New Fashioned Onions and Cucumbers
2 large sweet onions, peeled and thinly sliced
2 cups English cucumbers (or small pickling cucumber), thinly sliced
3/4 cup cider vinegar
3/4 cup sugar
½ cup water
1 TBSP salt
1 stalk fresh dill (or 1 tsp dried dill weed)

Combine onions and cucumbers in a large bowl. If using fresh dill, immerse the stalk of
dill in the mixture. Mix vinegar, sugar, water, and salt (and dried dill is using) in a small
saucepan. Heat to boiling. Stir to dissolve sugar and pour mixture over cucumbers and
onions. Toss to coat. Cover and chill at least 8 hours before serving.
This is a new variation of a very old Southern treat. Traditionally, the cucumbers and
onions were sliced, and vinegar, sugar, and salt was heated and poured over them.
They were sometimes refrigerated and sometimes not. The dill is such a natural that
we should have thought of it years ago.

Couscous Salad with Fruit and Chicken
2 1/4 cups water
2 TBSP chicken bouillon granules
1 3/4 cups couscous, uncooked
2 cups (about 3 to 4 halves) boneless skinless chicken breast, cooked, cut into
bite-sized pieces
1 cup red bell pepper, chopped (one pepper)
1 carrot, chopped
½ cup dried cranberries (Craisins)
1 green apple, chopped
3 green onions, chopped
1/4 cup parsley sprigs, finely minced
½ cup lemon juice
3 TBSP olive oil
1 clove garlic, minced
½ tsp curry powder

½ tsp cumin
1/4 tsp Tabasco sauce
1/4 tsp black pepper, freshly ground

In a jar or small bowl, blend together lemon juice, oil, garlic, curry powder, cumin, Tabasco, and black pepper. Set aside. In a medium sauce pan, bring water to a boil, stir in chicken bouillon and add couscous. Mix couscous with a fork; cover and remove from heat. Let stand until broth is absorbed, about 15 minutes. Fluff couscous with a fork and transfer to a large bowl. Place bowl in refrigerator for about 5 minutes to cool. When couscous has cooled, mix in cooked chicken, red pepper, carrots, dried cranberries, apple, green onions, and parsley. Add lemon dressing and toss well. Chill at least one hour before serving.

Champion Chili Salad
    1 ½ lbs lean ground beef
    1 medium onion, chopped fine
    2 TBSP chili powder
    1 tsp ground cumin
    salt and pepper to taste
    2 or 3 large Grainger County tomatoes, chopped
    4 or 5 cups lettuce, shredded
    cheddar cheese, grated to taste
    ranch dressing

In a heavy skillet, fry the ground meat with the skillet until fully cooked. Drain COMPLETELY. Stir in chili powder and cumin. Add salt and pepper to taste. In a large salad bowl, place the lettuce and top with chopped tomatoes. Spoon the hot meat over the top of tomatoes. Sprinkle generously with grated cheddar cheese. Serve immediately with ranch dressing.

Ms. Essie's Summer Salad
Fred Williams, Jr.   Morristown
    4 hard boiled eggs, peeled and chopped
    3 or 4 cucumbers, chopped fairly fine
    3 green onions
    3 or 4 medium sized tomatoes
    ½ cup mayonnaise (Fred says Ms. Essie used Hellmann's), approx.

Mix eggs and vegetables lightly and add mayonnaise. Stir, cover, and let sit in the refrigerator 5-6 hours or overnight to get cold. This waiting period is important to allow the taste to develop. There are those who say it is better the second day.

One Potato, Two Potato Salad
    1 ½ lbs small red potatoes, halved or quartered

1 ½ lbs sweet potatoes, peeled and cut into 1" pieces
3 TBSP unseasoned rice vinegar (Or white vinegar)
3/4 cup sour cream
1/4 cup fresh chives, chopped
3/4 tsp salt
1/4 tsp black pepper

Place potatoes in a large pot and cover with water. Bring to a boil, reduce heat, and simmer until just tender (about 15 to 20 minutes). Drain. Place potatoes in a large bowl and drizzle with vinegar. Allow to cool to room temperature. Mix sour cream with remaining ingredients and pour over potatoes. Toss just to coat. You may serve the potatoes at room temperature or you can cover and chill them. Toss lightly before serving cold.

Roasted New Potato Salad
2 TBSP olive oil
2 lb small red potatoes, diced
½ medium sweet onion, chopped
2 tsp minced garlic
1 tsp freshly ground pepper
8 to 10 bacon slices, cooked crisp and crumbled
3/4 cup prepared ranch dressing
salt and pepper to taste

Place oil in a 15x10" jellyroll pan. Add potatoes and the next 4 ingredients, tossing to coat. Arrange potato mixture in a single layer. Bake at 425 deg for 30 to 35 minutes or until potatoes are tender, stirring occasionally. Transfer to a large bowl. Toss together potato mixture, bacon bits, and dressing. Add salt and pepper to taste. Serve immediately or cover, and chill until ready to serve.

Red Potato Salad
5 lbs red potatoes, unpeeled, cut into 1-inch cubes
2 cups ranch salad dressing
1 cup mayonnaise
3 TBSP apple cider vinegar
3 TBSP sugar
1 ½ TBSP Dijon mustard
1 cup purple onion, finely chopped
1 cup celery, thinly sliced
1 cup green pepper, diced
3/4 tsp salt
½ tsp black pepper
1 TBSP dill, chopped, or 1 tsp dried dill

Cook potatoes in boiling salted water until just barely tender (about 10 to 15 minutes).

Drain and let cool. Place all other ingredients in a large mixing bowl, and mix thoroughly. Add potatoes to bowl and mix well. Cover loosely and chill.

Fiesta Corn Salad
>1 lb pkg frozen whole kernel corn
>1 15.5 oz can black beans, drained and washed
>1 lb pkg baby lima beans
>3/4 cup salsa
>2 green onions, sliced thin
>3 TBSP fresh cilantro, chopped
>1/4 tsp garlic powder
>1/4 tsp cumin

Prepare corn and limas according to pkg directions. In a bowl with a tight cover, mix hot vegetables with canned beans and all remaining ingredients. Toss to mix. This is good served still warm or allow to chill overnight before serving.

Broccoli Salad
>6 cups broccoli, chopped
>1 ½ cups each, raisins and dry-roasted salted peanuts
>2 to 3 TBSP onion, grated fine
>1 cup mayonnaise
>1/3 cup red wine vinegar
>1/4 cup sugar

Place broccoli, raisins, and peanuts in a mixing bowl. Mix together the remaining ingredients and pour over broccoli mixture.   Toss to mix completely. Place in a covered bowl, and refrigerate several hours or overnight before serving.

Chapter 3
Soups

Left Over Lamb Stew
>2 to 3 cups roasted lamb, cut into cubes (See page 202)
>2 potatoes, peeled and cut into cubes
>2 onions, peeled and cut into 6 wedges each
>2 carrots, peeled and cut into slices
>1 TBSP dry thyme
>1 TBSP parsley
>1 can chicken stock
>salt and pepper to taste

In a heavy pot, put the potatoes, onions, carrots, and herbs. Pour chicken stock over and bring to a boil. Reduce heat and simmer, covered, about 20 minutes or until carrots are tender. Add lamb and bring back to boil. Allow to simmer another 15 minutes. Serve hot. This is also good with Irish soda bread (see recipe). It is also very good with cornbread.

Easy Slow Cooker Chicken Stew
>2 cans diced tomatoes, undrained
>1 can cream of mushroom soup
>1 can cream of celery soup
>1 bag of frozen mixed veggies
>4 boneless, skinless chicken breast halves, cut into bite sized pieces
>1 cup milk
>salt and pepper to taste

Mix the cans of soup and the milk in a Crock Pot. Add the tomatoes, spices, and chicken and stir. Add the veggies and stir. Cook on low heat until the chicken is cooked (approx 5 - 6 hours). Add salt and pepper to taste.

Ham and Potato Chowder
>1 pkg au gratin potato mix
>1 ½ cups diced cooked ham
>½ cup chopped carrots
>1/4 tsp pepper (or to taste)
>3 cups water
>2 cups milk
>1/4 cup chopped parsley (optional)

In a large pan, combine potato slices from mix, seasoning packet, ham, carrot, pepper, water, and milk. Bring to a boil. Reduce heat, and cook 15 minutes or until potatoes are tender. Stir in parsley (if using) and serve immediately

Taco soup
Sheila Shuler   Halls Crossroads
    2 lbs ground beef
    1 cup onion, chopped
    1 pkg taco seasoning mix
    1 pkg ranch dressing mix
    3 16 oz cans diced tomatoes
    1 16 oz can pinto beans
    1 16 oz cans kidney beans
    2 can whole kernel corn, drained
    1 4 oz can chopped green chilies

Cook beef and onion together until beef is browned. Drain thoroughly, and pour into a slow cooker. Add all remaining ingredients, and stir to mix. Cook on low for at least 6 hours (more will not hurt). Serve with a dollop of sour cream and shredded cheddar cheese.

Bean and Pasta Soup
    2 TBSP olive oil
    1 onion, chopped
    2 tsp each chopped garlic and dry oregano
    2 cans Italian flavor diced tomatoes
    1 8 oz can tomato sauce
    2 cups chicken stock
    2 cans white kidney beans, undrained
    1 cup uncooked pasta (any small variety)

In a heavy saucepan, saute onion and garlic in oil until starting to brown. Add tomatoes, tomato sauce, oregano, chicken stock, and beans. Bring to a boil, reduce heat, and allow to simmer about 20 minutes. Bring back to a full boil. Add pasta, and cook about 10 minutes or until pasta is tender. Serve hot with Parmesan cheese. If you like, you can thin this soup a little with about 1 cup water just before you bring it back to a full boil to add the pasta.

Cheese and Sausage Chowder
    1 lb reduced-fat smoked sausage, sliced into thin slices
    1 14 ½ oz can whole-kernel corn, drained
    1-2 TBSP butter
    3 TBSP flour
    1 15 oz can chicken stock
    1 envelope onion soup mix

8 oz Cheddar cheese, shredded
1 cup milk

Cook sausage and corn in butter over medium heat 4-5 minutes. Stir in flour; cook 1 minute, stirring constantly. Add chicken stock and onion soup mix and heat to boiling; Reduce heat to low and add cheese, stirring until melted. Add milk; cook until hot (about 4 or 5 minutes). Do not allow to come to a boil.

A Whole New Kettle of Stew
2 lbs lean beef cut into bite sized pieces
3 potatoes, peeled and cubed
2 carrots, peeled and cut into chunks
1 onion, peeled and cut into 8 wedges
2 stalks celery, sliced
3 cups spicy V-8 juice
4 TBSP instant tapioca

Place the meat in the bottom of the slow cooker. Layer vegetables over meat. Mix V-8 juice with tapioca, and pour over layered beef and vegetables. Cover and cook on low about 8 hours. Serve in pot on the table and stir to serve.

Winter Vegetable Soup
4 TBSP olive oil
1 medium onion, peeled and chopped
1 leek, white and light green part only (about ½ to 3/4 cup)
1 TBSP minced garlic
2 carrots, peeled and sliced diagonally
2 medium potatoes, peeled and cubed (Yukon Gold are nice)
1 parsnip, peeled and diced
2 turnips, peeled and diced
8 cups chicken stock (or water with 4 tsp chicken bullion)
1 can garbanzo beans, drained
1 bay leaf
2 tsp Italian seasoning
salt and pepper to taste
1 bunch kale greens, washed carefully and chopped

In a large soup pot, add 2 TBSP of the olive oil, and heat to medium hot. Add onion, leek, and garlic. Saute, stirring, a couple of minutes. Add carrots, potatoes, parsnip, and turnips and cook, continuing to stir about 5 minutes. Add beans, stock, bay leaf, and Italian seasoning. Cook about 30 minutes. Add salt and pepper to taste. In a large skillet, heat the remaining 2 TBSP olive oil and add the kale greens. Cook, stirring, until they are wilted. Stir into soup and allow to cook about 5 minutes. Taste and adjust salt and pepper if needed. If you wish, Remove a couple of cups of the vegetables into a food processor and puree them. Stir back into the soup to thicken it.

Serve hot.

Butternut Squash Soup
     1 medium onion, chopped
     1 garlic clove, minced
     1 TBSP olive oil
     2 cans (14 oz or thereabouts) chicken broth
     2 to 3 cups butternut squash puree (see note below)
     2 tsp sugar
     1/4 tsp dried thyme
     1/4 tsp salt
     1/8 tsp ground sage
     1 cup sour cream

Saute onion and garlic in olive oil about 5 minutes. Stir in broth, squash puree, sugar, and spices. Bring to a boil, then reduce heat, and simmer for 15 minutes. Stir sour cream into pumpkin mixture. Heat through but do not allow to boil. Serve with an added dollop of sour cream on the top.

Note: You can make the puree very easily. Just split a butternut squash lengthwise. Place on a baking dish, and put into a preheated 325 deg oven. Allow to bake about one hour or until the flesh of the squash can be easily peeled from the peel. Place into food processor with just a little of the broth and puree. You can use any kind of winter squash puree (including a can of pumpkin) to make this soup.

Italian Sausage and Cheddar Cheese Soup
Cook your favorite cheddar cheese soup recipe. Serve the cheddar cheese soup in a bread bowl, and top it with Italian sausage which has been fried crisp and chopped fine.

In case you do not have a favorite Cheddar Cheese Soup, here is one from Dollywood:

Cheddar Cheese Soup & Italian Sausage
     2 cups cheddar cheese, shredded
     3 TBSP butter
     4 Scallions (including some of the green part), chopped
     1 small onion, chopped
     1 rib celery, chopped
     3 TBSP flour
     1/8 tsp nutmeg, grated
     1/8 tsp black pepper
     2 cups chicken broth
     1 quart milk
     1 tsp salt
     1 TBSP Worcestershire sauce
     1 TBSP Italian Sausage, cooked

In a large pot, melt the butter. Add scallions, onion, and celery. Cook until the onion softens. Sift in the flour, nutmeg, and pepper and cook for 2 or 3 minutes longer. Gradually stir in the broth. Bring the mixture to a boil and simmer for 15 minutes. Cool the mixture slightly. Strain into a bowl and return it to the pan. Add the milk, and bring soup just to a boil. Gradually add cheese, stirring to melt each batch before adding more. Return the soup to a boil, stirring often. Taste for seasoning, and add salt and Worcestershire. Serve cheddar cheese soup in a bread bowl, and top it with Italian sausage.

Chicken Corn Chowder
A recipe from the kitchens of Walt Disney World at the Animal Kingdom Lodge
    1 cup chicken stock
    1 chicken bouillon cube
    2 chicken breasts, cooked and diced
    2 baking potatoes, cooked and diced
    2 cups frozen corn kernels
    1/8 cup medium onion, diced
    1/8 cup red bell pepper, diced
    1 cup milk
    1 cup heavy cream
    2 tsp sugar
    2 tsp hot sauce
    1/8 cup fresh parsley

Bring chicken stock to a boil, add chicken bouillon cube, and dissolve. Add all other ingredients except parsley and hot sauce. Simmer for 40 minutes. Add parsley and hot sauce and simmer for 5 minutes.

Chicken & White Bean Stew
    1 TBSP cooking oil
    2 medium carrots, sliced (about 2 cups)
    1 medium onion, thinly sliced
    2 cloves garlic, finely chopped
    1 pound boneless, skinless chicken thighs, cut into chunks
    1 jar (1 pound 10 ounces) pasta sauce
    2 cans (15 ounces each) white kidney beans, drained
    ½ tsp Tabasco sauce (optional)

In a large pot, heat oil over medium heat and cook carrots, onion, and garlic, stirring occasionally, about 5 minutes or until vegetables are tender. Add chicken to same skillet and thoroughly brown chicken medium-high heat. Stir in pasta sauce, beans, and Tabasco sauce. Bring to a boil over high heat. Reduce heat to medium, and simmer covered, stirring occasionally, 15 minutes or until chicken is thoroughly cooked.

100% Guaranteed To Be As Good Or Better Than Nationally Advertised Brands And Priced To Save You Money

London Particular (Split Pea) Soup
This great, thick, flavorful soup is named for London because the fogs which used to cover that great city were said to be as thick as pea soup. The fogs are gone, but this fine soup will warm your heart.

    1 TBSP butter (15 grams)
    2 oz Streaky Bacon (50 grams) rind, removed and chopped
    1 medium onion, chopped
    1 medium carrot, chopped
    1 stick celery, chopped
    1 lb dried split peas
    3 pints ham or chicken stock (3 cans with a little water)
    4 TBSP yogurt (optional)
    salt and pepper to taste

Melt the butter and add the bacon, onion, carrot, and celery in a pot with a good lid. Cook for 5 to 10 minutes, stirring occasionally, until the vegetables start to soften. Add the peas and stock. Bring to a boil, cover, and reduce heat. Simmer about 1 hour or until the peas are cooked. Liquidize (run in the blender or food processor) thoroughly. Add yogurt and reheat gently without boiling. Serve garnished with bacon pieces if you wish.

To make this soup, I use salt bacon. I have also substantially reduced the amount of liquid I use. I like the soup THICK. If you want thinner, you may add up to twice as much liquid.

5-Bean Soup
Sylvia Spurling   Friendsville, Tn.
    1 can pinto beans
    1 can pork & beans
    1 can lima beans
    1 can great Northern beans
    1 can red kidney beans
    1 jar Bulls Eye Barbecue sauce
    1 green pepper, chopped
    1 onion, chopped
    1 to 1 ½ lbs. Ground beef, browned and drained

Combine all these ingredients in a large soup pot. Then add:
    1/4 tsp red pepper
    1/4 tsp white pepper
    1/4 tsp black pepper

(If you do not want this as spicy, reduce pepper to 1/8 tsp.) Let simmer on low heat for about two hours.   Very good with cornbread.

Potato and Cauliflower Soup with Cheese
5 or 6 potatoes, peeled and cubed
3 cups cauliflower, chopped
2 cans chicken stock
water
½ lb Cheezy Does It Cheese
1 cup cheddar cheese, grated
salt and pepper to taste

Place potatoes and 2 cups cauliflower into a large pot. Pour chicken stock over and add water to almost cover. Bring to a boil and reduce heat. Simmer about 25 minutes or until potatoes are soft. Mash lightly with a potato masher. Add remaining cauliflower and cook an additional 10 to 15 minutes on low heat. Stir in cheeses and cook, stirring until cheese is melted. Add salt and pepper to taste. Serve hot.

Collard Greens, Potato and Black Eyed Pea Soup
2 slices hog jowl bacon, cubed
2 ½ cups peeled and cubed potatoes
1 cup thinly sliced celery
1 onion, chopped
6 cups shredded collard greens
2 cans chicken broth
1 bay leaf
½ teaspoon ground black pepper
2 (15 ounce) cans black eyed peas

Fry bacon in a medium size saucepan until brown. Remove bacon with a slotted spoon reserving the grease. Add potatoes, celery, and onion; saute for 5 minutes. Stir in collards. Cover and cook over medium heat, until greens are tender. Add broth, bay leaf, pepper, and black eyed peas. Heat until soup boils. Reduce heat and allow to simmer for 15 minutes. Remove bay leaf and serve with cornbread.

Quick Tortellini Soup
4 cups chicken broth (2 cans plus ½ cup water)
1 medium onion, chopped
1 cup carrots, diced fine
1 4 oz can green chiles, diced
2 tsp garlic, minced (2 cloves)
1 tsp basil, dried or 1 TBSP fresh, finely chopped
2 cups (150g) tortellini, cheese-filled, fresh or frozen
2 TBSP freshly grated Parmesan cheese

In a large soup pot, bring broth, onion, carrot, green chiles, garlic, and basil to a simmer.

Cover, reduce heat, and simmer 10 minutes. Turn heat up and bring broth to a boil.
Add tortellini and cook uncovered until tender to bite, 4 to 8 minutes. Ladle into bowls
and sprinkle with Parmesan cheese.

Harvest Soup

Inez Elmore   (Who sent it anonymously, but I found her out)
  1 lb ground beef (or ground turkey)
  1 onion, chopped
  2 large cans Veg-all (do not drain)
  1 large can V-8 juice
  I large can crushed tomatoes
  Pasta (if desired)

Brown the ground beef and onion together and drain. Mix all remaining ingredients
together, and bring to a boil. Reduce heat, and simmer 15 to 20 minutes.   If using
pasta, add in last 10 min of cooking time.

A couple of notes about this hearty, heartwarming soup. How much pasta you use
depends on how thick you want the soup to be. 4 oz will make it thick, but still soupy. 8
oz will make it more like a stew. You get to decide. You may also want to consider
adding some dried parsley or dried oregano or both. Some folks would like some hot
peppers added. Lots of folks would like it just the way it is above. About salt and
pepper: most of the ingredients are salted, and the finished soup is salty enough for me
without any added. You should make the soup and taste it before adding any
additional.

Vegetarian Black Bean and Corn Soup

  2 15 oz cans black beans, drained and rinsed
  2 14 ½ oz cans Mexican style diced tomatoes, undrained
  1 11 oz can whole kernel corn
  4 green onions, sliced thin
  2 TBSP chili powder
  1 tsp cumin
  ½ tsp minced garlic

Combine all ingredients in the slow cooker. Cover and cook on low for 7 or 8 hours.
This is good served with grated cheese and nacho chips.

Chapter 4
Breads

Hot Fried Cornbread
> 3 cups self rising corn meal mix
> 2 ½ cups milk (approx)
> ½ lb hot cheese grated
> oil for frying

Mix the corn meal mix with enough milk to make a loose batter. Stir in grated cheese. Heat a small amount of oil in a non stick skillet over medium heat. Use about 1/4 cup batter for each fried corn cake. Cook until bubbly and starting to brown around edge. Turn and cook until brown and firm to the touch. This is great served hot with some pinto beans.

White Lily Sweet and Spicy Rolls
Belinda Ellis   White Lily Foods
> ½ cup granulated sugar
> 1 tsp ground ginger
> ½ tsp ground cinnamon
> 1/4 tsp ground cloves
> ½ cup (1 stick) butter, melted and cooled to room temperature
> 1 bag (27 oz.) White Lily Frozen Yeast Rolls

Preheat oven to 150° to 200° F., then turn oven off. In small bowl, stir together sugar and spices; set aside. Pour about 3 tablespoons melted butter in a 13x9x2-inch baking pan to coat bottom. Dip frozen rolls in butter, then in sugar mixture, turning to coat all sides and place about 1 inch apart in baking pan. (Combine remaining sugar mixture and butter; set aside.) Cover rolls with plastic wrap. Place in warmed oven to rise. Let rise until doubled, about 1 ½ to 2 hours. Remove from oven; remove plastic wrap. Heat oven to 375° F. Drizzle remaining butter-sugar mixture over top of rolls. Bake for 12 to 15 minutes or until golden brown. Serve warm. Makes 12 servings.

White Lily Savory Herb Rolls
> ½ cup (1 stick) butter
> 1 tsp dried parsley leaves
> 1 tsp dried rosemary leaves
> ½ tsp dried sage leaves
> ½ tsp dried thyme leaves
> 1 bag (27 oz.) White Lily Frozen Yeast Rolls

Preheat oven to 150° to 200° F., then turn oven off. In 1-cup glass measure, melt butter in microwave on High for 30 seconds. Stir in parsley, rosemary, sage, and thyme. Pour about 3 tablespoons mixture into 13x9x2-inch baking pan to coat bottom. Allow mixture to cool to room temperature. Dip frozen rolls in butter mixture to coat all sides and place about 1 inch apart in baking pan. Cover with plastic wrap. Place in warmed oven to rise. Let rise until doubled, about 1 ½ to 2 hours. Remove from oven; remove plastic wrap. Heat oven to 375° F. Drizzle remaining herb-butter mixture over top of rolls. Bake for 12 to 15 minutes or until golden brown. Serve warm. Makes 12 servings.

White Lily "Light" Biscuits
     2 cups White Lily Self Rising Flour
     1/4 cup shortening
     2/3 to 3/4 cup milk or buttermilk

Preheat oven to 500 deg. Lightly spray on baking sheet with non-stick cooking spray. Measure flour (spoon into measuring cup and level off) and place in bowl. Cut in shortening until mixture resembles coarse crumbs. With a fork, blend in just enough milk until dough leaves sides of bowl. (Too much milk makes dough sticky, while too little makes biscuits dry). Knead gently 2 or 3 times on lightly floured surface. Roll dough to ½ inch thickness, cutting without twisting biscuit cutter. Place on baking sheet, 1 inch apart for crisp sided biscuits, almost touching for softer sided biscuits. Bake 8 to 10 minutes or until golden brown. Brush with melted butter if desired. Serve warm. If you happen to not have self rising flour, you can use 2 cups White Lily All Purpose Flour and add 1 TBSP baking powder and 1 tsp salt before cutting in the shortening. Makes 12, 2 inch biscuits.

"Stickies"
     2 cups White Lily Self Rising Flour
     1/3 cup shortening
     3/4 cup milk
     ½ cup butter, softened
     1 cup sugar (white or light brown)
     1 TBSP (approx) cinnamon

Using flour, shortening, and milk, make a dough exactly like the former recipe. Turn dough out onto a heavily floured board and knead several turns until it is still and easily rolled.   On a floured surface, roll the dough very thin (about 1/8 inch or less). Spread with the butter. Sprinkle about 1/4 cup of the sugar over the dough and sprinkle with cinnamon. Roll dough up from the long side jelly roll fashion and slice into slices about 1/4 inch thick. Spray a 9x13 inch pan with cooking oil spray and sprinkle with the remaining sugar and cinnamon. Lay the slices, cut side down, into the pan leaving a little space between each slice. Pour 1 cup water over the slices and immediately place in a 375 deg oven and bake about 25 to 30 minutes or until browned. Do not overcook. Serve warm, spooning the syrup which will have formed over the rolls. A little whipped cream or a dollop of ice cream would not be a bad idea.

Beginner's (Top-Choice) White Bread
One of Fleischmann's Yeast's Best recipes for a loaf of bread.
>   5-1/2 to 6 cups bread flour
>   3 TBSP sugar
>   2 pkg Fleischmann's RapidRise Yeast
>   2 tsp salt
>   11/2 cups water
>   ½ cup milk
>   2 TBSP butter

In large bowl, combine 2 cups flour, sugar, undissolved yeast, and salt. Heat water, milk, and butter until very warm (120° to 130°F); stir into dry ingredients. Beat 2 minutes at medium speed of electric mixer, scraping bowl occasionally. Stir in 1 cup flour; beat at high speed for 2 minutes, scraping bowl occasionally. Stir in enough remaining flour to make soft dough. Knead on lightly floured surface until smooth and elastic, about 8 to 10 minutes. Cover; let rest 10 minutes. Divide dough in half. Roll each half to 12 x 7-inch rectangle. Beginning at short end of each rectangle, roll up tightly as for jelly roll. Pinch seams and ends to seal. Place, seam sides down, in greased 8-1/2 x 4-1/2 inch loaf pans. Cover; let rise in warm, draft free place until doubled in size, about 45 minutes. Bake at 400°F for 25 to 30 minutes or until done. Remove from pans; cool on wire rack.

To Make Whole Wheat Bread: Substitute 2 cups whole wheat flour for part of bread flour and add 3 TBSP honey to the water, milk, and butter mixture.

"Mamaw's Banana Bread"
Shellie Fellers   Owner   Sweet Sinsations   Oak Ridge

1 ½ cups all purpose flour	3/4 cup oil
3/4 tsp soda	3 TBSP buttermilk
1/4 tsp salt	3 large bananas mashed (about 1 cup)
1 cup white sugar	½ cup chopped pecans
2 eggs, lightly beaten	1 tsp cinnamon
1 tsp baking powder	

Preheat oven to 325 degrees. Grease and flour an 8 ½ x 4 ½ x 2 ½ inch loaf pan; set aside. Sift together flour, soda, baking powder, cinnamon, and salt. Add sugar, oil, and buttermilk; stir to blend. Fold in bananas and nuts. Pour into prepared dish. Bake 1 hour 10 minutes. Makes one 2 lb. loaf.

* I also add a powdered sugar glaze over the top to make a prettier presentation. Just a bit of water, maybe 2 TBSP, mixed with about 3/4 cup of powdered sugar.

Cheddar Cheese Scones

1 ½ cups flour
2 tsp baking powder
½ tsp salt
2 tsp dry mustard
1/4 cup unsalted butter
1 ½ cups (8 ounces) shredded sharp cheddar cheese
1 large egg, beaten
1/4 to 1/3 cup milk

Preheat oven to 425 deg. Lightly grease a baking sheet; set aside. In a mixing bowl, stir flour, salt, baking powder, and mustard powder together. Using a pastry blender, cut in the butter until the mixture is crumbly. Stir in cheese, mixing well. Combine the egg with 1/4 cup of milk and stir into flour mixture to make a soft dough, adding more milk only if it is needed. Turn dough out onto a lightly floured work surface. Knead several times and then pat dough out into an 8-inch circle onto the prepared baking sheet. Cut into 8 wedges. Brush scones with milk. Bake until tops are just starting to brown, about 9 to 12 minutes. Serve immediately.

Chelsea Buns
In 18th century London, the Chelsea area was famous for its buns. George II, George III (you remember him from the American revolution), and George IV all bought them from the celebrated Chelsea Bun House, which was in Grosvenor Row. With a little work, you can make them in your own home.

Yeast Batter:
> 3 oz plain flour
> 1 tsp granulated sugar (the original recipe calls for caster sugar which is super fine.)
> 2 tsp dry yeast
> 4 oz (½ cup) milk, hot to the touch (about 108 to 110 deg)

Dough:
> 6 oz plain flour
> 1 oz (about 2 TBSP) butter, diced
> 1 egg beaten

Filling:
> 2 oz Demerara (brown) sugar
> 2 oz each currants and sultanas
> 1 oz cut mixed peel
> Golden syrup (to glaze)

Place the batter ingredients in a large bowl. Beat well with a wooden spoon until smooth. Cover with a tea towel and leave in a warm place until frothy (about 20 minutes). Place the flour for the dough into a bowl and rub in the butter until it resembles fine bread crumbs. Add the rubbed mixture and egg to the batter and mix well. Turn out onto a lightly floured surface and knead for about 10 minutes or until the dough feels firm and elastic, You may need to work a little more flour into it. Place the dough in a lightly floured bowl and cover with clingfilm (plastic wrap) and leave to rise in a warm place about 1 hour or until the dough has doubled in bulk and will spring back when lightly pressed. Knead the dough lightly. Roll into an 8x12" rectangle on a lightly floured board. Spread with softened butter and sprinkle the sugar evenly over. Sprinkle evenly with the fruit and peels. Roll up like a Swiss Roll (Jelly roll) from the long side. Seal seam. Cut into 9 slices. Place 8 slices around a greased 9" cake tin, and place the 9th slice in the center. Cover and allow to rise about 1 hour or until doubled in bulk. Uncover and bake about 30 to 35 minutes in a 400 deg oven or until golden brown. Brush lightly with golden syrup. Allow to cool a few minutes in the pan, and then turn out and allow to cool completely on a wire rack.

Upside-Down Onion Zucchini Cornbread
>1 onion, peeled and sliced thin
>1 zucchini, sliced thin
>2 ½ cups cornmeal mix
>1/3 cup vegetable oil
>2 TBSP solid shortening
>1 cup milk
>1 egg

Melt shortening in a 9-inch oven-proof skillet over medium heat. Arrange onion and zucchini slices over bottom of skillet in an attractive pattern. Cook 2 to 3 minutes or until onion and zucchini is partially cooked. Meanwhile, place cornmeal mix in bowl. Beat together milk, oil, and egg. Stir into dry ingredients. Pour batter over onion and zucchini slices. Bake in 350 deg oven for 20 to 25 minutes or until bread is done. Invert onto serving plate. Cut in wedges, serve.

Sausage Bread
Amy Shubet   Loudon, TN
>2 lbs. sausage, 1 hot and 1 mild
>1/4 cup green pepper, chopped fine
>1/4 cup onion, chopped fine
>1 lb pkg cheddar cheese, shredded
>Pillsbury hot roll mix

Prepare roll mix according to package directions. Let set for five minutes. Then divide. Press half into a lightly buttered 9x13 pan and the other half on a lightly buttered piece of wax paper. Shape into size of pan. Let rise for 15-20 minutes (covered). Cook sausage chopped up. Add green pepper and onion and cook until done. Drain off all grease, and put in pan on bread mixture. Add cheddar cheese then put on the top piece of bread dough and tuck in around edges. Bake 25 minutes at 400 degrees. Cut into squares to serve.

Broccoli Cornbread
Ed Nicewanner at NHC Fort Sanders

1 10 oz pkg frozen chopped broccoli
1 medium onion, chopped
2 cups sharp cheddar cheese, shredded
4 eggs, beaten
1 stick butter, melted
1 box Jiffy Cornbread mix

Thaw and drain broccoli, but do not cook. Mix all ingredients together, and turn into a hot, greased 9" pan. Bake at 400 deg for 25 to 30 minutes. Serve hot.

Eggnog Bread
2 eggs
1 cup sugar
1 cup dairy eggnog
½ cup butter, melted
1/4 tsp nutmeg
2 tsp rum extract
1 tsp vanilla
2 1/4 cup flour
2 tsp baking powder

Preheat oven to 350 deg. Grease bottom of a loaf pan. Beat eggs and add sugar, eggnog, butter, rum extract, and vanilla. Blend well. Add flour, baking powder, and nutmeg. Stir until just moistened. Pour into greased pan. Bake at 350 deg for 45 to 50 minutes or until toothpick inserted comes out clean. Cool 10 minutes and remove from pan. Cool bread completely before slicing.

Zucchini Bread
1 ½ cups plain flour
1 tsp ground ginger
1 ½ tsp baking powder
1/4 tsp salt
1 cup sugar
1/4 cup vegetable oil
2 eggs, slightly beaten
2 TBSP fresh lemon juice
1 tsp freshly grated lemon peel
1 cup shredded zucchini
½ cup chopped walnuts

Grease and flour a 9x5x3-inch loaf pan; set aside. In a large mixing bowl, stir together flour, ginger, baking powder, salt, and sugar. Add oil, eggs, lemon juice, and peel shredded zucchini and chopped walnuts. Stir to blend. Do not over mix. Spoon batter into prepared loaf pan. Bake at 350 deg for 45 to 55 minutes, or until a wooden pick inserted into the center of the loaf comes out clean. Cool zucchini bread in pan on wire rack for 5 to 10 minutes. Turn zucchini bread out of pan and cool completely on rack.

Carrot Bread from <u>Cook Book</u>
Published by Fountain City Methodist Church in 1966
> 1 stick butter
> 1 TBSP oil
> 2 TBSP water
> 1 cup sugar
> 1 ½ cups flour
> 2 eggs
> 1 tsp cinnamon
> 1 tsp soda
> ½ tsp salt
> 1 cup carrots, grated

Cream together oil, butter, water, sugar, and eggs. Mix all dry ingredients and stir into butter mixture. Stir in carrots. Bake in a greased loaf pan at 350 deg until done (which will be about 45 minutes). You may add a cup of chopped nuts if you wish.

Pumpkin Nut Bread
> 1 cup pumpkin puree (canned works fine)
> 2 cups flour
> 1 cup sugar
> 2 eggs
> ½ cup milk
> 1/4 cup butter, softened
> 1 cup chopped nuts (walnuts or pecans will work well)
> 2 tsp baking powder
> ½ tsp baking soda
> 1 tsp nutmeg
> ½ tsp cinnamon
> 1 tsp salt

Preheat oven to 350 deg. Mix the flour, baking powder, baking soda, and spices. In a separate large bowl, combine pumpkin, sugar, milk, and eggs. Beat in softened butter. Add dry ingredients to pumpkin mixture until well blended. Mix in chopped nuts. Pour into greased loaf pans(9x5x3). Bake in oven for 45 to 55 minutes. Check with a toothpick. It is done when it comes out clean. Allow to stand in pans 5 minutes and turn out onto a rack to cool. This is good warm or cold. It is also nice toasted and spread with a little softened cream cheese.

Irish Soda Bread
> 1 cup whole wheat flour
> 1 cup plain flour
> 2 tsp soda

½ tsp cream of tarter
½ cup butter
buttermilk to make a dough (about 3/4 cup)

Mix all dry ingredients. Work in the butter until no large lumps still show. Add milk to form a dough that will hold its shape. Do not get it too wet. Turn out onto a floured surface and knead for a couple of minutes. Place on a lightly greased baking sheet and shape into a round cake shape. With a sharp knife, cut a cross into the top. If you wish, you may brush the top with some milk. Bake in a 400 deg oven about 40 minutes or until nicely browned. Serve hot.

New Fashioned Irish Soda Bread
2 cups plain flour
1 cup whole wheat flour
2 tsp baking powder
1 tsp soda
3/4 cup salted butter, cold, cut into small pieces
1 ½ cups golden raisins or currants
1 egg
½ cup honey
1 cup buttermilk

Mix the flours, baking powder, and soda. Cut in butter until mixture is like coarse crumbs. Mix in raisins. In another bowl, beat egg and add honey. Beat to mix. Beat in buttermilk. Stir into dry ingredients. Turn into a heavy iron skillet which has been heavily greased with solid shortening. Smooth the top. Bake in a 350 deg oven about 45 to 50 minutes or until brown and cook through. Serve warm with butter and lemon curd or jelly or to go with a hearty stew.

Double Quick Dinner Rolls
1 pkg active dry yeast
1 cup warm water (110 deg)
1/4 cup potato flakes
2 TBSP sugar
1 tsp salt
1 egg
2 TBSP vegetable oil
3/4 tsp onion powder (optional)
2 1/4 cups all-purpose flour

In a large bowl, dissolve yeast in warm water. Add potato flakes, sugar, salt, egg, vegetable oil, onion powder (if using), and one cup of flour. Beat until smooth. Stir in remaining flour. Continue stirring until smooth, scraping batter from sides of bowl. Cover and let dough rise in warm place until doubled in bulk (about 20 to 30 minutes). Punch down dough. Spoon dough into 12 greased muffin cups, filling each about half full. Let rise until batter reaches tops of cups (about 20 minutes). Bake in a preheated 400 deg oven for about 15 minutes or until brown. Serve immediately.

Easy Whole Wheat Bread
 1 cup milk
 1 pkg yeast
 2 TBSP molasses
 ½ tsp salt
 2 TBSP butter, melted
 1 egg, beaten
 1 cup all purpose flour
 1 cup whole wheat flour

Warm milk to about 105 deg. Stir in yeast, molasses, and salt. Allow to stand about 5 minutes or until it starts to bubble. Stir in butter, egg, and flour until smooth. Turn into a well greased 8 or 9" cake pan. Allow to rise about 30 minutes or until doubled in bulk. Bake at 350 deg for about 30 minutes or until brown. Brush with melted butter and serve hot.

Corn Yeast Rolls
 2/3 cup milk, warmed
 2 TBSP vegetable oil
 2 TBSP butter, melted
 1 egg
 ½ cup cornmeal
 1 tsp salt
 2 TBSP white sugar
 3 cups all-purpose flour
 1 pkg active dry yeast

Mix yeast and sugar in milk and allow to stand about 5 minutes. Mix flour, corn meal, and salt and form a well in the center. Pour in oil, butter, and yeast mixture. Stir until a dough forms. Turn out onto a floured board and knead about 10 or 12 turns or until smooth. Shape dough into 8 to 10 balls and arrange in a greased 9 inch pie pan. Allow to rise in a warm spot until doubled in size. Bake in a preheated 400 degree oven for about 30 to 40 minutes, or until the rolls are lightly browned.

May-o Rolls
Barbara Yoakum   New Tazewell, Tn.
 2 cups self rising flour
 1 cup milk
 1/4 cup mayonnaise
Mix all ingredients thoroughly and drop into greased muffin tins. Bake at 350 deg about 15 minutes or until brown.

Chapter 5
Muffins, Hotcakes, and Breakfast Stuff

Enchantress's Spellbinding Scones
>1 1/4 cup all purpose flour
>3/4 tsp baking powder
>1 ½ tsp sugar
>1/8 tsp salt
>1/4 cup butter
>½ cup light cream
>1/4 cup golden raisins, shopped
>1 TBSP finely grated orange rind
>1 small egg yolk
>2 tsp water
>1 TBSP sugar

Mix flour, baking powder, sugar, and salt together. Blend in butter with a pastry cutter until the mixture is the size of small peas. Gently mix in cream, raisins, and orange rind. Gather the dough together and pat it out on a lightly floured board until it is 3/4" thick. Cut into 2" circles with a floured cutter. In a small bowl, stir the egg yolk and water together until well blended. Lightly brush the scones with the egg yolk mixture. Sprinkle with sugar. Place 1 inch apart on an ungreased cookie sheet. Bake in a preheated 400 deg oven for about 15 minutes or until golden. Cool on a wire rack.

Beauty's Banana Mini-Muffins
>1/3 cup shortening
>½ cup sugar
>2 eggs
>1 3/4 cups sifted all purpose flour
>1 tsp baking powder
>½ tsp soda
>½ tsp salt
>1 cup mashed ripe banana
>½ cup chopped walnuts or pecans

Cream together the shortening and sugar: add eggs and beat well. Mix together dry ingredients; add to creamed mixture alternately with banana, blending well after each addition. Stir in nuts. Fill well greased or lined miniature muffin pans half full. Bake in a preheated 350 deg oven 8 to 10 minutes or until done. Remove muffins from pans and place on rack to cool completely.

Handy Pumpkin Muffins
>1 ½ cups sugar
>1 cup cooking oil
>1 16 oz can pumpkin
>2 1/4 cups plain flour
>1 ½ tsp each, salt, baking powder, soda, and nutmeg
>3 eggs
>1 tsp vanilla
>½ cup chopped nuts
>1 cup raisins

Beat together the sugar, eggs, oil, pumpkin, and vanilla. Stir together flour, salt, baking powder, soda, and nutmeg. Mix with oil mixture just enough to blend. Stir in nuts and raisins. Fill cups of muffin pans about 2/3 full. Bake in a preheated 350 deg oven about 20 minutes or until lightly browned. Makes about 2 dozen muffins. This batter will keep in the refrigerator for up to 2 weeks. It is very handy to premix it and have it ready to bake when needed.

Savory Ham Muffins
Ms. Patty Williams sent this to me. She said the start of it was a recipe in the Knoxville Journal several years ago. She added the cornmeal for texture. I agree with her.
>2 eggs
>1 TBSP sugar
>1 cup sour cream
>2 TBSP butter, melted
>2 tsp honey mustard
>1 cup self-rising flour
>1/4 cup self-rising cornmeal mix
>½ cup chopped ham
>½ cup cheddar cheese, shredded

Beat eggs with sugar until fluffy. Stir in sour cream, butter, and mustard. Add remaining ingredients and stir until just mixed. Do not overmix. Fill greased muffin cups 3/4 full. Bake at 400 deg about 20 minutes. Serve hot with orange juice and coffee for breakfast.

Big Orange Muffins
>1 stick butter, melted
>1 cup sugar
>2 eggs
>1 cup buttermilk
>2 ½ cups plain flour
>1 tsp baking powder
>1 tsp soda
>1/4 tsp salt

1 TBSP orange zest, minced (optional)
½ cup orange marmalade

Mix butter, 3/4 cup sugar, and eggs. Beat in buttermilk. Mix flour with baking powder, salt, and soda. Stir into liquid ingredients. Stir in zest and marmalade. Divide evenly into 12 muffin tins which have been fitted with paper liners. Sprinkle remaining sugar on top of muffins. Bake at 375 deg about 15 to 20 minutes or until brown. Remove to a plate and serve warm.

Zu-Key-Ni Dill Muffins
From the Baldpate Inn near Estes Park, Colorado
3 ½ cups plain flour
1/3 cup sugar
2 TBSP baking powder
1 TBSP dill weed
2 tsp salt
2 cups grated unpeeled zucchini
2 eggs
1 ½ cups milk
½ cup oil
½ cup grated Parmesan cheese

In a large bowl combine flour, sugar, baking powder, dill, and salt. Stir in the zucchini until it is fully coated. Combine the milk, eggs, and oil and stir into dry mixture just until moistened. Fill greased or paper lined muffin tins 2/3 full. Sprinkle with Parmesan cheese. Bake at 400 deg about 18 to 20 minutes or until they test done. Allow to cool in the pan about 5 minutes before removing to a wire rack to cool completely.

Cherry Corn Muffins
1 cups all-purpose flour
1 cup yellow self-rising corn meal
2/3 cup dried tart cherries
½ cup granulated sugar
1 cup milk
1/4 cup vegetable oil
1 egg, slightly beaten
1 teaspoon vanilla extract

Combine flour, corn meal, cherries, and sugar in a medium mixing bowl; mix well. Stir in milk, vegetable oil, egg, and vanilla just until dry ingredients are moistened. Fill paper-lined muffin cups 3/4 full with batter. Bake in a preheated 400-degree oven 20 to 25 minutes, or until wooden pick inserted in center comes out clean. Let cool in pan 5 minutes. Remove from pan and serve warm or at room temperature.
Makes 12 muffins.

Southwestern Corn Muffins
1/4 cup butter
½ cup onion, chopped very fine
1 11 oz can Mexican style whole kernel corn, drained
1 cup self rising meal
1 cup flour (plain or self rising will work)
1 cup cheddar cheese, grated
2 TBSP sugar
½ tsp each, baking powder and salt
1 1/4 cup buttermilk
1 egg

Heat butter and add onion. Saute until onion is tender. Stir all remaining ingredients together and stir in onions. Divide evenly into 12 greased muffin tins and bake at 375 for about 20 minutes or until brown. Remove from pan and serve warm.

Sunny Pull-Apart Coffee Cake
1/4 cup sugar
1/4 cup nuts (walnuts, almonds or pecans all work well)
2 tsp grated lemon zest
2 TBSP butter melted
1 12 oz pkg flaky biscuits

Line bottom of an 8 or 9" cake pan with waxed paper. In a bowl, mix all ingredients except biscuits. Mix well. Separate dough into 10 biscuits and cut each into quarters. Place biscuits in sugar mixture and toss to coat completely. Arrange in a single layer in prepared pan. Sprinkle any remaining sugar mixture on top of biscuits. Bake in a preheated 375 deg oven about 20 to 25 minutes or until brown. Run knife around sides of pan to loosen, and invert coffee cake on a serving plate. Remove pan and waxed paper. Serve warm. Pull out pieces to serve.

Sausage and Grits Casserole
2 lbs mild pork sausage
4 cups water
1 1/4 cups quick cooking grits
4 cups shredded sharp cheddar cheese
1 cup milk
1/8 tsp garlic powder
4 large eggs, beaten
paprika (optional)

Brown sausage, crumble, drain, and set aside. Cook grits in water according to package. Stir cheese and next two ingredients into grits, until cheese is melted. Add eggs and sausage, stirring well. Place in a 9"X13" greased pan. Bake 1 hour at 350 degrees. Let stand 5 minutes before serving.

Sweet Potato Biscuits
    2 cups flour
    2 tsp baking powder
    ½ tsp baking soda
    1 tsp salt
    1 tsp sugar
    12 TBSP cold butter
    1 cup mashed roasted sweet potatoes
    ½ cup ground pecans
    1/3 cup half and half

Preheat oven to 450 deg. Grease a baking sheet. In a mixing bowl, combine the flour, baking powder, baking soda, salt, and sugar together. Add the butter, and with you hands, work the butter into the flour mixture until the mixture resembles a coarse cornmeal. Stir in the sweet potatoes and pecans. Add the half and half a little bit at a time until a soft dough forms. Lightly flour a surface, place the dough onto the surface and dust the top with flour. Lightly press the dough out to ½ inch thickness. Using a 2 inch biscuit cutter, cut the dough into rounds. Place the biscuits on the greased baking sheet and bake for 15 minutes or until the biscuits are a golden brown.

Biscuits with Ham and Cheese
    3 cups self rising flour
    1 ½ to 1 3/4 cups milk
    1/3 cup cooking oil
    1 cup chopped country ham, cooked
    1 cup cheddar cheese, grated

Mix the flour, milk, and cooking oil to make a batter that will just hold its shape. Stir in cheese and country ham. Drop by teaspoonfuls onto a lightly greased baking sheet. Bake at 400 deg until brown (about 12 to 15 minutes). Serve hot.

Light Cinnamon French Toast
Matthew Hope   Clinton, Tn.   Age 9
    1/4 cup fat free egg substitute
    1 tsp milk
    1/4 tsp cinnamon

Mix all ingredients. Soak two slices of reduced calorie bread in mixture. In a nonstick pan, sprayed with cooking oil spray, cook toast until done. Sprinkle top with Splenda and cinnamon or light syrup.

Bread Pudding Pancakes

    3/4 cup self rising flour
    2 TBSP sugar
    7 oz (about 7 slices) white bread with crust trimmed
    2 cups whole milk
    2 large eggs, lightly beaten
    3 TBSP butter, melted
    butter (or oil) for frying
    syrup

Place bread in a large bowl with milk. Let stand about 15 minutes or until bread starts to fall apart. Add flour, eggs, and melted butter and blend. Let batter stand an additional 15 minutes. Drop batter by 1/4 cupsful into nonstick skillet which has been buttered. Cook until bubbles form on top and edges are brown. Turn and cook on other side. Transfer finished pancakes to a baking sheet and keep warm until all are cooked. Serve with syrup.

Green Eggs and Spam Quiche

SPAM Kid Chef of the Year Recipe competition   Peter Shankles, age 13 1st Place

    1 (12 oz) can SPAM, diced
    1 cup shredded Gruyere or cheddar cheese, divided use
    3 large eggs, lightly beaten
    1 ½ cups half and half
    3 TBSP refrigerated, prepared pesto
    1 tsp dry mustard
    1/4 tsp salt
    1/4 tsp ground black pepper
    6 slices white and/or whole wheat bread, toasted and edges trimmed if desired
    fresh basil leaves, for garnish

Preheat oven to 350 deg. Grease six 6 oz custard cups. Divide the cubed SPAM and cheese evenly among the cups. In a medium bowl, combine eggs, cream, pesto, dry mustard, salt, and pepper. Beat until well blended and pour over spam and cheese in the custard cups. Place custard cups in a 13x9x2" baking pan on an oven rack. Pour boiling water around the cups in the pan to a depth of 1 inch. Bake in a preheated 325 deg oven and bake for 18 to 22 minutes or until the filling is slightly puffed and the top is golden brown. A thin knife blade inserted near the center should come out clean. Run a thin knife blade around the edges to loosen. Cool on a wire rack for 3 to 5 minutes. Invert quiches onto toasted bread slices and garnish with fresh basil leaves. Yields 6 servings.

Spam Muffins

SPAM Kid Chef of the Year competition Jonathan Shankles (age 8) 2nd place

    2 cups self-rising cornmeal mix
    3 TBSP sugar

1 cup grated cheddar cheese
½ cup sour cream
3/4 cup milk
2 TBSP prepared yellow mustard
4 TBSP butter, melted and cooled
2 eggs
1 12 oz can SPAM

Preheat oven to 400 deg. Grease muffin pans or line with paper muffin liners for 18 muffins. In a large bowl, mix together cornmeal mix, sugar, and grated cheese. In a medium bowl, combine sour cream, milk, mustard, butter, and eggs; beat well. Add to dry ingredients along with diced SPAM and stir gently until just blended. Spoon into prepared muffin pan and bake in preheated oven for 18 to 20 minutes, or until a toothpick inserted into muffins comes out clean. Yields 18 muffins.

Country Ham Scramble
½ lb country ham, chopped (I use the ham seasoning pieces)
½ cup green onions, sliced
2 tsp cooking oil
1 large can white hominy, drained
1 can cream of celery soup
½ cup milk
1 cup grated cheddar cheese

In a heavy skillet, heat the oil, and cook the chopped country ham, stirring, until it starts to brown. Add the green onion and cook about a minute more. Stir in the drained hominy and allow to heat through. Stir in the celery soup and milk and bring back to a boil. Stir in the cheese and allow to melt. Serve hot.

Grits Deluxe from Holiday Hostess
Published by the Knoxville Utilities Board (undated)
1 ½ quarts boiling water
1 ½ cups grits
2 tsp salt
2 tsp seasoned salt
dash tabasco
½ cup butter
1 lb American cheese, grated
3 eggs, lightly beaten

Preheat oven to 300 deg. Grease 9x13" baking dish. In large sauce pan, combine water and grits. Cook over medium heat, stirring frequently for 20 minutes. Remove from heat; stir in all remaining ingredients except eggs. Stir until blended. Stir in eggs, and mix well. Pour into pan and bake in preheated oven for 1 hour.

Hot Tomato Grits
2 sliced bacon, chopped
2 14 ½ oz cans chicken broth
½ tsp salt
1 cup quick cooking grits
2 large, ripe Grainger County tomatoes, peeled and chopped
2 TBSP canned chopped green chilies
1 cup cheddar cheese, grated

Cook bacon in a large heavy saucepan until crisp. Add broth and salt, and bring to a boil. Stir in grits, tomatoes, and chilies. Return to a boil, stirring constantly. Reduce heat and allow to simmer about 15 minutes stirring often. Add cheese and stir to mix. Allow to cook until cheese melts and serve hot.

Toad In the Hole
1 TBSP butter
1 lb well flavored link sausages
4 oz flour
1 egg
300 ml milk (about 1 1/4 cup)

Preheat oven to 425 deg (220 C). Place butter and sausages in a 9x13" roasting tin. Cook for 10 minutes (or longer if you like your bangers very well done). Sift the flour into a bowl. Break in egg. Gradually add half the milk, beating to form a smooth batter. Pour in remaining milk, and beat until quite smooth. Alternatively, add the flour, milk and egg to the liquidizer (blender) and blend until smooth. Pour the batter into the hot pan with the sausages and continue to bake for 40 to 45 minutes or until the batter is well risen and golden. This traditional dish is just Yorkshire Pudding with Sausages. It is a delight for a late breakfast or a summer supper.

Sunday Morning Souffle
1 lb sausage
1 medium onion, chopped
6 cups bread, cubed
2 cups cheddar cheese, grated
6 eggs
3 cups milk
½ cup Parmesan cheese

Fry the sausage and onion together until the sausage is browned. Drain. Toss sausage with the bread and cheese. Turn into a 9x13" dish which has been sprayed with cooking oil spray. Beat together eggs and milk and pour evenly over the sausage mixture. Sprinkle with the Parmesan cheese. Cover with plastic wrap and refrigerate for several hours or overnight. Remove plastic, and place in a preheated 350 deg oven

and bake about 45 minutes or until puffed and brown. Serve immediately.
This dish has an almost infinite number of variations. For example, you may use ham instead of the sausage. Or you can use half sausage and half ground beef. With either ham or sausage, it is very nice to add a couple of peeled and thinly sliced apples. For the cheese, it is nice to use half cheddar and half processed cheese like Velveeta.

Chapter 6
Entrees

<u>Beef:</u>

Autumn Gold Pot Roast

1/4 cup all-purpose flour
1 teaspoon salt
1/4 teaspoon pepper
1 (4-pound) chuck roast
2 tablespoons vegetable oil
3/4 cup water
½ teaspoon dried oregano
3/4 teaspoon celery seed
1 1/4 cups water
1 (6-ounce) can frozen concentrated orange juice
4 sweet potatoes, peeled
4 onions, sliced
1 tablespoon packed brown sugar

Combine flour, salt, and pepper. Dredge a chuck roast in the flour mixture, reserving the rest of the flour mixture. Brown the chuck roast on all sides in oil. Combine 3/4 cup water, oregano, and celery seed; pour over the roast. Cover and cook at 325 deg for 2 hours. Combine 1 1/4 cups water and ½ cup frozen concentrated orange juice (undiluted); pour over the roast. Add peeled sweet potatoes and sliced onions. Cover and continue to cook at 325 deg for 1 hour, or until the roast and vegetables are tender. Remove the roast and vegetables to a serving platter and keep warm. Combine the remaining flour mixture, the remaining orange juice concentrate, and brown sugar; mix well. Cook over medium heat, stirring constantly, until thickened. Serve with the roast. Makes 6 servings.

Oven Barbecued Pot Roast

1 lean chuck roast, about 3 pounds
1 can (10 1/2 ounces) condensed cream of mushroom soup
1 envelope Lipton onion soup mix.

<u>Barbecue Sauce:</u>

1 cup ketchup
2 TBSP prepared mustard
1/4 cup cider vinegar

1/3 cup dark brown sugar
2 tsp Worcestershire sauce
1/2 tsp salt
1/4 tsp Tabasco sauce

Place a large double thickness of heavy-duty foil in a 9x13x2-inch pan -- enough foil to cover and seal foil around the chuck roast. Place chuck roast on foil in pan. Mix the cream of mushroom soup, onion soup mix, and barbecue sauce (directions below) together. Pour over meat. Seal foil tightly, leaving about 1" clearance between meat and foil. Bake chuck roast for 2 1/2 to 3 hours, or until meat is very tender. Let chuck roast sit for 10 minutes before slicing. Serve with the pan drippings over noodles.

Barbecue Sauce: Combine all ingredients in a small pan and bring to a boil; reduce heat and simmer for 2 to 3 minutes.

All Day Crock Pot Delight

2-3 lb boneless chuck, cut into 1 inch cubes
½ cup flour
1/4 cup cooking oil
1 onion, sliced
8 oz mushrooms, sliced
1 tsp salt
1/4 tsp pepper
1 clove garlic, minced
12 to 16 oz beer
1/4 cup flour (optional)

Coat beef cubes with the ½ cup flour. Brown in hot oil. Drain off excess fat. In Crock Pot, combine browned meat with onion, mushrooms, salt, pepper, garlic, and beer. Cover and cook on low 5-7 hours (all day) until meat is tender. If you wish the gravy to thicken, turn control to high. Dissolve remaining 1/4 cup flour in small amount of water. Stir into meat mixture, cook on high 30-40 minutes. Serve with rice and salad.

Cheeseburger Pie

3/4 lb ground beef
½ onion, chopped
1-1/2 slices bread, cubed
½ cup Original Ragu sauce
salt, pepper and oregano to taste
1 egg
½ cup milk
1 cup cheddar cheese, shredded
9" deep dish pie shell, unbaked

Saute beef and onions in butter. Add Ragu, bread and seasonings. Pour into 9 inch unbaked pie shell. Beat egg, add milk, and grated cheddar cheese. Spread over beef mixture. Bake ½ hour at 350 F.

Parmesan Round Steak
    1 ½ pounds round steak
    1 egg, beaten
    1/3 cup milk
    ½ cup fine dry bread crumbs
    1 tsp salt
    1/8 tsp pepper
    3 TBSP cooking oil
    ½ cup water
    1/4 tsp Oregano
    1/4 cup Parmesan cheese
    1/4 tsp salt
    1/4 tsp paprika
    3 onions, peeled, quartered and sliced thin

Cut steak into 6 serving-size pieces. Pound to ½-inch thickness. combine egg and milk. Mix bread crumbs, salt and pepper. Dip steaks in egg mixture; dredge in seasoned crumbs. Brown meat in cooking oil and remove to a baking dish in a single layer. Add water. Sprinkle oregano on steaks. Place 2 tsps Parmesan cheese on each steak. Combine salt and paprika. Sprinkle onions with salt mixture and add to meat. Cover tightly and bake at 325° for 1 1/4 to 1 ½ hours or until meat is tender. Serves 6.

Italian Meatballs
Prepared with Meatball Magic
    2 ½ lbs ground beef
    2 eggs
    1/8 cup dry minced garlic
    1/4 cup dry parsley
    1/4 cup water
    ½ cup Italian breadcrumbs
    1 medium onion, chopped fine

In a bowl, combine all ingredients and knead together. When all mixed, thoroughly shape into 2" meatballs. Place meatballs on baking sheet. Preheat oven to 425 deg and bake for 20 to 25 minutes or until firm. Take out of oven and simmer in your favorite sauce for about 30 to 45 minutes. Serve over spaghetti with Parmesan cheese. Raw meatballs can also be put into your favorite sauce and simmered for about 2 to 2 ½ hours or until meatballs are cooked through.
Walter's note: If you intend to use this alternative method of cooking (which is easier), be sure to use very lean ground beef or your sauce will be greasy.

Easy Enchilada Casserole
    1 pound ground beef
    1 cup chopped onion
    2 cloves garlic, finely chopped
    1 16 oz jar salsa
    1 16 oz can refried beans
    1 10 oz can enchilada sauce
    ½ cup sliced ripe olives
    10 6 inch corn tortillas, sliced in half, divided
    2 cups shredded Mexican cheese blend, divided
    sliced green onions

Preheat oven to 375 degrees. Cook beef, onion and garlic in large skillet until beef is browned; drain. Stir in salsa, beans, enchilada sauce, and olives. Bring to a boil. Reduce heat to low; cook, stirring frequently, for 5 to 6 minutes.   Layer half of corn tortillas on bottom of greased 13x9" baking dish. Cover with half of meat sauce. Sprinkle with 1 cup cheese. Repeat layers. Bake, covered, for 20 minutes. Remove cover; bake for additional 5 minutes or until bubbly and cheese is melted. Sprinkle with green onions
to serve.

Slow Cooker Corned Beef
    1 3 to 5 lb corned beef brisket
    3 to 4 potatoes, peeled and quartered
    2 onions, peeled and quartered
    3 to 4 carrots, peeled and cut into chunks
    1 small head cabbage, quartered
    2 cups water

Place potatoes, onions, and carrots in slow cooker. Lay corned beef on top of them and sprinkle with the spices if a spice package is included with your corned beef. Pour water over. Place cover on pot and cook on low for 6 to 8 hours. Open and lay cabbage wedges on top. Cover again and cook an additional 2 hours. Salt the cabbage lightly. Serve hot.
I like to serve this in a large soup plate and spoon the great broth that will have formed over it. It is terrific with Irish Soda bread.

Nearly Instant Noodle Stove Top Casserole
    1 lb lean ground beef
    1 onion, chopped
    1 can green peas, drained
    1 can whole kernel corn, drained
    1 can condensed tomato soup
    2 cups water
    2 pkg beef flavored ramen noodles

In a large pot cook beef and onion over high heat until beef has lost all pink color and onion is translucent. Stir in peas, corn, and tomato soup and bring to a full boil. Stir in water and bring back to a boil. Break up noodles by laying the package on the counter and hitting it a couple of times. Stir in noodles and contents of flavor package. Bring back to a boil and cook about 3 minutes. Turn off, remove from heat, cover, and allow to stand about 5 minutes before serving.

Note that I did not give a size for the cans of peas and corn. I use 15 oz cans, but if you like less use smaller cans, more use larger cans. By the way, if you do not like peas and corn use carrots, or green beans, or something you do like. I have given you a starting point. You can fill in the blanks. Oh, and this will double or triple nicely.

Stir Fry Beef and Vegetables
Executive Chef Keith Andreasen   Harrah's Cherokee Casino
        12 oz small-diced beef (sirloin)
        ½ cup bias cut Zucchini
        ½ cup bias cut yellow squash
        ½ cup sliced mushrooms
        ½ cup sliced carrots
        ½ cup all purpose flour
        ½ cup soy sauce
        1/4 cup canola oil

Toss beef in flour. Heat skillet with oil. Blanch carrots. When oil in skillet is hot, toss in beef. When beef is 3/4 cooked add vegetables. Add soy sauce to beef and vegetables when they are cooked to taste. Sauce will thicken and glaze beef and vegetables. Serve with steamed white rice.

Quick Cheesy Chili and Rice Skillet
        1 lb lean ground beef
        1 can (15 ounces) chili with beans
        1 can (14-1/2 ounces) diced tomatoes, undrained
        1 cup water
        2 cups instant white rice, uncooked
        ½ lb pasteurized cheese (Like Cheezy Does it or Velveeta), cut up

Brown meat in large pot on medium-high heat; drain. Add chili, tomatoes and water to skillet; stir. Bring to boil. Stir in rice and cheese; cover. Remove from heat. Let stand 5 minutes. Stir until cheese is melted and serve hot.

This is a fairly small recipe which will serve four. It doubles easily.

Ground Beef and Rice Casserole
        1 lb lean ground beef
        1 onion, chopped

2 TBSP soy sauce
1 can mushroom soup
1 cup uncooked Uncle Ben's converted rice
1 can beef broth
salt and pepper to taste

In a heavy skillet with a cover, brown the ground beef and onion until no red remains. Stir in soy sauce, soup, and rice. Add beef broth and bring to a boil. Reduce heat to a simmer, cover pan, and allow to cook about 20 minutes. Turn off heat and allow to stand 5 minutes before serving.

Grilled Steak with Mango Salsa
A Southern Living Recipe from Dollywood
1 lb top round steak cut 3/4 inch thick
salt and pepper
4 cups hot cooked couscous
2 cups sugar snap peas, steamed

Marinade:
1/4 cup lime juice
2 TBSP green onions, minced
2 TBSP water
2 tsp fresh ginger, minced
2 cloves garlic, minced
1/4 tsp salt

Mango Salsa:

1 to 1 ½ cups finely diced fresh mango
2 TBSP minced green onion
1 TBSP lime juice
1 TBSP cilantro, minced
1 Serrano or red jalapeno pepper, seeded and finely chopped

Combine marinade ingredients. Place beef steak and marinade in a plastic bag. Turn to coat. Place bag in refrigerator for at least 6 hours or even overnight, turning occasionally. Just before grilling steak, combine salsa ingredients in medium bowl. Cover and refrigerate until ready to serve. Remove steak from marinade; discard marinade. Place steak on grid over medium, ash-covered coals. Grill covered about 19 to 24 minutes for medium rare doneness, turning occasionally. Carve steak into thin slices across the grain. Season with salt and pepper as desired. Serve with salsa, couscous, and sugar snap peas.

All American Meat Loaf
1 ½ lb lean ground beef

1 10 oz pkg chopped frozen spinach, thawed and squeezed dry
1 cup dry bread crumbs
2 eggs
3 TBSP soy sauce
1 can cream of mushroom soup
½ tsp each salt and pepper

Mix all ingredients thoroughly and shape into a loaf. Place in a flat pan which has been sprayed with cooking oil spray. Bake in a 350 deg oven about 1 hour or until brown and juices run clear. I often cut two potatoes in half and place in each corner of the pan with the meat loaf. You may want to spray the cut surface of the potato lightly with cooking oil spray and sprinkle lightly with salt and pepper.

Slow Cooker Lasagna
From the good looking Bigelows of Crossville
1 lb ground beef
1 onion, chopped
1/8 tsp garlic powder
2 15 oz cans tomato sauce
1 6 oz can tomato paste
1 ½ tsp salt
1 tsp dried oregano
1 12 oz carton cottage cheese
½ cup Parmesan cheese, grated
12 oz Mozzarella cheese, shredded
12 oz lasagna noodles, uncooked (look for the kind which says it does not need to be precooked)

Brown ground beef and onion in a skillet. Drain. Add garlic powder, tomato sauce, tomato paste, salt, and oregano. Cook until hot through. Mix all cheeses. Spoon a layer of meat sauce onto bottom of slow cooker. Cover with a double layer of uncooked lasagna noodles (break to fit) and top with a layer of cheeses. Repeat with sauce, noodles and cheeses until all used up. Cover and cook on low for 6 to 8 hours. Great with Garlic Rolls.

By the way, I have it on good authority that when Mrs. Bigelow doesn't have time to make the meat sauce, she uses a canned sauce like Ragu. But don't tell anyone I told you.

Easy Pasta Skillet
Diana Brock   Cumberland Gap
1 lb ground beef
3 cups mostaccioli (or other similar pasta), uncooked
1 28 oz jar spaghetti sauce
1 8 oz pkg mozzarella cheese, shredded

½ cup grated Parmesan cheese

Brown meat in a large skillet with a lid. Drain. Add 2 ½ cups water. Bring to a boil and stir in pasta. Reduce heat to maintain a simmer. Cover and allow to cook about 15 minutes or until pasta is tender. Stir in spaghetti sauce and 1 cup of mozzarella cheese. Sprinkle with remaining cheese. Cover and cook about 3 minutes or until cheese is melted.

Meat Balls from Mary Dunbar's Favorite Recipes
Published by the Jewel T company (undated but probably from the 1930's based on pictures)
>1 lb ground steak (I would suggest Food City's 93/7 ground beef)
>½ cup uncooked rice
>1 green pepper, chopped
>1 onion, chopped
>1 tsp salt
>½ tsp pepper
>flour
>tomatoes   (The recipe did not specify how many, but I use two 15 oz cans of diced tomatoes)

Mix steak, rice, green pepper, onion, salt and pepper. Shape in balls the size of a walnut (about 1 ½ inch). Roll in flour. Bring tomatoes to a boil. Drop in meat balls. Reduce heat and cook one hour without stirring.

Spicy Steak
>1/4 cup flour
>1 tsp salt
>1/4 tsp pepper
>2 pounds round steak -- ½-inch thick
>3 TBSP shortening
>1 cup ketchup
>½ cup water
>1 medium onion -- thinly sliced
>1 lemon -- thinly sliced
>1 green pepper -- sliced
>5 whole cloves

Combine flour, salt and pepper; pound into steak. Melt shortening in a skillet and brown steak. Place in baking dish. Blend ketchup and water; pour around steak and add onion, lemon, green pepper, and cloves. Cover with aluminum foil; place on lower rack of oven. Bake at 350 degrees for about 1 hour.
Serves 6 to 8.

Herbed Round Steak In Slow Cooker

2 Pounds Round Steak
1 TBSP cooking oil
1 Large onion, sliced
2 or 3 large potatoes, peeled and sliced
½ cup small carrots or regular carrots, peeled and cut into chunks
1 Can cream of celery soup--10-3/4 oz. size
1 Can cream of broccoli soup--10-3/4 oz. size
1 tsp dried oregano
1 tsp dried parsley
1 tsp garlic powder
1 TBSP Worcestershire sauce
½ Cup red or white wine   (Or beef stock)
3/4 tsp salt
½ tsp pepper

Trim all the fat that you can off the steak. Cut meat into serving size portions. In a skillet brown meat in hot oil. Place sliced onion and potatoes in bottom of a 4 quart slow cooker. Sprinkle carrots over top.   Place browned meat on top of the vegetables. In a bowl, combine remaining ingredients; pour over meat. Cook on HIGH setting for 5 hours or LOW for 8 to 9 hours.

Tennessee Beef
        2 cups Tennessee Hickory Jack Daniel's Grilling Sauce
        2 TBSP oil
        1 brisket of beef (about 5 lbs.)
        1 tsp dry mustard
        1 tsp garlic powder
        1 tsp paprika
        1 tsp salt

Combine the salt and spices in a small bowl and mix well. Rub this into the brisket. Heat the oil in a heavy pan with a tight fitting lid. Sear the brisket in the oil, brushing with the Tennessee Hickory Jack Daniel's Grilling Sauce while browning. Reserve remaining sauce.   Cover the pan and place in a preheated 325 deg oven. Bake about 3 ½ hours until fork tender. Remove the pan from the oven, and, using 2 forks, pull the meat apart in the pan juices, shredding it coarsely. Heat the remaining Tennessee Hickory Jack Daniel's Grilling Sauce to a boil. Mound the shredded beef onto a platter and spoon the hot sauce over the meat. This is a fine tailgating recipe.

Spaghetti Casserole
Anita G. Hawkins   Oak Ridge
        1 lb hamburger
        1 cup chopped onion
        1 15 oz tomato sauce
        1 ½ cups water

1 ½ tsp salt
¼ tsp pepper
1 tsp chili powder
8 oz spaghetti – broken, cooked, & drained
1 cup shredded cheese

Lightly brown hamburger in skillet. Add onions, cook until tender. Stir in sauce, water, and seasonings. Simmer 25 minutes. Place half the spaghetti in a 2 quart casserole; cover with half the sauce, then half the cheese. Repeat layers. Bake at 350 degrees for 30 minutes.

Southwestern Beef Stew
1 ½ to 2 lbs beef stew cut into small pieces
2 cans hominy, drained
1 medium onion, chopped
1 1.25 oz taco seasoning mix
1 15.25 oz can whole kernel corn, drained
1 14.5 oz can diced tomato, undrained
1 4.5 oz can diced green chilies
1 cup water

Combine all ingredients in a large slow cooker. Stir to mix. Cover and cook on low for 10 to 12 hours before serving.

Oven Barbecued Pot Roast
1 lean chuck roast, about 3 pounds
1 can (10 ½ ounces) condensed cream of mushroom soup
1 envelope Lipton onion soup mix.

Barbecue Sauce:
1 cup ketchup
2 TBSP prepared mustard
1/4 cup cider vinegar
1/3 cup dark brown sugar
2 tsp Worcestershire sauce
½ tsp salt
1/4 tsp Tabasco sauce

Place a large double thickness of heavy-duty foil in a 9x13x2-inch pan -- enough foil to cover and seal foil around the chuck roast. Place chuck roast on foil in pan. Mix the cream of mushroom soup, onion soup mix, and barbecue sauce (directions below) together. Pour over meat. Seal foil tightly, leaving about 1" clearance between meat and foil. Bake chuck roast for 2 ½ to 3 hours at 300 deg, or until meat is very tender. Let chuck roast sit for 10 minutes before slicing. Serve with the pan drippings over noodles.

Slow Cooker Nearly Irish Stew
>2 Lbs. Stewing beef , cubed
>1 envelope dry onion soup mix
>2 cans tomato soup
>1 soup can water
>1 tsp salt
>½ tsp pepper
>2 cups diced carrots
>2 cups diced potatoes
>1 cup diced parsnips (optional)

Place all ingredients in a slow cooker and stir to mix. Cook on low about 8 hours or until vegetables are tender. If you wish, you may add a 10 oz pkg of frozen peas and 1/4 cup of water to the stew about 1 hour before the stew is finished.

Tomato Free Meat Loaf
>1 ½ lbs lean ground beef
>1 pkg dry onion soup mix
>1 cup dry bread crumbs
>2 eggs
>4 TBSP soy sauce

Blend all ingredients together and shape into a loaf. Place in a 5x7" dish which has been sprayed with cooking oil spray. Bake at 350 deg about 45 minutes or until brown and juices run clear. Remove from pan and allow to cool before slicing to serve.

If you wish, potatoes roast quite nicely if you wash and quarter them. Spray lightly with cooking oil spray and sprinkle with salt and pepper. Place around meat loaf and allow to cook. Remove immediately when the meat loaf is finished.

Cheesy Sloppy Joe's
>2 lbs lean ground beef
>½ cup ketchup
>2 tsp onion salt
>2 tsp garlic powder
>1 lb Cheezy Does It (or other Velveeta type) cheese
>hamburger buns

Brown the ground beef and drain. Stir in the ketchup and the onion and garlic. Pour into a slow cooker. Cut the cheese into cubes and sprinkle it over the top. Cook on low for 3 to 4 hours. Stir thoroughly and serve on buns. While this is good on buns, it can also be made into a main dish casserole by stirring in 8 oz of macaroni which has been cooked according to package directions. You may stir in a drained can of whole kernel corn if you wish. Finally, if you want to turn this into a mild spaghetti sauce, add 2 tsp dry oregano and a 8 oz can of tomato sauce and a cup of tomato juice. Cook as described above and serve over cooked spaghetti sprinkled with Parmesan cheese.

Coca Cola Roast
    1 (3 to 4 pound) boneless beef roast
    1 (12-ounce) can of Coca Cola
    1 to 2 garlic cloves, minced
    ½ cup catsup
    1 (1.5-ounce) package dry onion soup mix

Place beef in a slow cooker. Pour cola over the roast. Cut slits in roast and placing the minced garlic into the slits. Pour the catsup over the roast, and sprinkle the onion soup mix on top of the catsup. Cover and cook on low for 7 to 8 hours.

Jiffy Meat Loaf
Janie Robinson   Knoxville
    11/2 lb ground beef
    1 can Spanish rice
    1 egg
    1 onion, chopped fine (or 1 TBSP onion powder)

Combine ingredients, shape into loaf, and bake in 325 deg. oven for 1 hour. This meat loaf is very moist and flavorful. If desired, top with a mixture of ½ cup catsup and ½ cup light karo syrup during last 15 minutes of baking.

Sweet and Savory Meat Loaf
    3 lbs extra lean ground beef
    1 stack saltine crackers, crushed
    2 eggs
    1 tsp salt
    1 tsp black pepper
    1 medium onion, chopped
    1 tsp Worcestershire sauce
    2 8 oz cans tomato sauce, divided
    ½ cup brown sugar

In a large bowl, mix the first 8 ingredients well (using only one can of tomato sauce). Spray a 9x13" baking dish with cooking oil spray. Shape meat to create two equal loaves and place side by side in the baking pan. Mix the remaining can of tomato sauce with ½ cup brown sugar, and heat until sugar dissolves. Spread all over the meat loaves covering well. Bake for about one hour and thirty min at 350 deg. Top should be brown and juices should run clear if pierced with a thin knife.

Crock Pot Chili
    2 lbs ground beef

½ cup chopped celery
½ cup chopped mushrooms
1 medium onion, chopped
3 to 4 TBSP chili powder
1 tsp garlic powder
1 tsp salt
1 can diced tomatoes (Mexican style is nice)
8 oz tomato sauce
2 15 ½ oz cans kidney beans

Brown beef, drain fat & put in Crock Pot. Add rest of ingredients, except kidney beans. Cook on low 8-10 hours or on high for 5-6 hours.   Add beans about 1 ½ hours before you serve.

Savory Swiss Steak - Low Carbohydrate Recipe
3 TBSP oil
2 lbs round steak
1/4 cup Atkin's bake mix
1 pkg dry onion soup mix
½ tsp garlic powder
8 oz can Hunt's tomato sauce
1/4 cup water plus more if needed

Preheat oven to 325. Heat oil in heavy fry pan. Pound steak on both sides with heavy meat mallet, and cut into serving size pieces. Combine bake mix and garlic and rub into meat pieces. Fry in hot oil til browned on all sides. Layer in 13x9x2 baking dish and sprinkle soup mix over meat. Mix tomato sauce and 1/4 cup water and pour over all. Cover tightly with foil. Bake 2-3 hours til tender. Check each hour, may need to add water.

Mighty Mexican Meal in a Minute
1 16 oz jar taco sauce
1 12 oz can flaky biscuits (10 biscuit size)
2 cups Mexican cheese blend
1 2 1/4 oz can sliced ripe olives, drained
½ lb lean ground beef
1 4 oz can chopped green chilies
½ cup onion, chopped
1 4 oz jar mushroom stems and pieces, drained

Spray a 9x13" baking dish with cooking oil spray. Spread ½ of taco sauce in bottom of pan. Cut biscuits into quarters and spread evenly over taco sauce. Stir to coat. In a skillet, combine ground beef and onions and cook, stirring until beef is no longer pink. Drain any excess fat. Stir in green chilies, remaining taco sauce, black olives and mushrooms. Spread evenly over biscuits. Sprinkle cheese over top. Bake at 400 deg about 15 to 20 minutes or until brown and bubbly. Serve hot.

Beef Stroganoff
    2 TBSP vegetable oil
    1 lb beef sirloin, cut into 2x1x1/8" strips
    kosher salt and freshly ground black pepper
    6 TBSP unsalted butter
    12 oz button mushrooms, quartered
    1 medium yellow onion, sliced thin
    1 TBSP tomato paste
    2 TBSP all purpose flour
    2 cups beef broth, homemade or canned
    1/4 cup sour cream
    2 tsp Dijon mustard
    2 tsp lemon juice
    1 TBSP chopped flat leaf parsley leaves

Noodles:
    kosher salt
    12 oz pkg wide egg noodles
    2 TBSP butter
    fresh ground black pepper

Preheat a large skillet over medium heat for 3 to 4 minutes. Raise the heat to high, and heat 1 TBSP oil. Season half the beef with salt and pepper. Add to the skillet, arranging it in a single layer and saute, without stirring, until well browned and pinkish inside. About 1 to 2 minutes. (It is key to only partially cook the meat at this stage, since it will be finished cooking later in the sauce.) Transfer to a large plate and set aside. Repeat with the remaining oil and beef. Discard any excess oil. Return the skillet to medium high heat. Melt 2 TBSP butter and when the foaming begins to subside, add the mushrooms and cook, stirring occasionally, until well browned, about 7 minutes. Season with salt and pepper to taste. Using a slotted spoon, transfer the mushrooms to the plate with the beef. Heat 4 TBSP butter and just as the foaming begins to subside, add the onion and cook, stirring, until lightly caramelized, about 5 minutes. Add the tomato paste and cook, stirring, until lightly browned, about 1 minute more. Whisk in the flour and cook, stirring, for 1 minute. Pour in the beef broth and whisking constantly, bring to a full boil. Remove from the heat. Whisk in the sour cream, mustard, lemon juice and season with pepper to taste. Set the sauce aside covered. Bring a large pot of water to a boil, salt generously, and cook the noodles until tender but not mushy. Drain and transfer to a large bowl. Toss with the butter and season with pepper to taste. Add the beef and any juices, mushrooms, and parsley to the sauce and reheat over medium heat until just hot. DO NOT BOIL. Divide the noodles among 4 plate and top with the stroganoff. Serve immediately.

Slow Cooker Christmas Chili

1 lb lean ground beef
1 lb mild country sausage
1 onion, chopped
2 15 oz cans diced tomatoes (seasoned for chili ones work nicely)
1 8 oz can tomato sauce
2 tsp ground cumin
3 TBSP chili powder
1 15 oz cans white beans, undrained
1 10 oz cans pinto beans, undrained
sour cream
shredded cheddar cheese
sliced green onions

Cook ground beef, sausage, and onion, breaking up the meat. Drain. Place into a slow cooker with all remaining ingredients except sour cream, cheese, and green onions. Cover and cook on low heat for 8 to 10 hours. Serve hot with sour cream, cheese, and green onions.

Stuffed Flank Steak
This comes from "Quick Cooking" magazine and makes a great company dinner right from the slow cooker. And besides, flank steak is cheap.
1 beef flank steak (about 2 lbs)
1 medium onion, chopped fine
1 garlic clove, minced
1 TBSP butter
1 ½ cups soft bread crumbs (about 3 slices, toasted and broken into crumbs)
½ cup fresh mushrooms, chopped
1/4 cup parsley, minced
1 egg
3/4 tsp rubbed sage
½ tsp salt
1/4 tsp pepper
½ cup beef broth (canned will work fine)
2 tsp cornstarch
2 TBSP water

Use the back of heavy knife or a meat mallet to flatten steak to ½ inch thickness. Set aside. In a nonstick skillet, saute onion and garlic in butter until tender. Add bread crumbs, mushrooms, parsley, egg, sage, salt, and pepper. Mix well. Spread over steak to within 1 inch of edge. Roll up jelly roll style from long edge. Tie with kitchen string. Place in a slow cooker. Add beef broth. Cover and cook on low for 8 to 10 hours. Remove meat to a platter and keep warm. Pour cooking juices into a small pan and skim off as much fat as possible. Combine cornstarch and water until smooth and stir into juices. Bring to a boil, stirring constantly. Cook and stir until thick. Remove string and slice steak and serve with gravy.

Quick Porcupine Meatballs
    1 ½ lbs lean ground beef
    1 pkg Beef Rice-a-roni
    1 tsp salt
    2 tsp black pepper
    2 cups water

Thoroughly mix the ground beef with the rice and pasta from the rice-a-roni. Shape into 1" meat balls. Arrange in a pot with a tight fitting lid. Sprinkle on the salt, pepper, and the beef flavor pack from the rice-a-roni. Pour the two cups water over. Bring to a full boil. Reduce heat and simmer for about 30 minutes or until the liquid is almost absorbed and is thick. Serve hot.

Calico Chili
    2 lbs lean ground beef
    1 medium onion, chopped
    2 cans Food Club Mexican Style diced tomatoes
    1 can each, great Northern, Pinto, and black beans, undrained
    4 to 6 TBSP chili powder
    1 TBSP cumin
    salt to taste

In a large pan, saute the beef and onion until the onion is translucent. Drain off any excess fat. Add all remaining ingredients. Stir to mix completely. Bring back to a boil, reduce heat, and simmer about 20 minutes to blend flavors. Serve hot with grated cheese, sour cream, and oyster crackers for a nice Christmas antidote.

Slow Cooker Beef Stew
    2 to 2 ½ lbs lean beef cut into cubes
    1 TBSP cooking oil
    2 TBSP soy sauce
    1/4 cup minute tapioca
    3 to 4 potatoes, peeled and cut into large chunks
    3 to 4 onions, peeled and left whole if small or in halves if large
    3 to 4 carrots, peeled and cut into chunks
    1 or 2 parsnips, peeled and cut into chunks (optional)
    2 or 3 ribs celery, washed and cut into chunks (optional)
    1 8 oz can tomato sauce (optional)
    1 can beef or chicken stock

In a heavy skillet, heat the cooking oil and add the beef. Cook hot, stirring, until the beef is brown. Add soy sauce and stir to coat beef. Place in slow cooker. Sprinkle tapioca over beef. Add vegetables. Stir together the tomato sauce and the stock and pour over. Cook on low 10 to 12 hours. Stir to mix before serving.

Beef with Greens and Red Potatoes
    1 pound beef round steak
    1 ½ to 2 tsp Tabasco sauce
    vegetable oil spray
    8 medium red skinned potatoes, halved
    2 cups onions, finely chopped
    2 cups beef broth
    2 large cloves garlic, minced
    1 large carrot, peeled, cut in very thin strips about 2 inches in length
    1 pound (about 2 bunches) mustard greens, collard, or turnip greens, stems
        removed and torn in bite-size pieces

Thinly slice the beef across the grain into long strips 1/8-inch thick. The beef will slice nicely if partially frozen. Thoroughly coat each strip with Tabasco. Spray a large heavy skillet with vegetable oil spray. Preheat pan over high heat. Add meat; cook, stirring, for 4 to 5 minutes. Add potatoes, onion, broth, and garlic. Cook, covered, over medium heat for 20 minutes. Stir in carrots and greens and cook, covered, until carrots are tender, about 15 minutes. Serve with crusty bread or cornbread.

Food City often has beef cut for stir fry. That beef will work nicely in this recipe. Instead of Tabasco, any of the Cajun seasonings will work nicely. Just sprinkle it over the strips of beef and stir to coat. Then proceed as above.

Italian Beef
This recipe was given to us by a former Channel 8 employee Kevin Summers and his wife Linda
    4 lbs very lean beef (chuck or bottom round works well)
    2 pkg onion soup mix
    2 bay leaves
    1 tsp oregano
    1 12 oz jar pepperoncini peppers with juice
    2 cups water

Put the beef in a slow cooker and pour all remaining ingredients over it. Start on high until boiling and turn down to low. Allow to cook overnight. When ready to serve, shred the meat, and mix with the broth to serve on rolls.

San Juan Pueblo Steak
    1/2 cup flour
    1 TBSP chili powder
    1 tsp salt
    2 lbs round steak, 1-inch thick (I suggest you buy this pre tenderized)
    2 TBSP olive oil
    1 clove garlic, minced
    1 onion, minced

1 cup tomato sauce
2 cups water

In a small mixing bowl, combine flour chili powder, and salt. Using the edge of a plate, pound steak and flour mixture. (If you use pre-tenderized steak, simply work the flour mixture into the steak.) In a heavy skillet, heat oil, and sauté garlic and onions for 3 minutes. Remove and set aside. Add the steak to the skillet and brown on both sides. Add the tomato sauce, water, and garlic and onions. Cover and cook over low heat for 1-1/2 hours.

Baked Spareribs with Barbeque Sauce
Favorite Recipes Home Style   Jeanna Gardner
2 lbs pork spareribs (lean)
1 clove garlic minced
3 TBSP vinegar
1 8 oz can tomato sauce
1/3 cup chopped onion
1 ½ tsp chili powder
1 tsp salt
1/4 tsp pepper
½ tsp oregano
½ cup water

Trim excess fat from ribs. Cut into 6 serving portions. Place in baking pan. Combine remaining ingredients; pour over the ribs. Cover and let stand for 15 minutes. Preheat oven to 350 deg. Bake, covered, for 1 ½ hours. Remove cover; baste. Bake ½ hour. Spoon off excess fat before serving.

Chili Layered Casserole
1 large bag original Fritos
4 15 oz cans chili with beans
1 medium onion, chopped
1 lb Cheezy Does It, cubed (or Velveeta)

In a 9x13" pan which has been sprayed with cooking oil spray, pour half of the Fritos. Empty 2 cans of chili evenly over chips. Sprinkle with onions and cheese. Pour on remaining two cans chili and sprinkle remaining chips on top. Bake in a 350 deg oven about 45 minutes or until nicely browned and bubbly in the center. Serve hot.

Company Casserole
Katy Brown   Oak Ridge "Secret City" Celebration
1 lb ground beef
½ cup green onions, sliced
3 TBSP green pepper

2 8 oz cans tomato sauce
½ cup sour cream
1 8 oz pkg cream cheese
1 cup cottage cheese
1 small pkg wide noodles, cooked
2 oz melted butter (optional)

Begin cooking noodles, set aside. Brown ground beef, onions, and green peppers. Add tomato sauce. In separate bowl mix sour cream, cream cheese, and cottage cheese. Layer in 2 quart casserole dish noodles, cheese mixture, then meat. Over this, you may want to pour 2 oz of melted butter. Bake at 350 deg for 30 minutes.

Jalapeno Cornbread Shortcake With Black Bean Chili
Linda Carman, Martha White Cornmeal   (Sometimes called the Cornbread Lady)
Cornbread Shortcake:
        1 egg, beaten
        1 (6 oz.) pkg. Martha White 'Cotton Pickin' or Buttermilk Cornbread Mix
        2/3 cup milk
        ½ cup shredded sharp Cheddar cheese
        1 to 2 tablespoons chopped pickled jalapeno peppers

Chili:
        ½ lb. lean ground beef
        1 ½ cups chunky salsa, divided
        3/4 cup water
        2 tablespoons chili powder
        1 teaspoon ground cumin
        1 (15 oz.) can black beans, drained and rinsed
        Salt to taste, if desired
        2 tablespoons chopped cilantro, if desired
        Toppings: Sour cream, salsa, cheese and/or sliced green onions

Preheat oven to 450˚ F. Place 8-inch cast iron skillet in oven for 7 to 8 minutes or until hot. Combine egg, cornbread mix and milk in medium bowl; mix well. Stir in cheese and jalapeno peppers. Pour into hot skillet. Bake at 450˚ F. for 13 to 17 minutes or until golden brown. Meanwhile, brown ground beef in a medium cast iron skillet. Drain, if necessary. Stir in 1 cup salsa, water, chili powder, and cumin. Reduce heat and simmer 10 minutes or until slightly thickened. Stir in black beans and remaining ½ cup salsa; heat 5 minutes or until hot. Before serving stir in salt and cilantro, if desired.

Cut cornbread into wedges and split horizontally. Place bottom of each wedge on a serving plate. Top each with about 1 cup chili and top of wedge. Add toppings, if desired. Makes 4 servings

Chicken:

Coca Cola Chicken

     4 to 6 boneless, skinless chicken breasts
1 cup Coca Cola (not diet Coke)
1 cup barbeque sauce
1 tsp salt

Place chicken in a 9x13" dish which has been sprayed with cooking oil spray. Mix coke, barbeque sauce, and salt and pour over chicken. Bake uncovered in a 350 deg oven until chicken is tender and sauce has cooked down very thick. Baste chicken while baking and spoon sauce over chicken to serve.

Chicken and Dumplings

     1 3 to 5 lb baking or stewing hen
1 carrot, cut into large pieces
1 stalk celery, cut into large pieces
1 onion, peeled and left whole
salt
water

Place the chicken in a large Dutch oven with a tight fitting lid. Add the vegetables and cover with water. Bring to a full boil and skim off any gray foam which forms. Reduce heat and allow to cook slowly until chicken is pulling away from the bones. Add salt to taste. Remove chicken from broth and allow to cool. Remove the meat from the bones and discard the skin and the bones. Cut the meat into bite sized pieces and set aside. Remove the vegetables from the broth and discard.   There should be about 8 cups of broth. If not, add enough water to have 8 cups. Bring broth to a full boil and add the dumplings (see below) slowly enough that the broth never stops boiling. Reduce heat, cover and allow to cook slowly until the dumplings are tender and the broth is thick. Stir the chicken back into the dumplings and serve hot.

Dumplings:
     3 cups plain flour
1/3 cup shortening
2 tsp baking powder
1 tsp salt
1 cup milk

Stir the baking powder and salt into the flour. Work in the shortening thoroughly into the flour mixture. Add the milk and stir to form a firm dough. Turn out onto a heavily floured surface and knead until smooth (about 1 minute). Shape the dough into an even ball and flatten. Roll very thin (about 1/8 inch). Cut crosswise into strips about 2 inches wide. Tear the strips into pieces about 2 inches long. Drop into boiling broth as described above.

Capt'n Crunch Chicken

6 to 8 pieces of chicken, skin removed
1 egg, beaten
½ cup milk
2 to 3 cups Capt'n Crunch Cereal, crushed

Beat together the egg and milk. Place in a flat dish. Place cereal into a plate or other flat dish. Dip each piece of chicken in the egg wash and roll in the cereal crumbs. Place on a baking pan that has been sprayed with cooking oil spray. Place so that pieces do not touch. Bake in a 350 deg oven about 35 minutes or until brown and juices run clear if pierced. Serve hot.

Chicken Tetrazzini
1 can cream of mushroom soup
1 can cream of celery soup
1 cup milk
3 cups cooked chicken meat, cut into small pieces
1 lb. spaghetti, cooked, drained and lightly buttered
Bread crumbs (about 3/4 cup)
Parmesan cheese (about 3/4 cup)

In a saucepan, mix the soups and the milk and heat to almost boiling. Remove from heat and blend in chicken. Place spaghetti in a baking dish sprayed with cooking oil spray. Pour chicken mixture evenly on top. Sprinkle bread crumbs and Parmesan on top. Bake at 350 deg for 30 minutes or until bubbly and brown on top. Makes about 6 servings.

Curried Chicken Skillet
2 to 3 tsp curry powder
1 1/4 tsp salt, divided
1/4 tsp black pepper
6 boneless, skinless chicken breast halves
1 ½ cups orange juice
1 cup uncooked rice
3/4 cup water
1 TBSP brown sugar
chopped fresh parsley

Combine curry, ½ tsp salt, and pepper, and rub over both sides of the chicken. In a skillet with a tight fitting lid, combine orange juice, rice, water and brown sugar with remaining salt. Mix well. Top with chicken. Bring to a boil. Reduce heat to a simmer. Cover and cook about 25 minutes. Remove from heat and allow to stand 5 minutes to absorb any remaining liquid. Sprinkle with parsley to serve.

White Chicken Chili with Cheddar Hushpuppy Crust

Gaynell Lawson   National Cornbread Festival Winner   Maryville, Tn
1 TBSP olive oil
1 cup finely chopped onion
2 cloves garlic, minced
1 green pepper, seeded and chopped
½ tsp cumin
1 TBSP chili powder
2 TBSP lime juice
1 can cannellini beans (white kidney beans)
4 cooked chicken breast halves, cut in bite-size pieces
2 cans chicken broth
1 small can chopped mild green chilies, drained

Cheddar Hushpuppy Crust:
1 pkg Martha White Cotton Pickin' Cornbread Mix
1/4 cup finely chopped onion
½ cup milk
1 egg
3 TBSP melted butter or margarine
1 cup shredded cheddar cheese

In 11" Lodge Iron skillet, heat olive oil, add the 1 cup onion, garlic, green pepper, cumin, and chili powder. Saute until tender. Add lime juice, beans, chicken, chicken broth and chiles. Simmer about 10 minutes. In a medium bowl, mix the cornbread mix, 1/4 cup onion, milk, egg, butter, and cheese. Pour over the chicken chili in the hot skillet. Place in preheated oven for 20 to 25 minutes or until cornbread crust is golden brown. Serve with garnishes of sour cream, cilantro and salsa as desired.

Cran-Orange Turkey
1/4 cup sugar
2 tablespoons cornstarch
3/4 cup orange marmalade
1 cup fresh cranberries, ground or finely chopped
1 frozen boneless turkey roll, partially thawed
salt and pepper

In small saucepan, blend sugar and cornstarch. Stir in marmalade and cranberries. Cook and stir til mixture is bubbly and slightly thickened. Place partially thawed turkey roll in slow cooker. Sprinkle lightly with salt and pepper. Pour sauce over turkey. Cover and cook on low for 9 - 10 hrs. Slice turkey roll. Spoon sauce over turkey.

An Excellent Chicken Dish
1 can (10 oz) white chicken, drained
1 can cream of chicken soup
1 10 oz pkg frozen chopped broccoli, thawed

1 can (15 oz) chicken stock
1 tsp each salt and ground black pepper
2 cups stuffing mix

Mix the chicken, soup, broccoli, salt and pepper, and chicken stock. Pour into a lightly greased 9x9" dish. Sprinkle stuffing mix evenly over the top. Bake at 350 deg about 40 minutes or until bubbly and brown.

What makes this an excellent chicken dish? Well, it is made entirely from things you can keep on hand all the time. Second, it is very versatile. If you do not like broccoli, use frozen French style green beans. If you want crunch, add some sliced water chestnuts or some chopped celery. You starting to get the picture?

Chicken Piccata
4 chicken breast halves
½ cup flour
1 tsp salt
4 TBSP butter
1/4 cup lemon juice
1 TBSP sugar
3 TBSP capers
1 TBSP Italian parsley, chopped (optional)

Place each chicken breast between two pieces of wax paper and pound with a meat hammer or the back of a heavy knife until it is flat. Mix the flour and salt and dredge the chicken pieces in the flour. Melt the butter in a large flat skillet. Saute the chicken in the butter about 5 to 7 minutes on each side until brown and cooked through. Cook in batches if necessary the chicken should never be stacked in the pan. Remove the chicken to a platter and add all remaining ingredients to the pan. Bring to a boil and cook a couple of minutes until it starts to thicken. Pour over chicken and serve.

Cherry-Glazed Chicken
1 (2 ½- to 3-pound) broiler-fryer chicken, cut up (or 6 chicken breast halves)
½ cup milk
½ cup all-purpose flour
1 teaspoon dried thyme
Salt and pepper, to taste
1 to 2 tablespoons vegetable oil
1 (16-ounce) can unsweetened tart cherries
1/4 cup brown sugar
1/4 cup granulated sugar
1 teaspoon prepared yellow mustard

Rinse chicken; pat dry with paper towels. Pour milk into a shallow container. Combine flour, thyme, salt, and pepper. Dip chicken first in milk, then in flour mixture; coat evenly. Heat oil in a large skillet. Add chicken; brown on all sides. Put chicken in a 13x9x2-inch baking dish. Bake, covered with aluminum foil, in a preheated 350-degree oven 30 minutes. Meanwhile, drain cherries, reserving ½ cup juice. Combine cherry juice, brown sugar, and granulated sugar in a small saucepan; mix well. Bring mixture to a boil over medium heat. Add mustard; mix well. Cook 5 minutes, or until sauce is slightly thickened. Stir in cherries. (Sauce will thicken more as it is baked on chicken.) After chicken has cooked 30 minutes, remove from oven and uncover. Spoon hot cherry mixture over chicken. Bake, uncovered, 15 to 20 minutes, or until chicken is tender. Serve immediately.

Slow Cooker Adobo Chicken

    1 small sweet onion, sliced
    8 cloves garlic, crushed
    3/4 cup soy sauce
    ½ cup vinegar
    3 lbs chicken, cut into pieces (legs and thighs work nicely for this recipe)

Place chicken in a slow cooker. In a small bowl mix the onion, garlic, soy sauce, and vinegar, and pour over the chicken. Cook on Low for 6 to 8 hours. Serve with rice.

Traditional Fried Chicken

    3 to 4 lbs chicken (use your favorite parts)
    ½ cup flour
    1 tsp salt
    1 tsp pepper
    oil for frying

Mix salt and pepper with flour. Place in a one gallon, heavy plastic bag. Place several pieces of chicken in the bag and seal. Shake carefully to completely coat the chicken in the seasoned flour. In a heavy skillet with a lid, add oil to about 1/4 inch deep. Heat until fairly hot. Add chicken in a single layer. Keep the oil hot. Cover and cook about 10 to 15 minutes (depending on how large the pieces of chicken are) or until brown on the bottom. Turn and cook until brown on the other side. Remove from oil and drain on paper towels before serving.

Mexican Chicken and Rice

    2 lbs boneless, skinless chicken breasts, cut into 1" cubes
    1 pkg taco seasoning
    2 TBSP cooking oil
    1 cup uncooked Uncle Ben's converted rice
    1 cup salsa (Mild, medium or hot to your taste)
    1 cup water
    salt and pepper to taste

Toss the chicken cubes with taco seasoning. In a heavy skillet with a tight fitting lid, heat the oil and add the chicken and cook, stirring, until it changes color. Stir in rice and stir to mix. Add salsa and water. Bring to a boil and reduce heat to a simmer. Cover and allow to cook about 20 minutes. Remove from heat and allow to stand about 5 minutes before serving. If you like, you may sprinkle with chopped cilantro.

White Chili
> 1 TBSP olive oil
> 2 medium onions, chopped
> 1 TBSP garlic (about 4 cloves), chopped
> 3 15 ½ oz cans Great Northern beans
> 2 lbs (approx) cooked chicken, cubed
> 2 4 oz cans chopped green chilies
> 2 tsp ground cumin
> ½ tsp ground cayenne pepper
> 2 cups chicken stock (or water), approx

In a heavy pan with a tight fitting lid, heat the oil, add the onion and garlic and cook on medium heat, stirring until onion is soft. Add all remaining ingredients and stir to blend. Bring to a boil, reduce heat and simmer about 20 minutes to blend flavors. Serve hot with grated Monterey Jack cheese or salsa or both. As a matter of interest, this is the second most requested recipe in the history of this program. Frances' Strange Fudge is number one.

Boneless Chicken Breasts with Red Chili Sauce
> 2 TBSP nonfat plain yogurt
> 2 large garlic cloves, minced and mashed to a paste with ½ teaspoon salt
> ½ tsp ground cumin
> four skinless boneless chicken breast halves
> 1 tsp vegetable oil
> 1 TBSP coarsely grated white cheese
> 1 bottle chili sauce

Preheat oven to 400 deg. In a bowl stir together yogurt, garlic paste, cumin, and salt to taste. Add chicken and coat with marinade. Marinate chicken, covered and chilled, at least 15 minutes and up to 1 day. In a 10-inch nonstick skillet heat oil over moderately high heat until hot but not smoking. Add chicken with marinade clinging to it and saute 1 minute on each side, or until golden-brown patches appear. Add chili sauce to skillet and bring to a simmer, uncovered, scraping up any brown bits. Transfer chicken mixture to a shallow baking pan just large enough to hold chicken in one layer and bake, covered, 15 minutes. Remove cover and sprinkle cheese over chicken. Remove pan from oven and let stand 1 minute to melt cheese.

Chicken-Cornbread Casserole
> 3 to 4 cups chicken, cooked and cubed

2 pkgs frozen chopped broccoli
1 medium onion, chopped
1 can each mushroom soup and cream of chicken soup
1 tsp salt
2 cups self-rising cornmeal mix
1/4 cup grated Parmesan cheese
1 can chicken stock (or 2 cups water)

Mix first 5 ingredients and turn into a 9x13" dish which has been sprayed with cooking oil spray. Smooth the top of the chicken mixture in the pan. Mix together the cornmeal mix, cheese, and stock. Pour evenly over the chicken mixture. Bake at 350 about 45 minutes or until hot through and the cornbread is brown. Serve hot.

Chicken Casserole Supreme
1 2 lb bag frozen hash brown potatoes, thawed
2 lb chicken breast halves, cooked and sliced
1 (8 ounce) pkg cream cheese, thinly sliced
½ lb deli-sliced ham coarsely chopped
2 cups shredded Swiss cheese
2 (10 ounce) pkg frozen chopped broccoli, thawed
2 cans condensed soup, undiluted (Use Chicken, Celery, or Mushroom)
1/4 Teaspoon pepper

Preheat oven to 350. Slice chicken breasts into bite-sized strips and brown in oil; season if desired. While chicken is cooking, spray the bottom of a 9x13 pan and layer bottom with potatoes. Layer browned chicken, cream cheese slices and ham over potatoes. Sprinkle with 1 cup shredded Swiss cheese. Top with broccoli. Combine soup and pepper; spoon over broccoli. Top with remaining cheese. Bake uncovered at 350 deg for 50 to 55 minutes or until bubbly.

Savory Chicken Casserole
2 to 3 lbs boneless chicken (breasts or thighs work well)
1 medium onion, chopped
3 carrots, peeled and cut into chunks
1 can cream of chicken soup
1 can cream of celery soup
1 soup can milk
2 cups cornbread dressing mix
2 cups (1 can) chicken stock
1 stick butter, melted

Mix the chicken, onion, carrots, soups, and milk and pour into a slow cooker. Mix dressing mix with chicken stock and spoon onto top of chicken mixture. Drizzle butter over the top. Cover and cook on low 6 to 8 hours. Serve hot.

10 Minute Chicken and Mushroom Dinner
    1 TBSP cooking oil
    1 6 oz pkg Monterey Baby Bellini mushrooms, sliced
    1 (10 ½ oz) can cream of chicken soup
    ½ c milk
    2 chicken breast, halves, cooked and sliced
    ½ tsp rubbed sage
    1/4 tsp salt
    dash of ground black pepper
    cooked rice

Heat oil in a heavy skillet. Stir in mushrooms and cook until they release their liquid. Stir in remaining ingredients (except rice) and cook 10 minutes or until hot. Serve over hot cooked rice.

Caribbean Chicken Wraps
    12 inch flour tortilla shell
    4 oz grilled Caribbean chicken
    1 oz red onion rings
    1 oz shredded lettuce
    1 oz sliced tomato
    ½ oz Caribbean Sauce

Place the sandwich ingredients on the flour tortilla just off center and drizzle the Caribbean Sauce over. Fold over the ends of the tortilla and fold over the short side. Roll to enclose filling.

Slow Cooker Jambalaya
    8 chicken thighs
    1/4 pound cooked ham, cut into one inch cubes
    1 (16 ounce) can diced tomatoes
    1 green bell pepper, chopped
    1 medium onion, chopped
    1 (6 ounce) can tomato paste
    1 tsp salt
    2 dashes hot pepper sauce (or to taste)
    2 cups water
    1 cup uncooked long grain white rice
    ½ pound Polish sausage, sliced diagonally (use chorizo or andouille if you can
        find it)

In a slow cooker, place the chicken, ham, tomatoes, bell pepper, green onions, tomato paste, salt, and hot pepper sauce. Cover, and cook on Low for 4 to 5 hours. Combine water and rice in a medium saucepan. Bring to a boil. Reduce heat, cover, and simmer for 20 minutes. Mix the cooked rice and sausage into the slow cooker. Cover, and cook on High for 15 to 20 minutes, or until the sausage is heated through

Here is another take on this popular dish.

Slow Cooker Jambalaya
    1 pound skinless, boneless chicken breast halves - cut into 1 inch cubes
    1 pound andouille sausage, sliced (any good smoked sausage will work)
    1 (28 ounce) can diced tomatoes with juice
    1 large onion, chopped
    1 large green bell pepper, chopped
    1 cup chopped celery
    1 cup chicken broth
    2 tsp dried oregano
    2 tsp dried parsley
    2 tsp Cajun seasoning
    1 tsp cayenne pepper
    ½ tsp dried thyme
    1 pound frozen cooked shrimp without tails
    3 cups uncooked long grain white rice
    6 cups water

In a slow cooker, mix the chicken, sausage, tomatoes with juice, onion, green bell pepper, celery, and broth. Season with oregano, parsley, Cajun seasoning, cayenne pepper, and thyme. Cover, and cook 7 to 8 hours on Low, or 3 to 4 hours on High. Stir in the shrimp during the last 30 minutes of cook time. Cook the rice according to package directions. Stir the rice into the slow cooker mixture and serve. You may want to pass the Tabasco Sauce with this.

Three Cheese Chicken Casserole
    ½ cup chopped onion
    ½ cup chopped green pepper
    3 TBSP butter
    1 can cream of chicken soup
    1 can (8 oz) sliced mushrooms, drained
    1 jar (2 oz) chopped pimentos, drained
    ½ tsp dried basil
    1 8 oz pkg noodles, cooked and drained
    3 cups diced, cooked, chicken
    2 cups small curd cottage cheese
    2 cups cheddar cheese, shredded
    ½ cup grated Parmesan cheese
    1/4 cup buttered bread crumbs

Saute onion and green pepper in butter until tender. Remove from heat and stir in soup, mushrooms, pimentos, and basil.   In a large bowl, combine chicken, noodles and cheese. Add mushroom mixture. Turn into a 9x13" dish and bake for 40 to 45 minutes or until bubbly. Sprinkle with crumbs and bake an additional 15 minutes or until crumbs are browned.

Jambalaya Grits

> 1 half chicken breast, cut into strips
> 1 TBSP Cajun seasoning
> 1 tsp oil
> 8 oz smoked sausage, sliced thin
> ½ lb shelled shrimp
> 1/4 cup scallions, sliced thin
> 2 cloves garlic, minced
> ½ cup heavy cream
> 1 TBSP hot sauce (or to taste)
> ½ tsp Salt
> ½ cup Parmesan cheese
> ½ cup uncooked grits

Cook grits according to package directions and keep hot. Toss chicken strips with seasoning - heat oil in large skillet and add seasoned chicken and saute - add sausage - cook 1 minute - add shrimp, scallions, garlic, and cream - Cook 2 minutes stir in hot sauce, salt and 1/4 cup Parmesan cheese and simmer 3 minutes. Add cooked grits to the skillet - blend thoroughly. To serve put in bowls and sprinkle remaining Parmesan on top of each bowl.

Slow Cooker Asian Chicken

> 4 lbs chicken legs and thighs, skin removed
> ½ medium onion, chopped
> ½ cup soy sauce
> 1/4 cup apple juice
> ½ cup water
> ½ cup honey
> ground black pepper to taste

Place chicken into slow cooker. Stir together the onion, soy sauce, apple juice, water, honey, and pepper in a cup or small bowl. Pour over the chicken. Cover, and cook on high for 4 hours or low for 6 to 8 hours.   Serve hot with rice.

Chicken Casserole
Susie Sweany   Clinton, Tennessee

> 4 or 5 boneless, skinless chicken breast halves, cooked
> 1 can cream of chicken soup
> 1 can cream of mushroom soup
> 1 medium onion, chopped

84

Pepperidge Farm stuffing mix
1 cup shredded cheddar cheese
1 can chicken broth (or just enough to make it more moist)

Put a layer of the stuffing mix in the bottom of a 9 x 13 inch baking dish. Then shred the chicken to cover the stuffing. Mix the soups in a bowl and spread over the chicken. Put the onion, and cheese over the soups. Pour in some of the chicken broth using as much as you want. Top with another layer of stuffing. Bake in a 400 deg oven until hot and bubbly and the cheese is melted. This will take about 20 to 25 minutes. Serve hot.

Creole Crusted Chicken
4 whole wheat bread slices
½ cup all-purpose flour
½ cup 100% grated Parmesan cheese
2 tablespoons dried parsley flakes
1 ½ tablespoons Creole seasoning
½ teaspoon salt
½ teaspoon pepper
½ cup buttermilk
1/4 cup lemon juice from concentrate
6 boneless, skinless chicken breasts
2 tablespoons butter or margarine, melted
1 tablespoon lemon juice from concentrate

Process bread in a blender or food processor until finely ground. Add the next 6 ingredients. Sprinkle on a flat plate. Combine buttermilk and 1/4 cup lemon juice; brush mixture on both sides of chicken. Coat chicken pieces with the bread/flour mixture. Place chicken on a lightly greased rack in a broiler pan. Sprinkle with any remaining breadcrumb mixture. Stir together butter and 1 tablespoon lemon juice, and drizzle evenly over chicken. Bake at 375˚ for 45 to 50 minutes or until done.

Oven-Fried Corn Flake Chicken
3 lb chicken; Cut Up   (I use boneless, skinless chicken breasts)
2 eggs, slightly beaten
4 TBSP Milk
2 ½ cups corn flakes, crushed
2 tsp salt
½ tsp pepper
5 TBSP butter, melted

Preheat oven to 350 degrees F. Wash chicken and pat dry. Mix together eggs and milk. Separately mix corn flake crumbs, salt, and pepper. Dip chicken into milk and egg mixture then into the crumb mixture coating each piece evenly. Set in well-greased baking pan. Drizzle with melted butter. Bake, uncovered, for 1 hour.

When only the Best will do for You and your Family . . .

Creamy Turkey and Noodles

8 oz wide noodles
3 cups left over turkey cut into cubes
1 can cream of mushroom soup
1 can cream of chicken soup
3/4 cup sour cream
½ cup onion, chopped
½ cup celery, chopped
2 cups Mozzarella cheese

Cook noodles according to package directions and drain. Stir in all remaining ingredients except cheese. Pour into a 9x13 dish which has been sprayed with cooking oil spray. Cook in a preheated 350 deg oven about 40 minutes or until bubbly and top is lightly browned. Sprinkle with cheese and bake an additional 15 minutes or until cheese is melted. Serve warm.

Chicken Spectacular

3 cups cooked, cubed chicken breast meat
1 6 oz pkg rice and wild rice mix
1 can condensed cream of celery soup
1 4 oz jar diced pimento peppers, drained
1 onion, chopped
2 14.5 ounce cans French cut green beans, drained
1 cup mayonnaise
1 can sliced water chestnuts, drained
salt and pepper to taste

Cook rice mix according to package directions. Preheat oven to 350 degrees. In a large bowl combine the cooked chicken, cooked rice, soup, pimentos, onion, beans, mayonnaise, water chestnuts, salt, and pepper. Mix well and pour mixture into a 3 quart casserole dish. Bake in the preheated oven for 25 to 30 minutes, or until heated through.

Atkins Diet Worthy Chicken Divan

1 10 oz pkg frozen chopped broccoli, cooked
½ cup mayonnaise
½ cup sour cream
1 tsp chicken bouillon
½ tsp paprika
½ tsp dry mustard
1/4 tsp curry powder
12 oz chicken breasts, raw, cut in cubes
Parmesan cheese for topping

Preheat oven to 350 deg. Mix all ingredients except broccoli and chicken. Stir in chicken, then broccoli. Spoon into 9x13" pan and bake 25 min. Top with Parmesan and bake additional 5 min.

Pork:

Sausage Pie
Favorite Recipes Home Style   Barbara Plemmons
> 2 cans croissant rolls
> 1 lb sausage
> 16 oz cream cheese

Cook sausage. Lay half of the croissant rolls flat on a greased baking pan. (I press the seams together) Stir cream cheese into cooked sausage. Spread mixture on flat croissant rolls. Add a second layer of croissants. Bake for 30 minutes at 400 deg.

Caramel Apple Pork Chops
> 4 (3/4 inch) thick pork chops (or slices of pork loin)
> 1 tsp vegetable oil
> 2 TBSP brown sugar
> salt and pepper to taste
> 1/8 tsp ground cinnamon
> 2 tart apples - peeled, cored and sliced
> 3 tablespoons pecans (optional)

Heat a large skillet over medium-high heat. Brush chops lightly with oil, and place in hot pan. Cook for 5 to 6 minutes, turning occasionally.   Arrange apple slices around pork chops. Cover and cook on medium heat about 5 minutes or until apples are nearly cooked. In a small bowl, combine brown sugar, salt, pepper, and cinnamon.   Sprinkle over apples and chops and stir lightly to distribute brown sugar mixture evenly. Cover and allow to cook a couple of minutes or until sugar is melted. Remove cover and remove chops and apples to a platter.   If necessary, continue cooking mixture uncovered in skillet, until sauce thickens slightly. Spoon sauce over apples and chops. Sprinkle with pecans if desired.

Bubble & Squeak
> 1 medium onion, chopped
> 1 medium head of cabbage, chopped
> 1 lb bacon or ham, cut into small pieces
> salt and pepper to taste (do this last as the bacon or ham will lend saltiness to
> the recipe)
> 4 oz butter (margarine)
> 3 lbs potatoes (cooked and mashed)

In a large frying pan over medium heat, melt butter and sauté bacon, cabbage and onion, cooking until all is tender.   Add mashed potatoes to the frying pan, mix well, press down to give it the appearance of a giant pancake. Keep cooking on medium heat and checking to see when the potatoes are getting brown. Flip over, and flatten again. You don't have to flip the whole thing in one piece. You may do sections at a time. Keep up the flattening and flipping. You will hear the cabbage and potatoes actually squeaking while being cooked! The whole process of flattening and flipping will take about ½ hour. When you feel you have enough browning, you can stop and serve!

Mom's Saucy Pork Chops

Jennifer Brewer and Linda Clinard   NHC Fort Sanders

>4 to 6 pork chops
>1 large can cream of chicken soup
>1/4 cup catsup
>1 onion, chopped
>2 cloves garlic, chopped

Place pork chops into a slow cooker. Mix all remaining ingredients and pour over pork chops. Cook on low for 6 to 8 hours. Serve with mashed potatoes for the great gravy.

Ham and Egg Easter Left Over Casserole Pie

>3 to 4 cups cooked ham, cubed
>3 or 4 eggs, hard cooked, peeled, and cubed
>1 onion, chopped
>1 cup celery, chopped
>1 TBSP oil
>2 cans cream of celery soup
>1 cup milk
>1 13.25 oz can mushroom stems and pieces, undrained
>1 sheet, ready to bake pastry (I use Food Club brand)

In a heavy pan, heat the oil and saute the onion until translucent. Stir in celery and cook a couple of minutes. Add the ham and cook until ham starts to brown. Stir in the soup, milk, and mushrooms. When hot through, stir in eggs carefully. Turn into a 2 quart casserole and cover with pastry. Seal pastry to edges of dish. Cut holes in pastry to allow steam to escape. Bake at 350 deg about 35 minutes or until pastry is nicely browned. Serve hot.

Pork Tenderloin with Herbs

>4 slices pork loin cut about 3/4 to 1" thick
>1 cup milk
>1 egg
>1 cup crumbs
>1 tsp each, garlic powder, salt, pepper, oregano, parsley, and basil
>2 TBSP each, olive oil and butter

Hammer the pork with the back of a heavy knife and with a meat hammer until it is about one half of its original thickness. Beat together the milk and egg in a flat, shallow bowl. Mix the herbs and spices with the crumbs and spread on a flat plate.   Mix the oil and butter in a non stick skillet and heat to medium heat. Dip each slice of beaten pork in the milk mixture and then coat lightly with the seasoned crumbs. Place into the hot oil/butter mixture and fry about 4 or 5 minutes or until browned. Turn and brown the other side.   If necessary fry in more than one batch. Cutlets should not overlap. Serve immediately.

Apple City Barbecue
A Memphis in May BBQ winner
Dry Rub:
> 10 TBSP black pepper and paprika
> 5 TBSP chili powder, red pepper, and garlic powder
> 3 TBSP celery salt
> 1 TBSP dry mustard

Finish Sauce:
> 32 oz Hunt's Ketchup
> 8 oz soy sauce
> 4 oz Worcestershire sauce
> 1 TBSP garlic powder
> 8 oz Apple cider vinegar
> 4 oz apple juice
> 1 TBSP white pepper or to taste

Mix dry rub ingredients. Rub into pork ribs. Put rubbed ribs into the refrigerator for 4 to 10 hours before cooking. Bring sauce ingredients to a boil. Then add ! Finely grated onion, 1 grated medium Golden Delicious apple and 1/4 grated small bell pepper. Cook slowly until you reach desired thickness. Cook prepared ribs for about 5 ½ to 7 hours over charcoal kept at 180 to 200 deg. Baste occasionally with warm apple juice. Use soaked applewood chips in the fire to create a sweet flavor. About 30 minutes before serving, brush ribs with finishing sauce. Right before serving, sprinkle on more dry rub. Serve sauce on the side. Tip: Don't rush the cooking process.

Sweet and Tart Pork Chops with Cabbage
> 6 pork chops
> 2 TBSP cooking oil
> salt and pepper
> ½ cup chopped onion
> 1/4 cup vinegar
> 1 cup tomato juice
> 4 cups coarsely chopped cabbage
> 1 TBSP sugar
> 1 tsp salt
> pepper to taste

Trim excess fat from pork chops. Brown in a heavy skillet in hot oil. Pour off excess fat. Season chops with salt and pepper. Add onion, vinegar, and tomato juice. Cover and cook over low heat until pork chops are tender, about 30 minutes. Add cabbage; sprinkle with sugar, salt and pepper. Cover and cook 15 to 20 minutes longer, until cabbage is tender. Remove the pork chops and toss cabbage in the sauce before serving.

Sausage and Sweet Potato Casserole
1 can (20 ounces) pineapple chunks in juice
1 can (about 18 ounces) sweet potatoes, sliced 1-inch thick
12 to 16 ounces smoked sausage links
1/4 cup brown sugar
2 TBSP cornstarch
1/4 tsp salt
1 TBSP butter

Drain pineapple, reserving juice in a 2-cup measure. Add water to juice to make 1 ½ cups. Arrange pineapple chunks, sliced sweet potatoes, and sausage in a lightly greased shallow baking dish. In a small saucepan over low heat, combine brown sugar, cornstarch, and salt. Gradually stir in reserved pineapple juice. Cook, stirring constantly, until thickened and bubbly; cook and stir for 1 minute longer. Remove from heat; stir in butter. Pour mixture over sausage and sweet potato mixture. Cover and bake at 350° for 30 to 40 minutes, until heated through.

Tennessee Skillet Supper
½ lb sausage
1 medium onion, chopped
2 cans pinto beans, undrained
2 TBSP flour
1 cup sour cream
1 cup Martha While Corn Meal mix
1 cup milk
1 cup cheddar cheese, shredded

In a heavy iron skillet, brown the sausage with the onion. Drain. Stir in beans and bring to a boil. Stir in flour and then sour cream. Remove from heat. Stir together the corn meal mix and the milk and drop by TBSP fulls over top of hot bean mixture. Bake at 400 deg about 20 to 25 minutes or until bread is brown. Sprinkle cheese over top and return to oven about 5 minutes or until cheese is melted. Serve hot.

Country Italian Sausage Pie
Linda Carmen   Martha White and the National Cornbread Festival
1 tablespoon oil
1 lb. mild or hot Italian sausage links, cut into 1-inch pieces
2 large green or red bell peppers, cut into strips

1 large onion, cut into thin wedges
1 (14.5-oz.) can diced tomatoes, undrained
½ teaspoon salt
¼ teaspoon pepper
1 (6-oz.) pkg. Martha White 'Cotton Pickin' or Buttermilk Cornbread Mix
½ cup milk
1 egg, beaten
4 oz. (1 cup) shredded mozzarella

Heat oven to 400 degrees F. Heat oil in 10 ½-inch cast iron skillet over medium-high heat until hot. Add sausage; cook until browned, stirring occasionally. Add bell peppers and onion; cook until vegetables are tender, stirring occasionally. Stir in tomatoes, salt and pepper; cook 2 to 3 minutes, stirring occasionally. In a small bowl, combine cornbread mix, milk and egg; stir until smooth. Stir in cheese. Spoon batter around edge of mixture in skillet.   Bake at 400 degrees for 20 to 30 minutes or until topping is golden brown.

Tip: For more robust flavor, cook one clove minced garlic with vegetables and use diced tomatoes with basil, garlic and oregano.

Pork Chops with Honey-Mustard and Spice
1/4 cup honey
2 TBSP Dijon Mustard
½ tsp ginger
½ tsp cinnamon
4 pork chops
1 TBSP oil
½ tsp salt
½ tsp pepper

Heat the oil in a heavy skillet. Sprinkle pork chops with salt and pepper and brown on both sides. Mix remaining ingredients and pour over pork. Reduce heat and cook about 15 minutes, turning pork at least once.

Italian Sausage and White Beans
3/4 to 1 lb sweet Italian sausage
½ cup bell peppers, chopped
½ cup onion, chopped
½ tsp minced garlic
1 tsp oregano
1 tsp basil, dried
2 cans cannellini or great Northern beans
1 can diced Italian style tomatoes

Remove casing from sausage. In a non stick pan which has been sprayed with cooking oil spray, cook peppers, onion, and garlic. Add sausage and cook until browned, stirring to break it up. Stir in all remaining ingredients and heat over medium heat until it boils. Simmer about 10 minutes to blend flavors and serve at once.

Cabbage with Sausage
        1 TBSP oil
        6 or 8 cups cabbage, finely shredded
        1 cup onion, chopped
        1 apple, peeled and sliced thin
        1 lb smoked sausage cut into 1" pieces
        ½ cup water or chicken stock
        salt and pepper to taste.

Heat cooking oil in a large skillet or Dutch oven. Add onion and cook, stirring until soft and translucent. Stir in cabbage and apple and cook, stirring until the cabbage is wilted. Stir in the sausage and the water and bring to a boil. Reduce heat to a simmer and cook about 15 minutes or until cabbage is tender-crisp.   Add salt and pepper to taste. Serve at once with Dijon mustard.

Pork Chop Dinner
        6 pork loin chops
        1 TBSP vegetable oil
        1 large onion -- sliced
        1 medium green pepper, chopped
        1 can (4 ounces) mushroom stems and pieces, drained
        1 can (8 ounces) tomato sauce
        1 TBSP brown sugar
        2 tsp Worcestershire sauce
        1 ½ tsp cider vinegar
        ½ tsp salt
        Hot cooked rice, optional

In a skillet, brown pork chops on both sides in oil; drain. Place chops in a slow cooker. Add the onion, green pepper, and mushrooms. In a bowl, combine the tomato sauce, brown sugar, Worcestershire sauce, vinegar, and salt. Pour over meat and vegetables. Cover and cook on low for 4-5 hours or until meat is tender. Serve with rice if desired.

Peaches and Pork Chops
        4 to 5 pork chops (slices of pork loin roast work nicely as well)
        1 TBSP oil
        1 small onion, chopped
        3 to 4 peaches, peeled, pitted and sliced
        1 cup chicken stock
        ½ tsp nutmeg
        2 TBSP brown sugar

1 TBSP soy sauce

Brown pork chops in a heavy skillet with a lid. Remove and add onion to skillet and stir until translucent. Add all remaining ingredients and bring to a boil. Return pork chops and any juices to the skillet arranging them to be in the sauce. Lower heat to a light simmer, cover and cook about ½ hour. Remove lid, remove pork chops and peaches to a plate and keep warm. Increase heat and cook sauce until it is reduced and begins to thicken. Pour over pork and serve at once.

Pork Cooked in Milk
4 lb loin of pork roast
salt and pepper
1 TBSP dried rosemary, crumbled
2 TBSP butter
1 quart milk
½ lb sliced mushrooms
1 TBSP butter

Trim any excess fat from the loin. Rub on all sides with salt, pepper, and rosemary. Brown on all sides in butter in a heavy, covered pan. Add milk, bring to a boil. Reduce heat to a bare simmer. Cover and cook for 2 to 2 ½ hours. When cooked, the milk should have cooked into a thick, brown gravy. Heat 1 TBSP butter in a skillet and saute the mushrooms until they are cooked dry. Remove the roast from the gravy and place on a serving dish. Stir mushrooms into pork gravy. If the gravy is not thick enough for your taste, mix 1 to 2 TBSP flour with ½ cup water and stir into the mixture. Bring to a boil. Serve with sliced pork.

Orange Glazed Pork Chops
4 pork chops, about 3/4-inch thick
1 TBSP olive oil
salt and pepper to taste
½ cup orange juice
3 TBSP brown sugar
3 TBSP orange marmalade
1 TBSP vinegar

In a large, heavy skillet, brown pork chops on both sides in hot oil. Season pork chops with salt and pepper. Drain off excess fat. In a bowl, combine orange juice, brown sugar, marmalade, and vinegar. Pour over the pork chops. Cover and simmer for 35 to 45 minutes, or until pork chops are tender and glazed. You may turn the chops half way through to insure complete coverage of the glaze. Remove pork chops to a warm platter. Spoon sauce over pork chops. Garnish with orange slices.

Potato Paprikash

    1 TBSP vegetable oil
    1 medium onion, chopped
    3 cloves garlic, minced
    1 ½ lb potatoes, peeled and cubed (about 4 or 5 medium potatoes)
    1 can chicken broth
    1 can (14.5 oz) sauerkraut, drained
    1 8 oz can tomato sauce
    1 TBSP paprika
    1 lb Polish sausage, sliced

In a heavy pan with a good lid, cook the onion in the oil until translucent. Stir in garlic and allow to cook about 30 seconds. Stir in potatoes and all remaining ingredients except the sausage. Allow to simmer about 15 minutes or until potatoes are just tender. Stir in sausage and allow to cook about and additional 10 minutes or until sausage is hot through. Serve with crusty bread and a tossed salad for an excellent supper.

Chinese Pork Chops

    ½ cup soy sauce
    1/4 cup brown sugar
    2 TBSP lemon juice
    1 TBSP vegetable oil
    ½ tsp ground ginger
    1/8 tsp garlic powder
    6 boneless pork chops

In a bowl, mix the soy sauce, brown sugar, lemon juice, vegetable oil, ginger, and garlic powder. If grilling the chops, set aside some of the mixture in a separate bowl for marinating during cooking. Place the chops in a large resealable plastic bag, and cover with the remaining marinade mixture. Refrigerate 6 to 8 hours. If grilling, preheat the grill for high heat. Lightly oil the grill grate. Discard marinade, and grill pork chops 6 to 8 minutes per side, or to desired doneness, marinating often with the reserved portion of the marinade. If you choose to do the chops in the oven, pour all the marinade over the chops and allow to stand as described above. When ready to cook, remove chops and place in a flat pan overlapping as little as possible. Pour the marinade over. Bake in a 350 deg oven about 35 minutes or until pork is done and the marinade has started to thicken. Serve hot.

Slow Cooker Dinner

    2 lbs lean pork cut into cubes
    3 large sweet potatoes, peeled and cut into cubes
    2 apples, peeled and cut into cubes
    1 can mushroom soup

1 soup can milk
salt and pepper to taste

Place the sweet potatoes and apples into slow cooker. Layer meat over. Mix soup and milk and pour over. Cover and cook on low about 8 to 10 hours. Add salt and pepper to taste.

Slow Cooker Pork Roast with Vegetables
1 (3 pound) boneless pork shoulder roast
2 15 oz cans chicken broth
3 cups peeled, chopped potatoes
2 onions, peeled and quartered
1 cup carrots, cut into chunks
2 cups sliced fresh mushrooms
1 tablespoon dried rosemary
1 teaspoon ground black pepper
salt to taste

Place the pork roast in a slow cooker. Pour in the broth. Mix in the potatoes, onions, carrots, mushrooms, rosemary, and pepper. Cover, and cook on Low 8 to 10 hours. Season with salt to taste.

Big Orange Meatballs
1 lb mild pork sausage
1 lb lean ground beef
½ cup seasoned breadcrumbs
2 eggs, lightly beaten
¼ cup milk
½ cup finely diced onion
½ teaspoon each - salt and pepper

Combine all ingredients and shape into 1 ½ inch balls. Place on a lightly greased jelly roll pan or cookie sheet (Be sure it has an edge or you will have grease in the oven). Bake at 375° for 30 minutes, turning after 15 minutes.

Sauce:
3/4 cup orange marmalade
¼ cup spicy brown mustard
1 tsp each- Worcestershire sauce and Tabasco sauce

Combine sauce ingredients in a large skillet or wok over medium heat. Cook for one minute, then add meatballs and cook for 5 more minutes, stirring to make sure they all get coated. This is another good tailgating recipe.

Easy Italian One-Pot Supper

1 lb Italian sausage, casing removed and crumbled (either hot or mild)
1 medium onion, cut into wedges
1 medium green bell pepper, cut into strips
2 cloves garlic, minced
1 (6.8-ounce) package RICE-A-RONI® Spanish Rice
1 (14-1/2-ounce) can diced tomatoes, undrained
½ cup sliced pimiento-stuffed olives
1 teaspoon dried oregano

In large pot, saute sausage, onion, bell pepper, and garlic until sausage is well cooked. Add rice-vermicelli mix and saute until vermicelli is golden brown. Slowly stir in 2 cups water, tomatoes, olives, oregano, and Special Seasonings pack from Rice-a-Roni; bring to a boil. Reduce heat to low. Cover; simmer 15 to 20 minutes or until rice is tender.

Sausage with Cabbage and Apples
1 lb smoked sausage (buy whatever is on sale)
1 to 2 TBSP cooking oil
16 oz pkg cole slaw mix (in the prepared salad section)
1 15 oz can White House sliced apples
1 tsp salt

In a large pot with a good lid, heat the cooking oil until fairly hot. Stir in the cole slaw mix and toss to coat with oil, allow to cook, stirring, until cabbage starts to wilt. Stir in undrained apples. Stir to mix. Add salt and mix. Cut sausage into 4 or 5 pieces and lay on top of cabbage mixture. Reduce heat until mixture just simmers. Cover and allow to cook about 15 to 20 minutes. Serve hot.

Almost Lion's Heads
2 to 2 ½ lbs lean pork chops
3 to 4 cups Chinese cabbage, sliced
1 large onion, peeled and sliced thin
2 TBSP fresh ginger, chopped fine
3/4 cup soy sauce
1/4 cup white wine (or water)
1/4 cup sugar

Layer pork chops, cabbage, onion, and ginger in a slow cooker. Mix soy sauce, sugar and wine and pour over. Cover and cook on low 8 to 10 hours. If you wish, you may spoon the meat and vegetables out onto a platter with a slotted spoon. Then mix together 2 TBSP cornstarch with 1/4 cup water and stir into broth. Turn cooker on high and allow the mixture to come to a boil and thicken. Serve with meat and vegetables.

North Carolina Style Barbeque Sandwiches
2 pork shoulder roasts (Boston butt) totaling 6 to 8 lbs
3 to 4 cups vinegar

1 cup water
2 to 3 TBSP hot pepper flakes
1 TBSP salt
1 TBSP ground black pepper

Place the pork roast in a roaster with a tight fitting lid. Pour over them 2 cups vinegar and 1 cup water mixed with 2 TBSP hot pepper flakes and half the salt and pepper. Cover the meat and roast at 300 deg about 4 or 5 hours or until meat is falling off the bone. Drain the cooking liquid and reserve. Remove the meat from the bone and discard the bone and as much fat as possible. Chop the meat fine. Place the remaining vinegar, hot pepper flakes, salt and pepper in a large, heavy pot. Add the meat and stir to mix. Cook on medium heat until the liquid is evaporated. Serve on buns with cole slaw and baked beans. Please note: you may vary the amount to vinegar and hot pepper to suit your taste. This recipe gives a medium hot barbeque.

Corn Pudding with Country Ham
I stole this recipe (with minor revisions) from the Martha White folks. But I don't want anyone to know that.
1 TBSP oil
1 medium onion, chopped
½ cup green bell pepper
2 eggs, beaten
½ cup butter, melted
1 8 oz carton sour cream
1 7 oz pkg Martha White Sweet Yellow Cornbread Mix
½ tsp cayenne pepper, ground
1 14 3/4 oz can cream style corn
1 11 oz can whole kernel corn
1 cup country ham, cooked and chopped

Preheat oven to 375. Grease a 2 quart baking dish. Heat oil in a large skillet over medium heat. Add onion and bell pepper and cook until wilted (about 3 minutes). In a large mixing bowl, beat eggs. Add melted butter, sour cream, cornbread mix, and red pepper. Stir to blend. Stir in both cans of corn, ham and cooked vegetables. Pour into greased baking dish. Bake for about 50 to 55 minutes or until set and browned.

Seafood:

Quick Creamy Shrimp with Rice
1 lb Shrimp (I use pre cooked frozen shrimp)
1 12 oz container Alfredo sauce
1 10 oz can diced tomatoes with basil
cooked rice
shredded Parmesan cheese

In a heavy pan, heat Alfredo sauce and tomatoes to a boil. Stir in shrimp. Continue to cook, and stir about 5 minutes until shrimp is thawed and hot through. Serve over rice, sprinkled with Parmesan cheese.

The Perfect Tuna Casserole
       2 cans cream of mushroom soup
       2/3 cup Milk
       2 6 ½ oz cans tuna, drained and flaked
       4 eggs, hard Boiled, Sliced
       1 can peas, drained
       2 cups potato chips, crushed

Preheat oven to 350 degrees F. Blend soup and milk. Stir in tuna, eggs, and peas. Pour into a 9x13" casserole. Bake 30 minutes. Top with chips; bake 10 minutes longer.

Black Skillet Shrimp and Veggie Polenta
Finalist, National Cornbread Festival by Pam Sanford, New Market, Tn.
Shrimp and vegetables:
       1 lb uncooked shelled and deveined shrimp
       2 cups coarsely chopped red bell pepper
       2 cups coarsely chopped sweet onion
       1/4 cup (½ stick) butter (or margarine)
       1 tsp hot pepper sauce
       1 9 oz pkg fresh pre-washed spinach, chopped
       1/4 tsp seafood seasoning

Melt butter in a 12" Lodge cast iron skillet over medium heat. Add red pepper and onion. Stir often until vegetables are tender. Add spinach, shrimp, seafood seasoning and hot sauce. Cook 5 minutes or until shrimp are done. Drain veggie mixture and save juice for polenta. Cover and keep warm.

Polenta:
       1 cup Martha White Self-Rising Yellow Corn Meal Mix
       1 cup ½ and ½ or whole milk
       1 cup fat-free low sodium chicken broth
       1 cup juice from shrimp and vegetable mixture
       1 tsp hot pepper sauce
       1/4 cup (½ stick) butter (or margarine)
       1 ½ tsp salt
       ½ tsp black pepper
       1/4 tsp onion powder
       4 oz (1 cup) shredded cheddar cheese

Mix cornmeal and half and half in a small bowl. Set aside. Bring to a boil, chicken broth and juice in a 2 quart Lodge cast iron serving pot. Slowly pour in cornmeal mixture stirring constantly. Add hot pepper sauce, butter, salt, pepper and onion powder. Stir constantly with whisk until polenta begins to boil. Reduce heat to low. Stir in cheese. Turn off heat and cover. Bake polenta in 350 deg oven with secure lid for 10 minutes.

All dishes to rest 10 minutes before serving. Spoon a generous mound of polenta onto serving plate and top with shrimp and veggies. Garnish with a small spoon of polenta, fresh spinach, cooked shrimp and red bell pepper.

Salmon with Ginger-Orange Glaze
     1/4 cup orange juice
     1/4 cup soy sauce
     1/4 cup Dijon mustard
     2 TBSP grated fresh ginger
     2 TBSP honey
     4 salmon fillets (about 1 inch thick)
     Hot cooked rice
     Lemon slices

Combine first 5 ingredients in a shallow dish; add salmon. Cover and chill 30 minutes, turning once. Remove salmon from marinade, reserving marinade. Bring marinade to a boil in a small saucepan. If you wish, you may grill salmon, covered with grill lid, over medium-high heat (350 degrees to 400 degrees) about 6 minutes on each side or until fish flakes easily when tested with a fork, basting frequently with reserved marinade. You may also broil salmon about 4 minutes on each side in the oven about 3 inches from heat. When ready to turn, baste generously with marinade. Turn and just before removing, baste again. Be careful, marinade will burn easily. Arrange salmon over rice; drizzle with any remaining marinade. Serve with lemon slices, and garnish, if desired.

Please note that the marinade is brought to a boil before using to baste the meat or to serve over it. NEVER use a marinade in which meat or fish has stood bringing it to a boil first.

Fresh Fish Picatta
     ½ tsp salt
     1/4 tsp pepper
     2 lbs fresh fish fillets (flounder or tilapia work well)
     4 TBSP butter
     2 TBSP oil
     2 TBSP lemon juice
     ½ tsp grated lemon zest (optional)
     1 TBSP dried parsley
     1 TBSP capers
     protein powder, soy isolate or baking mix

Combine protein powder, salt and pepper in bowl. Dredge fish to coat both sides. Melt 2 TBSP butter with oil in skillet. Add fish and cook, turning once, til browned outside and cooked through (5-7 min.) Remove to platter and keep warm. Add remaining butter to skillet and cook over med high heat til browned, about 1 min. Stir in lemon juice, zest, parsley, and capers and pour over fish.

Baked Fish Parmesan

    3/4 cup dry bread crumbs
    3 TBSP grated Parmesan cheese
    2 TBSP fresh parsley, chopped
    ½ tsp salt
    1/4 tsp paprika
    1/8 tsp each, pepper, dried oregano and dried basil
    6 fresh fish fillets (3 to 5 ounces each)   Catfish works nicely as does tilapia.
    ½ cup butter, melted

In a shallow bowl, combine bread crumbs, Parmesan, parsley, and seasonings. Dip fish fillets in the butter and then coat completely in the crumb mixture. Arrange in a single layer in a 9x13" baking dish. Bake, uncovered, at 375 deg for 20 to 25 minutes or until fish flakes easily with a fork. Do not overcook.

Quick Shrimp and Noodle Dinner

    1 pkg Lipton Thai Sesame Noodles
    1 1/3 cup water
    1 TBSP cooking oil   (Or you may substitute Chinese sesame oil)
    ½ lb Food Club frozen, cooked and peeled shrimp

Bring water and oil to a boil in a 2 quart saucepan. Add noodle pkg. Reduce heat, cover and simmer for about 6 minutes. While noodles are cooking, cover the shrimp with cold water in a bowl and remove tails. Drain thoroughly and stir into noodles. Allow to cook 1 more minute. Turn off and allow to stand about 2 minutes before serving. This recipe makes only enough for 2, but doubles easily.

Five Can Casserole

    1 7 ounce can of tuna, drained and flaked
    1 10 3/4 ounce can of condensed chicken noodle soup
    1 10 3/4 ounce can of condensed cream of mushroom soup
    1 3 ounce can of Chinese noodles
    1 5 1/3 ounce can of can evaporated milk

Mix all together. Place in greased 1 ½ quart casserole and bake in 350 degree oven for 30 minutes. Serves 4.

Snapper Francese

At Harrah's, we were shown around by Executive Chef Keith Andriessen and Chef Brian Cress. Chef Cress prepared a lovely fish dish for us.

    2 8 oz snapper filet
    2 eggs
    1/4 cup milk
    ½ cup flour
    2 TBSP capers
    2 oz white wine
    1 oz fresh lemon juice
    1 TBSP whole butter
    salt and pepper to taste

Beat milk into eggs to prepare an egg wash. Season fish with salt and pepper. Dredge snapper in flour, then egg wash, and then flour again. In a hot skillet, pour a little olive oil. Saute fish, belly side down, until golden. Flip. Finish the snapper in a 350 deg oven until desired doneness is reached. Remove fish from oven and place on plate. Deglaze pan with white wine and lemon juice. Add capers and then finish with the butter. Pour sauce over fish and serve.

Walter's note: This is a great preparation for almost any kind of fish. If your fish filets happen to be thin, just finish in the hot pan. Remove to plate and finish as above. This also works great with chicken breast. Hammer a boneless skinless breast until it uniformly about ½ inch thick. Cook on both sides in the olive oil until just cooked through and brown on the outside. Remove to a plate and prepare sauce exactly as you did for the fish.

If you happen to be into beef more than fish, you can use the same technique to prepare a beef fillet. Sear the beef in very hot oil and remove to the oven to cook to desired doneness. In the pan, stir chopped shallots and finely chopped mushrooms until they cook down until liquid is thick. Add an ounce of Jack Daniels whiskey and light to burn off alcohol. Pour mushroom sauce over steak and serve at once.

You will notice that these are restaurant recipes for a single serving. You can double them easily. However, they do not work that well for a large quantity.

At the beautiful Inn at Biltmore Estates, we were greeted by Executive Chef Brian Ross who gave us this fine dish.

Sautéed Scallops with a Brandade of Celery and Fennel, Pernod Jus with Olives
(serves 4)
For the Brandade of Celery and Fennel :

    1 medium celery root
    2 fennel bulbs
    2 large white-fleshed potatoes
    juice of lemon

1 clove garlic minced
1/3 C olive oil
2/3 C heavy cream
salt and pepper to taste

Peel and cut the vegetables into chunks. Place in a steamer and sprinkle with salt. Squeeze the juice of half a lemon over the vegetables. Steam the vegetables until tender, about 20 minutes. Place the vegetables in a food processor and puree. Add the rest of the lemon juice. Heat up the olive oil with the garlic in it until hot, but do not color the garlic. Add the olive oil into the food processor while it is mixing. Add the cream to the food processor. Adjust seasoning with salt and pepper.

For the Pernod Sauce:
2 tomatoes roughly chopped
1 TBSP tomato paste
The reserved fennel tops, chopped
4 cups fish stock, chicken stock or water
2 ounces butter
1 tablespoon Pernod
salt and pepper to taste
16 slices tomatoes, fresh, oven dried or sun dried
¼ cup chopped assorted olives
2 tablespoons chopped chives

Place the fennel tops, tomato paste, and chopped tomato in a pot and cover with the stock or water. Bring to a boil for 20 minutes, then strain. Reduce the liquid to 1 cup. Whisk in the butter. Adjust the seasoning with salt and pepper.

For the Scallops:
16 jumbo scallops
clarified butter for sautéing
salt and pepper

Season the scallops with salt and pepper. Heat the butter until hot, then add the scallops and cook for 3 to four minutes on each side to color and to cook through.

To assemble the dish:
When the scallops are done, divide the celery-fennel mixture between four plates and divide the scallops over the puree. Add the chopped chives, tomatoes, and olives to the sauce and spoon around the scallops. Garnish with reserved fennel fronds.

Walter's Note: This dish looks a little complicated, but is really easy if you go step by step. Everything about it is good, however, the celery root, fennel and potato mixture is amazingly good. I was afraid the fennel would dominate, but it does not. In case you are familiar with fennel, it is the dill looking vegetable which you see regularly at food city which has a large bulb at the bottom. It has a light licorice flavor. The celery root is not as common but you can find it at food city or the produce folks can get it for you. It is an ugly, gnarled round root. It has to be peeled before it is sliced to put into this preparation. The lacy leaves of the fennel make a great garnish for the dish.

At The Grove Park Inn, Chef de Cuisine of Chops restaurant, Kelly Patton was our principal guide, but we were joined by several other members of the excellent cooking team. This dish was really choice

Spice Crusted Grouper with Dried Apple Slaw and Pistachio Pesto Creme Fraiche
Dried Apple Slaw :
    2 cups Dried Apples
    2 yellow tomatoes
    2 red tomatoes
    1 red onion
    ½ cup cider vinegar
    ½ cup sugar
    1 cup oil
    ½ cup parsley

Core and quarter the tomatoes, trim out the seeds so you are left with the outer meat and skin. Julienne the tomatoes, onions and apple. Add remaining ingredients and allow to marinate. Drain to serve.

Pistachio Pesto Crème Friache:
2 cup pistachio
2 cups basil
1 cup asiago cheese
2 tbsp lemon juice
1/4 cup garlic
1 ½ cups pomace oil
5 cups sour cream
1 cup buttermilk
1 cup heavy cream

In a food processor combine the basil, garlic, Pistachio, cheese, and lemon juice. After produces are smooth slowly add the oil to form the pesto. In a large mixing bowl combine the creams and fold in the combined the creams and fold in the pesto.

Seasoned Flour:
½ cup plain flour
spices to taste

Chef Patton used salt, white pepper, cumin, and ginger. You may experiment to find the one you like best.

To prepare this dish, Chef Patton dredged the beautiful grouper fillets in the seasoned flour and sautéed them hot in olive oil. He then placed creamed potatoes on the plate and placed the fish on top of them. He then spooned the drained dried apple slaw on the fish and dotted the Pistachio Pesto on the plate.

Fish Cakes
Imogene Turner   Newport,Tn.
      1 can salmon(drain save juice)
      1 TBSP lemon juice
      1 cup shredded mozzarella cheese
      1/4 cup finely chopped onion
      1 box stuffing mix
      3/4 cup mayonnaise

Add enough water to the salmon juice to make 3/4 cup. Mix with stuffing mix, then add all other ingredients.   Cover and refrigerate for 10 minutes. Make into cakes and fry in hot cooking oil until golden brown. Good served with tarter sauce or cocktail sauce.

Potato Latke
Addie Shersky
>4 large potatoes, peeled and grated fine
>1 medium onion, peeled and grated fine
>½ to 1 tsp salt
>1 tsp baking powder
>4 TBSP flour
>2 eggs, beaten
>oil for frying

Squeeze and drain any excess moisture from the grated potatoes. Mix in all remaining ingredients (except oil); blend well. Heat about ½" oil in a heavy skillet. Drop potato mixture into hot oil by tablespoons and fry until crisp and brown on each side. Serve hot with applesauce.

Apple Matzo Kugel
>4 Matzos
>½ tsp. salt
>1/4 cup margarine
>½ cup chopped nuts
>½ cup raisins
>3 eggs
>½ cup sugar
>1 tsp. cinnamon
>2-3 apples, pared and chopped
>Additional margarine as needed

Break matzo and soak until soft. Drain, but do not squeeze dry. Beat eggs with salt, sugar, margarine, and cinnamon. Add matzo. Stir in chopped nuts, apples, and raisins. Pour mixture into a greased casserole. Dot top with additional margarine. Bake in 350 degree oven for about 45 minutes.

Matzo Balls in Sauce
>6 eggs
>2 cups of seltzer (use club soda if you must)
>½ teaspoon garlic powder
>½ teaspoon onion powder

2 cups matzo meal or enough to make a mildly thick batter
Rapidly boiling water in medium stock pot
3 cans tomato sauce with mushrooms or you own favorite sauce

Mix first 5 ingredients till batter is just thick enough to barely hold its shape. Cover with plastic wrap and refrigerate for 20 minutes. Make balls and drop into boiling water. Cook over low heat until balls float and rise to top of pot. (Approx. 20 minutes of cooking.) Drain all balls and place in a baking dish in one or two layers but not more. Pour sauce over balls. Cover and bake in 350 degree oven until hot and bubbly. Serve with chicken, fish, or beef.

Following the advice of our good friend Jean Millis, I attempted another version of cooking these. Prepare them exactly as we did above. After they have stood in the refrigerator, take out and with oiled hands, shape into balls about 1 to 2" across and place in a single layer in a baking dish. Pour sauce over and bake in a 350 deg oven about 35 to 40 minutes. Serve hot as a side dish.

Alligator and Kangaroo Tail Sausage Jambalaya
 1 lb alligator fillet, cut into small pieces
 1 lb smoked or hot kangaroo tail sausage
 3 TBSP oil
 2/3 cup chopped bell peppers
 2 cloves garlic, crushed
 1/4 cup chopped celery
 2 16 oz cans diced tomatoes
 2 cups chicken stock
 1 cup chopped green onion
 1 ½ tsp dried thyme
 2 bay leaves
 2 tsp oregano
 salt to taste
 ½ tsp each red pepper, black pepper, and garlic powder
 2 cups uncooked rice

In a heavy 4 quart pot, saute bell pepper, garlic, parsley, and celery. Drain tomatoes and reserve liquid. Add onions to pot and saute. Stir in tomatoes and cook until hot. Stir in tomato liquid, stock, thyme, bay leaves, oregano, salt, red pepper, and garlic powder. Add rice, sausage, and alligator. Cook covered until liquid is absorbed. About 20 minutes. Transfer to a baking dish and bake in a 350 deg oven for about 25 minutes. Remove bay leaves and serve hot.

Note: If you happen not to have alligator and kangaroo tail sausage laying around your kitchen, do not let that stop you from cooking this fine dish. Substitute chunks of pork or chicken for the alligator and a good andouille sausage for the kangaroo. If you have trouble finding andouille, use smoked polish sausage. This is worth your time and effort.

Gingered Pork and Noodles with Peanut Sauce
> 1 3 oz package pork-flavored oriental noodles
> 1 lb pork tenderloin
> 1 TBSP vegetable oil
> ½ tsp dry red pepper flakes
> 1 TBSP fresh ginger, shredded
> 1/4 cup peanut butter
> 2 TBSP soy sauce
> 2 cups spinach, washed, drained, and torn into small pieces
> 1/4 cup sliced green onions

Cut tenderloin into 1/4-inch slices, trimming as necessary; cut each slice in half. Cook noodles as directed on package. Drain, reserving cooking water, and keep warm. Heat oil in a heavy frypan; add pork, red pepper flakes, and ginger. Cook and stir until pork is done, about 4-5 minutes. Remove pork and keep warm. In the skillet where you have cooked the pork, blend peanut butter, ½ cup reserved cooking water, and soy sauce; heat and stir until hot, adding more cooking water, if needed. Toss cooked pork, noodles, spinach, and green onions with peanut sauce. Serve immediately.

Sopa de Camaron
Hector Gomez   Los Amigos Restaurant,   Maryville, Tn.
> 2 ½ TBSP butter
> 4 oz white mushrooms, chopped
> 1 medium onion, peeled and chopped
> 2 green bell peppers, seeded and chopped
> 2 jalapenos, cut in half lengthwise (seeds left in)
> ½ tsp each, salt and white pepper
> ½ cup tomato sauce
> 10 oz water
> 22 oz chicken broth
> 4 TBSP Cilantro
> 1 lb medium sized shrimp, peeled and deveined

Melt the butter and saute the vegetables (including the jalapenos) with the salt and pepper until just about done. Add tomato sauce and stir until the sauce changes in color from red to orange (about 30 seconds). Add broth and water and bring to a boil. Add shrimp and cilantro. Turn off heat, cover, and allow to stand. Serve hot.

Layered Enchilada Casserole
> 2 lbs lean ground beef
> 1 large onion, chopped
> 1/4 cup chili powder
> 1 jalapeño chili, seeded and chopped

12 5- to 6-inch-diameter corn tortillas
1 15-ounce can chili beans
1 ½ cups (packed) grated Mexican cheese blend
2 14 1/2-ounce cans Mexican-style diced tomatoes

Preheat oven to 350°F. Spray a 13x9 inch baking dish with cooking oil spray. Saute beef and onion in heavy large skillet over high heat until brown, about 10 minutes. Reduce heat to low. Mix in chili powder and jalapeños, and saute 5 minutes. Season mixture with salt and pepper to taste. Overlap 6 tortillas on bottom of prepared dish, covering completely. Spoon beef mixture, then beans evenly over tortillas. Cover with remaining 6 tortillas. Sprinkle cheese over. Pour tomatoes with their juices over cheese. Bake until casserole is heated through and bubbling at edges, about 1 hour.

Carnitas with Pico de Gallo
2 pounds boneless pork, cut into 3/4-inch cubes
Zest (colored rind only) of one lime, removed with vegetable peeler
2 cloves garlic
2 tsp TABASCO Sauce
½ teaspoon ground cumin
½ teaspoon salt
12 corn tortillas
Pico de Gallo

In 5-quart Dutch oven, place pork, lime peel, garlic, TABASCO sauce, and cumin; add water to barely cover. Heat to boiling; reduce heat to low, cover and cook 2 ½ hours or until water has evaporated. Add salt and continue cooking pork in its own juices until browned. Remove lime zest and garlic. Drain off all excess fat. Adjust seasonings with salt and TABASCO Sauce.   To serve, place warm meat in center of tortilla and spread with commercial Pico de Gallo sauce. Roll up and enjoy.

Hoppin' Juan with Chili Chicken
This was part of a page of neatly copied recipes mailed to me and I do not know who sent them. Thanks, whoever you were.
4 boneless, skinless chicken breast halves
1 tsp hot sauce
2 tsp chili powder
1 TBSP butter
4 green onions, sliced
3 cups cooked rice
1 16 oz can black-eyed peas, rinsed and drained
½ tsp salt
½ tsp ground cumin
salsa

Sprinkle chicken with hot sauce and chili powder. Let stand 15 minutes. Melt butter in a non stick skillet over medium heat. Add chicken and cook about 5 minutes on each side or until done. Remove from skillet and keep warm. Saute green onions a couple of minutes in the same skillet. Add rice, peas, salt and cumin. Cook 3 or 4 minutes or until hot through. Slice chicken crosswise at an angle and stir into rice mixture. Serve with salsa.

Mediterranean Medley
>   1 ½ lbs ground beef
>   4 cloves garlic, minced
>   1 large onion, chopped
>   1 8 oz box sliced mushrooms, broken up
>   1 14.5 oz can diced tomatoes with garlic
>   1 envelope dried onion mushroom soup
>   1/4 tsp thyme
>   3 TBSP flour
>   2 1/4 cups Martha White Buttermilk Self-Rising Cornmeal Mix
>   1 large egg, beaten
>   1 2/3 cup milk
>   6 oz pkg crumbled feta cheese
>   2/3 cup sliced green olives with pimentos
>   2/3 cup sliced ripe olives
>   1 tomato sliced thin
>   8 oz block hot pepper cheese, grated and divided

Cook ground beef, onion, and garlic in large frying pan until ground beef is cooked through. Drain and return to pan. Add mushrooms, tomatoes, thyme, and dried soup. Cook for about 15 minutes. Stir in flour. Combine cornmeal mix, egg, and milk. Stir in olives and feta cheese. Grease 12 inch iron skillet and heat in oven. Spread a layer of cornmeal mixture on the bottom of the pan. Then 1/3 of the beef mixture, layer of pepper cheese, layer of cornmeal mixture, layer of beef mixture, layer of pepper cheese and ending a layer of cornmeal mixture. Bake at 425 deg for 10 minutes. Place tomato slices and remaining hot pepper cheese on top and continue cooking for about 20 minutes or until cornbread is done. Remove from oven and let stand a few minutes. 8 to 10 servings.

Crockpot Arroz Con Pollo
>   4 boneless, skinless chicken breast halves
>   1/4 tsp salt
>   1/4 tsp pepper
>   1/4 tsp paprika
>   1 TBSP oil
>   1 medium onion, chopped
>   1 small red pepper, chopped
>   1 clove of garlic, minced
>   ½ tsp dried rosemary leaves

1 14 ½ ounce can crushed tomatoes
1 10 oz package frozen peas

Season chicken with salt, pepper, and paprika. In a medium skillet, heat oil over medium-high heat. Add chicken and brown. Put chicken in the Crock-pot. In a small bowl, combine remaining ingredients except the peas. Pour over chicken. Cover: cook on Low 7-9 hours (High 3-4 hours) One hour before serving, add peas. Serve over rice.

German Meatloaf
1 ½ lbs lean ground beef
1 cup bouillion
1/4 cup onion, chopped
1 tsp caraway seed
1/4 tsp pepper
3 slices rye bread, torn up
1 large egg
1 tsp salt
½ tsp celery seed

Heat the oven to 350 deg. Mix all of the ingredients together. Spread the mixture into an ungreased 9x5x3" loaf pan. Bake uncovered for 1 to 1 1/4 hours. Drain off excess fat and let stand for 5 to 10 minutes before slicing. Serve hot.

Australian Meat Pie
3 lbs beef chuck, diced into ½ inch cubes
½ cup flour
3 TBSP vegetable oil
2 cloves garlic, chopped
1 onion, diced
1 TBSP freshly ground black pepper
1 TBSP ground coriander
1 TBSP celery seed
1/4 cup Worcestershire sauce
1/4 cup soy sauce
4 cups beef or chicken stock
4 sheets puff pastry (you will find this frozen at Food City)
1 egg, beaten
Black pepper

Dredge beef in flour and sear in oil in a hot pan. Add the garlic and onion and saute for 4 more minutes. Add the spices, Worcestershire, and soy sauce and cook until the liquid is almost absorbed. Add the stock, and cook until the meat is coated in this gravy. Transfer to a container and cool.

Roll pastry to ½ " thickness and cut into circles of any desired size. Divide filling evenly onto pastry to one side of circle and fold over and seal. Bake at 350 deg until pastry is puffed and brown, about 20 to 30 minutes.

Note: These are fine made with plain pastry. Again, cut circles (I cut them about 4" across) and place about 2 TBSP filling to each circle. Fold over and seal edges. Bake as above.

Olie Bolen
Olie Bolen, small, round Dutch doughnuts, are a traditional food consumed over the Christmas season in the Netherlands.

> 1 envelope dry yeast
> 3 TBSP sugar
> 1 cup warm water, divided
> 2 eggs, room temperature
> ½ tsp vanilla
> 4 cups all purpose flour
> 3 cups fruit (diced apples, raisins, currents, or a combination)
> oil for frying
> confectioners sugar for dusting.

Pour ½ cup of water (about 85 to 115 deg) into the bowl of a large food processor. Sprinkle the yeast and sugar over the water and mix at a low speed. Let stand for 5 minutes. Slowly mix in remaining water, eggs, vanilla, and salt. Slowly add flour a cup at a time. Mix on high for about one or two minutes. The dough should turn into a ball and roll around the processor. (If the dough does not ball up because it's too dry, add water one TBSP at a time. If your mixture is more like batter, add flour one TBSP at a time.) Mix in fruit. Remove from processor. Place in a bowl, cover with a clean towel, and let rise until doubled, approximately 1 ½ hours. Roll the dough into small balls about 2 inches in diameter. Fry until golden brown, turning as needed. Remove from oil and drain. Dust with confectioners sugar.

Chapter 8
Vegetables

Zesty Black Eyed Peas
> 1 lb. cleaned and sorted dry black eyed peas, cooked until tender, or 5 to 6 cups
> cooked black-eyed peas
> 6 cups water
> 1 whole med. onion, diced
> 1 whole med. green bell pepper, diced
> 2 to 4 cloves garlic, finely diced
> ½ lb smoked hog jowl bacon, left in one piece
> black pepper and salt to taste

Combine all ingredients in the slow cooker or crockpot. Cover and cook on low for 6 to 8 hours. You may remove the meat and discard the skin and fat portion, returning the lean meat to the peas. It is best if you do this about one hour before the peas are tender.

Broccoli Casserole
> 4 cups cooked, chopped broccoli (about 3 large stems)
> 1 lb Cheezy Does It cheese (or Velveeta, if you insist)
> 1 can cream of mushroom soup
> 1 small onion, chopped
> 2 TBSP butter
> 12 soda crackers, crushed

In a saucepan, melt butter and cook onion until it is translucent. Stir in soup and heat to boiling. Stir in cheese, cubed, and continue to stir until cheese melts. Place half of broccoli in a 7x11" pan which has been sprayed with cooking oil spray. Pour half of the cheese mixture over. Repeat. Sprinkle cracker crumbs on top. Bake at 350 deg about 20 to 25 minutes or until crackers are brown and the mixture is bubbly.

Creamy Deluxe Macaroni and Cheese
Pennie Brown in Our Best Recipes from Tate's School of Discovery
> 1 3/4 cup elbow macaroni (uncooked)
> 2 cups small curd cottage cheese
> 2 cups shredded Cheddar cheese
> 1 8 oz carton sour cream
> 3 TBSP finely chopped onion

1 egg, beaten
3/4 tsp salt
1/4 cup soft bread crumbs
1 ½ TBSP butter or margarine, melted

Cook macaroni according to pkg directions. Drain. Combine macaroni and next 6 ingredients, stirring well. Spoon mixture into a greased 2 quart casserole. Combine bread crumbs and butter, stirring well. Sprinkle bread crumb mixture evenly over casserole. Bake, uncovered at 350 deg for 45 minutes or until thoroughly heated.

Quick Zucchini Skillet
3 to 4 cups zucchini, sliced
2 tsp salt
1 lb Swaggerty Farms pork sausage
2 cups prepared spaghetti sauce
1 cup grated cheddar cheese

Place zucchini in a bowl and sprinkle with the salt. Allow to stand about 30 minutes. Drain thoroughly squeezing to remove excess water. In a heavy skillet, cook pork sausage until it is brown, breaking it up as it cooks. Drain. Add zucchini and stir to mix with the sausage. Add spaghetti sauce and allow to come to a boil. Reduce heat and cook about 10 minutes or just until the squash is barely tender. Turn into a bowl and sprinkle with the cheese to serve.

Backyard Black Bean Burgers
This recipe was developed for our good neighbor the Bush's Best Beans folks
2 (15 ounce) cans BUSH'S BEST Black Beans, rinsed and drained
½ cup whole wheat or all-purpose flour
1/4 cup yellow cornmeal
½ cup chunky salsa
2 tsp ground cumin
1 tsp garlic salt
Hamburger buns

Place beans in food processor; process until fairly smooth. Add flour, cornmeal, salsa, cumin, and garlic salt. Process until well combined. Spoon mixture into 6 balls on a large plate and refrigerate at least 1 hour or up to 4 hours before cooking. These may be cooked on a hot grill or broiled in the oven. If grilling, heat barbecue grill or ridged grill pan over medium heat. Coat grill or pan lightly with oil. Form each ball into a 4-inch patty about 1/2-inch thick. Place the patties on the grill or in pan and cook until browned and heated through, 4 to 5 minutes per side. If broiling, place on a broiler pan which has been greased. Cook about 3 inches from the heat until browned (about 4 minutes on a side). Serve on hamburger buns with your favorite toppings.

Fresh Tomato Pie

1 deep dish pie crust
2 extra-large red ripe tomatoes
salt & pepper to taste
fresh basil
2 cups sharp cheese, grated
½ cup mayonnaise

Bake the crust for 5 minutes at 450 deg. Slice the tomatoes put in pie shell; sprinkle with salt, pepper, and fresh or dried basil. Mix the cheese and mayonnaise together and spread over top of pie. Bake pie for 30-35 minutes at 400.

You could substitute ANY vegetable and ANY herbs for a personalized combination. It has a very fresh flavor. Try zucchini with oregano, for example. You can also add thinly sliced Vidalia onion with the tomatoes.

Unstuffed Cabbage
1 lb lean ground beef
1 TBSP cooking oil
1 large onion, chopped
3 cloves garlic, minced
1 16 oz can tomato sauce
1 tsp salt, nutmeg and black pepper
4 to 6 cups cabbage, shredded

In a large, heavy skillet with a tight fitting lid, heat the oil and add the onion and garlic. Saute at high heat until the onion starts to brown. Crumble the ground beef into the skillet, and fry, stirring constantly until the beef starts to brown as well. Drain off all fat. Add salt, pepper, nutmeg, and tomato sauce. Add the shredded cabbage and mix. Reduce heat until the mixture just simmers. Cover and cook, stirring occasionally, about 25 minutes or until cabbage is tender but still crisp. Serve hot with rice.

Onion Casserole
Brenda Moore   Whitesburg, Tenn
4 large sweet onions, sliced
1 cup milk
1/4 cup butter
50 Ritz crackers
1 [8 oz] pkg cheddar cheese, grated
1/4 cup butter, melted
3 eggs
salt and pepper to taste

Saute onions in 1/4 cup butter. Crush crackers and mix with 1/4 cup of melted butter. Spread 3/4 of crumbs in bottom of 9x13 inch dish. Put sauteed onions on top of crackers. Sprinkle with salt and pepper to taste. Sprinkle cheese evenly over onions.

Mix together 3 beaten eggs and milk. Pour over cheese.   Sprinkle remaining crackers crumbs over top. Bake at 350 deg 30 to 40 minutes or until brown and bubbly.

Savory Sweet Potato Casserole
    4 medium sweet potatoes
    1 lb Swaggerty Farms sausage, fried and drained
    3 cups milk
    2 TBSP flour
    4 eggs
    1 tsp salt
    sprinkle of nutmeg

Boil sweet potatoes until barely tender, peel and slice. Arrange half the slices in the bottom of a greased 9x13" pan. Sprinkle sausage over potatoes. Cover top with the remaining potato slices. Beat together eggs, salt, and flour. Beat in the milk. Pour over the potatoes. Sprinkle with nutmeg. Bake in a 350 deg oven about 45 minutes or until lightly browned.

Baked Sweet Potatoes with Ginger and Honey
    6 large sweet potatoes, peeled and coarsely grated
    ½ cup honey
    3 TBSP grated fresh ginger
    1 tsp ground cardamom
    ½ tsp ground black pepper
    4 eggs
    3 cups milk
    ½ cup white sugar

Preheat oven to 350 deg. In a large bowl, combine the sweet potatoes, honey, ginger, cardamom, and pepper. Transfer to a 2 quart casserole dish. Beat together the eggs, milk, and 1/4 cup of the sugar. Pour over sweet potato mixture. Bake about 45 minutes until potatoes are tender. Sprinkle remaining 1/4 cup sugar over top and return to the oven for 15 minutes or until the sugar is melted and browned.   Serve hot, warm, or cold.

Sweet Potatoes and Onions
    2 TBSP olive oil
    2 TBSP butter
    1 large onion, peeled & sliced
    1/8 teaspoon cinnamon
    pinch allspice
    salt and pepper to taste
    5 medium sweet potatoes, cooked, peeled, diced, (1/3-inch cubes)
    1/4 cup fresh chopped parsley

Heat a large frying pan and add the oil, butter, and onion. Saute for a few minutes until the onion is translucent, then add the spices and salt and pepper [to taste]. Add the diced potatoes and saute until lightly browned. Toss with the parsley just before serving.

Praline Yams Becky Dinkins
Rebecca Dinkins   Morristown, TN
        1 40 oz can cut yams, drained
        1 15 oz can cut yams, drained
        1 cup chopped pecans
        1 cup coconut
        1 cup firmly packed brown sugar
        ½ cup flour
        1 stick margarine or butter, melted

Heat oven to 350 deg. Place drained yams in ungreased 9x13 baking dish. (Yams should cover bottom in single layer).   In small bowl, combine remaining ingredients; blend well. Sprinkle over yams. Bake at 350 deg for 35-40 minutes or until bubbly and top is browning.

Sweet Potatoes with Butter and Maple Syrup
        4 medium sweet potatoes
        3 TBSP butter
        1/4 cup milk
        1/4 cup pure maple syrup
        1/4 tsp salt

Wash the potatoes, and place in a saucepan and cover with water. Boil until tender. Drain and allow to cool. As soon as they are cool enough, peel the potatoes and place back in a sauce pan with the milk and butter. While heating, mash the potatoes with a potato masher until the milk and butter are completely incorporated. Stir in salt and maple syrup. Serve hot with the pork which we prepared yesterday.

Picnic Baked Beans
        1 lb hot dogs, sliced
        2 TBSP mustard
        ½ cup catsup
        1/4 cup molasses (or brown sugar)
        1 large onion, chopped
        1/4 cup sweet relish
        2 cans baked beans

Mix all together and turn into a 9x13" dish. Bake at 350 deg about 1 hour or until thick and very brown. Serve warm.

Baked Green Tomatoes
> 4 large firm green tomatoes
> salt and pepper
> ½ cup brown sugar
> 3/4 cup coarse buttery cracker crumbs
> 4 tablespoons butter

Cut green tomatoes in ½ inch slices; arrange green tomato slices in a greased baking dish. Season sliced green tomatoes with salt and pepper and spread each with about ½ TBSP brown sugar. Cover sliced green tomatoes with crumbs and dot with butter. Bake at 350 deg until green tomatoes are tender but still firm, or about 25 to 35 minutes.

Wild and Crazy Rice
> 1 (6 oz) box long grain and wild rice blend (such as Uncle Ben's)
> 1 (10.5 oz) can beef consomme (broth)
> 1 (10.5 oz) can French onion soup
> ½ cup water chestnuts, sliced
> 1 (6 oz) can sliced mushrooms

Preheat oven to 350 deg. In a medium-size baking dish, combine rice and seasonings, soups, water chestnuts, and mushrooms. Using one of the opened soup cans, add one additional can of water to the mixture. Stir until combined. Cook uncovered for approximately 1 hour or until rice is tender. Stir a couple of times while cooking. Serve hot.

Green Rice Casserole
Julie Thompson Seymour, Tn
> 3 cups cooked rice
> ½ cup butter
> 4 eggs, beaten
> 1 lb sharp cheese, grated
> 1 cup milk
> 1 pkg frozen chopped spinach
> 1 TBSP chopped onion
> 1 ½ tsp soy sauce
> ½ tsp salt
> 1/4 tsp each of thyme, marjoram, rosemary

Cook spinach and drain well. Mix all ingredients together and pour into a large greased casserole dish. Bake in a 350 deg oven for 1 hour. Serves 8-10.

Pasta With Tomatoes, Green Beans & Feta

1 1/2 lbs. ripe tomatoes, seeded and diced
2 garlic cloves, minced or pressed
salt and freshly ground pepper, to taste, plus 1 T. salt for pasta water
1-2 TBSP olive oil, or to taste
1-2 TBSP balsamic vinegar, or to taste (optional)
2 TBSP chopped fresh chives
1 TBSP chopped fresh basil
4 oz. feta cheese, crumbled (about 1/2 C.)
1 lb pasta (fusilli, rigatoni, farfalle, or penne)
1/2 lb green beans, trimmed and broken in half

Start a large pot of water to boil with 1 TBSP salt. While water heats, toss tomatoes with garlic, salt, pepper, oil, herbs, and vinegar (if using) in a pasta bowl. Add feta. Let sit at room temperature 15 minutes or longer. Taste and adjust seasonings. Add pasta to boiling water. Cook 5 minutes. Add beans. Keep cooking until pasta is al dente, firm to the bite (see cooking time on package). Drain, toss with tomato mixture, and serve with shredded Parmesan cheese.

Marinated Carrots
Sent to us by M. Gibson of Seymour, Tn. From the Electric Co-op Newsletter
2 pounds carrots
1 large onion, chopped
1 large green pepper, chopped
1 cup sugar
1/4 cup cider vinegar
2 TBSP Worcestershire sauce
1 can tomato soup
½ tsp dry mustard
1/4 cup salad oil
salt and pepper to taste

Scrape, wash, and slice carrots. Cook until tender, drain well. Add chopped onion and green pepper to carrots in a large bowl. Mix together all remaining ingredients and pour over the carrots. Cover tightly. Chill several hours or overnight. To serve, remove to a serving bowl with a slotted spoon and serve cold.

Fresh Corn Pudding
6 ears fresh corn with kernels cut from cob (2 cups)
3 eggs, beaten
1 cup heavy cream
1/3 cup milk
1 teaspoon salt
1 tablespoon sugar

Preheat oven to 350 deg. In a large bowl, mix together eggs, cream, and milk. Add salt, sugar, and corn. Pour mixture into a buttered 1-1/2 quart shallow glass dish. Place in a pan of warm water and bake for about 1 hour or until a knife inserted in the center comes out clean. Serve with ham steaks or a roasted chicken and green salad.

Quick Corn Pudding
3 eggs
1 cup self rising corn meal mix
1 cup milk
1 each 15 oz can cream corn and drained whole kernel corn
1 10 oz can tomatoes with green chilies
2 cups cheddar cheese, shredded

Beat eggs and mix in corn meal. Then beat in the milk. Add all remaining ingredients and turn into a 9x13" dish which has been sprayed with cooking oil spray. Bake in a 350 deg oven about 45 minutes or until puffed and brown. Serve hot, warm, or cold. I include this because I absolutely love the creamy corn and snappy tomato tastes of it with sliced Easter ham. And I think that is reason enough.

Corn Casserole
Donna Madden   Pine Knot, Ky
½ cup butter
1 cup sour cream
1 egg
1 can whole kernel corn, drained
1 can cream style corn
1 box jiffy corn muffin mix

Mix first three ingredients, and stir in corn. Stir in muffin mix. Put into a greased casserole dish or cast iron skillet, and bake at 375 deg for about 1 hour.

Vegetarian Lasagna
1 15 or 16 oz container ricotta cheese
½ cup shredded or grated Parmesan cheese
2 eggs
2 26 oz jars meat free pasta sauce combined with 3/4 cup water
1 lb lasagna noodles
1 lb sliced mushrooms
1 TBSP olive oil
2 10 oz pkg chopped spinach
4 cups shredded Mozzarella cheese
chopped parsley

Heat butter in skillet and cook mushrooms at high heat until they have given up their moisture and are lightly browned. Mix ricotta cheese, Parmesan cheese, and eggs. Thaw spinach and squeeze dry. Mix 1 cup of cheese mixture with spinach. In a 9x13 pan, spread 1 cup pasta sauce.   Top with a single layer of uncooked lasagna noodles. Break them as necessary to cover bottom. Use about half of the noodles. Spread with half the spinach mixture, then half of the mushrooms, half of the pasta sauce and half the cheese. Repeat layers. Sprinkle parsley over top. Cover tightly and bake 1 hour or until hot and bubbly. Let stand covered about 15 minutes before serving.

Country Green Beans with New Potatoes
>3 lbs fresh green beans (white half runners are good if you can find them)
>salt pork
>salt to taste
>1 cup water
>6 to 8 small white or red thin skinned potatoes

Wash the green beans and then string and break them into pieces about an inch long. Wash again. Place in a pot with a tight fitting lid. Add a piece of salt pork bacon about 4 inches long and ½ inch thick cut almost through to the skin in several places. Pour water over the beans. Bring to a boil, reduce heat to just a simmer, and cook about an hour. Wash the potatoes and place on top of the beans. Do not peel the potatoes. Place the lid back on the pan and allow to cook about another ½ hour. Sprinkle potatoes and beans lightly with salt and allow to cook about another 15 minutes or until potatoes pierce easily with a thin knife. Taste beans and correct salt if necessary. Serve warm.

Tomato Pudding
>3 to 3 ½ cups cooked tomatoes (or a 29 oz can)
>3/4 cup sugar
>½ cup water
>4 TBSP butter
>4 to 6 cold biscuits

In a heavy saucepan, mix together the tomatoes, sugar, water, and butter. Bring to a boil. Crumble the biscuits into the boiling tomato mixture stirring constantly. Reduce the heat, and continue to cook until thick, stirring often. Serve hot or at room temperature.

Tomato Tarts
>1 pie crust, unbaked
>1-1/2 cups shredded mozzarella cheese
>4 Roma or small regular tomatoes, cut in wedges
>3/4 cup loosely packed fresh basil leaves, chopped
>4 cloves garlic, minced
>1/ 2 cup JFG Mayonnaise
>1/4 cup grated Parmesan cheese
>1/8 teaspoon ground white pepper
>Fresh basil leaves for garnish

Cut pie crust with biscuit cutter into large rounds. Press into muffin tins. Don't prick. Partially bake in a 375 degree oven for 5 minutes. Remove from oven and sprinkle with 1/ 2 cup of mozzarella cheese. Cool in pan on wire rack. Meanwhile drain tomatoes on paper towels. Arrange wedges over melted cheese in pie crust. Combine basil, garlic, mayonnaise, Parmesan, and pepper. Spread evenly over tomatoes. Sprinkle with remaining mozzarella cheese. Bake for about 25 minutes or until cheese is golden. Let stand 5 minutes before serving. Garnish with additional basil leaves and serve.

Steve's Aunt Gladys' Creamed Spinach

>2 pkgs frozen chopped spinach
>1 cup sour cream
>1 pkg onion soup mix
>1 cup sharp cheddar cheese, shredded
>3 TBSP butter
>1/3 cup Parmesan cheese

Cook frozen spinach as directed on the package. Drain well. Mix together sour cream, onion soup, and cheese. Add spinach. Place in a greased casserole. Top with buttered crumbs and Parmesan cheese.

Squash and Onion Casserole with Cheese

>5 or 6 zucchini, yellow squash, or a mixture of the two
>3 large onions, sliced
>1 ½ cups cheddar cheese, grated
>1 cup ricotta (or small curd cottage) cheese
>2 cloves garlic, minced
>salt and pepper to taste

Combine squash and onion in a large pot and almost cover with water. Cook about 20 minutes or until vegetables are tender. Drain in a colander removing just as much moisture as possible. Combine with all remaining ingredients. Turn into a 9x13" dish which has been sprayed with cooking oil spray. At this point, you may cover the dish with plastic wrap and refrigerate until you are ready to cook. When you are ready to cook the dish, remove plastic and place in a preheated 375 deg oven and cook about 30 to 40 minutes or until bubbly and brown.

Mockaroni & Cheese

>1 bag frozen cauliflower, cooked
>3 oz cream cheese
>2 TBSP heavy cream
>1 cup shredded cheddar cheese
>Parmesan cheese

Preheat oven to 350 deg. Pour a little cream in bottom of baking dish and add handful of cheddar. Place remaining cream, cream cheese, and remaining cheese in microwave safe dish and microwave until all can be stirred together easily. Pour drained cauliflower into baking dish (while cauliflower still hot). Pour cheese mixture over and stir well to mix. Sprinkle some Parmesan over top. Bake 35 min; allow to stand few minutes before serving as a main dish or as a side dish.

Total: 20 carb, 10 fiber (10 NET carbs), 963 Calories, 76 fat, 45 protein. Serves 2 as main dish and 4 as side dish.

Easy One-Pot Pasta Veggie Medley
        2 ½ quarts water
        1 tsp salt
        2 cups sun-dried tomatoes
        8 ounces vegetable spiral pasta or pasta twists
        2 cups broccoli florets
        1 large red bell pepper, sliced in strips
        1 bunch scallions, thinly sliced
        1 pkg prepared Alfredo sauce
        1/4 cup fresh basil or parsley, chopped finely
        Parmesan cheese, grated

Bring water and salt to a boil in a large pot over high heat while you wash, trim, and prepare the vegetables. When water reaches the boiling point, transfer 1 ½ cups to a small mixing bowl. Add the sun-dried tomatoes; soak for 5 minutes, then drain and slice in thin strips. Return water to a rapid boil over high heat. Add pasta gradually, stirring for 30 seconds or so to prevent sticking. Cook pasta 3 minutes less than manufacturer's recommended cooking time. Add broccoli, bell peppers, and scallions to the pasta and water; cook 3 minutes over high heat. When pasta and vegetables are just done, drain well in a colander, then return mixture immediately to the empty pot. Stir in the sun dried tomatoes, Alfredo sauce, and basil or parsley. Mix well. Serve immediately topped with Parmesan cheese.

Hominy and Three-Cheese Grits
        2 cups water
        ½ cup enriched quick grits
        1/4 teaspoon salt -- (optional)
        2 ounces shredded Swiss cheese
        2 ounces shredded cheddar cheese
        1/4 cup grated Parmesan cheese
        2 TBSP butter
        1 small can hominy, drained
        1 egg, beaten
        1 garlic clove, minced
        ½ tsp Worcestershire sauce

Heat oven to 350 F. Grease 1-qt. casserole. Bring water to a boil; slowly stir in grits and salt. Return to boil; reduce heat. Simmer 2 to 3 minutes or until thickened, stirring occasionally. Add cheeses and butter; stir until melted. Stir in remaining ingredients. Pour into casserole. Bake 30 to 35 minutes or until knife inserted in center comes out clean.

True AuGratin Potatoes

1 clove garlic, halved
2 lbs potatoes, peeled and sliced very thin (I like Yukon Gold best)
2 TBSP butter, melted
½ tsp salt
1/4 tsp black pepper
1 cup (4 oz) grated Gruyere cheese, grated
1 cup milk

Rub an 11x7" dish with the garlic. Spray with cooking oil spray. Layer half the potatoes evenly into the dish. Drizzle with half the butter. Sprinkle with half the salt and pepper and top with half the cheese. Repeat with potatoes and remaining salt, pepper, and cheese. Heat the milk and pour evenly over the dish. Bake at 425 deg about 40 minutes or until potatoes are tender.

Collards and Rice

2 cups chicken stock
1 cup Uncle Ben's long-grain rice, uncooked
4 TBSP butter or olive oil
½ teaspoon salt
3 cups chopped collard leaves, loosely packed
pepper

Melt the butter (or olive oil) in a medium sized pot with a tight fitting lid. Add the chopped collard greens, a handful at a time, stirring after each addition. Cook until the greens are just wilted. Add the rice and salt; stir. Bring back to the boil; cover and reduce heat. Cook approximately 20 minutes, or until rice is tender. Allow to stand about 5 minutes. Season with pepper before serving.

Mushroom Rice

2 teaspoons butter
6 mushrooms, coarsely chopped
1 clove garlic, minced
1 green onion, finely chopped
2 cups chicken broth
1 cup uncooked white rice
1/2 teaspoon chopped fresh parsley
salt and pepper to taste

Melt butter in a saucepan over medium heat. Cook mushrooms, garlic, and green onion until mushrooms are cooked and liquid has evaporated. Stir in chicken broth and rice. Season with parsley, salt, and pepper. Reduce heat, cover and simmer for 20 minutes.

Creamy Mashed Potato Bake
> 3½ lbs russet potatoes, peeled, cut into 1-inch cubes
> 1 8 oz package cream cheese, room temperature
> ½ cup sour cream
> ½ cup whole milk
> ¾ cup chopped fresh chives (about 3 bunches)
> ½ tsp salt
> ½ tsp white pepper
> 1 TBSP chilled butter, cut into small pieces
> ½ cup Parmesan cheese

Grease 6- to 8-cup ovenproof baking dish. Boil potatoes in salted water until tender, about 15 minutes. Drain potatoes and mash with cream cheese. Add sour cream, milk, chives, salt, and pepper. Transfer potatoes into prepared dish; dot with chilled butter. Sprinkle with Parmesan. (Can be made 2 hours ahead; let stand at room temperature.) Bake potatoes at 350°F until brown on top, about 35 minutes.

Creamed Potatoes with Parsnips
> 4 or 5 large potatoes, peeled and cut into chunks
> 2 parsnips, peeled and cut into chunks
> ½ stick butter
> ½ cup milk
> salt and pepper to taste

Place potatoes and parsnips into a large pot and cover with water. Bring to a boil, reduce heat, and allow to cook until potatoes are tender. Remove and drain. Add butter and milk and mash with a potato masher until you reach desired consistency. If necessary, you may add more milk. Add salt and pepper to taste and serve at once.

Slow Cooker Scalloped Potatoes
> ½ tsp cream of tartar
> 1 cup water
> 8 to 10 medium potatoes, peeled and sliced thin
> 1 medium onion, chopped
> salt and pepper to taste
> 1 cup grated cheddar cheese
> 1 cup grated (or finely chopped) Cheezy Does It Cheese
> 1 can cream of celery soup
> 1 tsp paprika

Dissolve cream of tartar in water and pour over potato slices. Stir to coat completely.

Drain. Place half the potatoes in the slow cooker. Sprinkle with onion, salt pepper and half of cheeses. Repeat with remaining potatoes and cheeses. Spread soup over the top. Cover and cook on low for 8 to 10 hours.

Bramborak (Garlic Seasoned Fried Potato Pancake)
Czech Republic
        8 large potatoes
        1 medium onion
        2/3 cup flour
        3 eggs
        1 tsp minced garlic
        salt and pepper to taste

Peel and cut potatoes. Cook until soft. Drain well. Whip potatoes until creamy. Add all ingredients and mix well. Scoop and shape into small pancakes about 3" in diameter. Fry in a skillet with hot oil until brown.

Roasted Root Vegetables
        2 or 3 carrots, peeled and cut into chunks
        2 or 3 turnips, peeled and cut into chunks
        2 or 3 parsnips, peeled and cut into chunks
        2 or 3 potatoes, peeled and cut into chunks
        2 or 3 onions, peeled and cut into chunks
        kosher salt and black pepper to taste

Spray a large, flat pan with cooking oil spray and arrange the vegetables on it in a single layer. Spray the vegetables with cooking oil spray. Sprinkle over them kosher salt and fresh ground black pepper to taste. Cook in a 400 deg oven about 25 to 30 minutes or until the vegetables are browned and the potatoes are tender. Serve at once.

Onion Casserole
The late Mary Rose
        5 or 6 onions, peeled and sliced very thin
        ½ cup slivered almonds
        1/4 cup butter
        1 can mushroom soup
        salt and pepper to taste
        paprika

In an 8" baking dish, place half the onions. Sprinkle with half the almonds and dot with half the butter. Spread the remaining onions in the dish. Sprinkle on remaining almonds, and dot with the remaining butter. Spread mushroom soup over top and all salt and pepper to taste. Sprinkle with paprika. Cover tightly with foil and bake at 300 deg for about 1 hour and 15 minutes. Remove foil, increase heat to 325 deg, and cook about 15 additional minutes to brown the top of the casserole. Serve warm.

Green Bean Casserole
> 1 TBSP butter
> 1 medium onion, chopped
> 2 cloves garlic, minced
> 8 oz sliced fresh mushrooms
> 2 10 oz pkg green beans (either snap beans or French style beans will work)
> 1 cream of celery soup
> 1 TBSP dry ranch style salad dressing
> 3/4 cup fresh bread crumbs
> ½ cup grated Parmesan cheese

Cook beans according to package directions. Drain and set aside. In a heavy skillet, heat butter and cook onion until translucent. Stir in garlic and cook a couple of minutes more. Remove onion to beans. In the same skillet, cook mushrooms until they give up their liquid and begin to brown. Mix in with onions and beans. Stir ranch dressing mix into celery soup and mix into beans. Turn into a casserole dish. Mix cheese with bread crumbs and sprinkle evenly over beans. Bake at 350 deg about 20 to 30 minutes or until heated through and the crumbs are brown.

Tomatoes Boheme
This is a recipe from a 1950's KUB recipe sheet
> 2 or 3 large tomatoes, peeled and chopped (or 1 15 ½ oz can diced tomatoes)
> 1 cup diced celery
> 1 large onion, chopped
> ½ cup green bell pepper, chopped
> salt and pepper to taste
> 1 cup Ritz cracker crumbs
> 1/4 cup butter, melted

Mix tomatoes, celery, onion, and bell pepper. Add salt and pepper to taste, and turn into a 2 quart casserole dish which has been sprayed with cooking oil spray.   Toss the cracker crumbs with the butter and sprinkle over the top. Bake at 350 deg about 45 minutes or until bubbly and brown.   This is a great side dish with a good slice of meat loaf.

Tempali (Deep Fried Version)
Jamie Franks   Oak Ridge Renaissance Faire
> 1 cup flour
> 5/8 to 3/4 cups water, depending on desired consistency
> 3 TBSP reddish-orange chicken seasoning (McCormick's)
> a sprinkle of pepper

1 tsp salt (or to taste)
3 medium sized potatoes
2 carrots, average size
½ lb zucchini or yellow squash

Combine flour, chicken seasoning, salt, and pepper in a bowl, then add water. Stir. Batter should have the consistency of pancake batter. Cut the zucchini, potatoes, and carrots into slices. Deep fryer should be heated. If using stove top deep frying, set the heat between medium and high. Dunk sliced vegetables into batter, completely covering the vegetables. Then submerge in deep fryer. Vegetables should float and be golden brown and somewhat puffed when ready to remove from oil.

Optional:
1. Substitute snow peas, cauliflower, or broccoli instead of the zucchini or squash.
2. Adjust the amount of seasoning, salt and pepper for desired spice flavor
3. Meat may also be added as traditional tempali.
4. For the pan fry method, a thicker batter is recommended
5. Use olive oil in the pan fry method for a Mediterranean accent.

Mexican Green Beans
1 lb fresh green beans
1 bell pepper
1 onion
2 TBSP cooking oil
1 can diced Mexican style tomatoes
1 clove garlic, crushed
½ tsp each, oregano and cumin
Salt and pepper to taste
1 cup grated Mexican style cheese

Break ends and strings from green beans and break into about 1 inch pieces. Chop onion and bell pepper. Stir-fry onions and pepper in oil until onions are translucent. Stir in beans and continue to stir until they change color. Add stewed tomatoes, about ½ can of water, and seasonings. Simmer until tender (about 15 to 20 minutes). Add cheese and stir until cheese is melted. Serve at once.

Greek Spinach Frittata
1 16-ounce container cottage cheese
4 ounces feta cheese, crumbled
2 TBSP flour
4 eggs, beaten
3 10-ounce pkg frozen spinach, thawed and well-drained
½ cup onion, diced
2 TBSP lemon juice
2 TBSP dried dill (or 4 TBSP fresh dill, snipped)

Black pepper to taste

Preheat oven to 350 deg. In a food processor, combine nonfat cottage cheese and flour until smooth. Add eggs, drained spinach, onion, lemon juice, dill, and pepper to taste and combine well. Stir in Feta cheese. Spray a 9-inch (23cm) round or square baking dish with nonstick cooking spray. Pour in spinach mixture and bake 40 to 45 minutes or until knife inserted in the center comes out clean. Cool 10 minutes before cutting. Garnish with lemon, if desired.

Chapter 8
Desserts

Lime Mousse Cake
Winner in the Cake Category
Vicki Denton Baptist Health System, Business Office
Crust:
2 cups crushed graham crackers
1/4 cup sugar
½ cup (1 stick) butter, melted

Mix together cracker crumbs, sugar, and butter. Press into the bottom and 1 inch on sides of a 10 in springform pan.   Set aside.

Filling:
6 TBSP fresh lime juice (approximately 3 limes)
(bottled juice can be used if fresh limes are unavailable)
1- 1/4 oz pkg (1 envelope) unflavored gelatin
2 ½ cups heavy cream
10- 1 oz. squares Baker's premium white chocolate, plus 1 to 1 ½ ounces, grated or shaved into curls
3- 8 oz. packages cream cheese, softened
1 cup sugar
1 ½ TBSP lime zest (can use squeezed limes for the zest)
1 lime cut in small strips and twisted, sprinkle with a little sugar for decoration (place in refrigerator over night) - optional

Squeeze lime juice into a bowl and sprinkle gelatin over juice. Bring ½ cup of the heavy cream to a simmer in a saucepan, remove from heat, and add the 10 ounces of white chocolate, stirring until smooth. Stir in gelatin and lime juice mixture and allow to cool. Using an electric mixer, blend together cream cheese, sugar, and lime zest. Slowly beat cooled white chocolate mixture into cream cheese mixture. Using clean, dry beaters, beat remaining 2 cups heavy cream until it peaks. Fold into white chocolate cream cheese mixture, then pour into crust. Cover and freeze overnight. Remove from freezer and run a sharp knife around inside of springform pan to help loosen cake. Release springform ring from pan, move cake to a serving plate, and grate or curl the 1 to 1 ½ ounces white chocolate over cake. Place twisted lime strips on top of cake. Let set for 15 minutes before cutting into wedges with a knife that has been dipped into hot water.

(Serves 12- 14)

Italian Creme Cake
Runner-up in the cake category
Laurie Alsup, Baptist Heart Institute
½ cup butter
1 tsp soda
½ cup Crisco
2 cups flour
2 cups sugar
1 cup buttermilk
5 eggs, separated
1 tsp vanilla
1 cup chopped pecans

Cream butter and crisco together. Add sugar, beat until smooth. Add egg yolks. Beat well. Sift flour and soda in a separate bowl. Combine flour to creamed mixture alternately with buttermilk. Mixing well. Stir in vanilla. Add pecans Beat egg whites until stiff. Fold in stiffly beaten egg whites to batter. Gently pour into 3 greased and floured 8-inch cake pans. Bake at 350 degrees for 25 min.

Icing:
1 8 oz pkg of cream cheese, softened
1/4 cup of butter, softened
1 box of confectioners sugar
1 tsp vanilla
½ cup chopped pecans

Beat cream cheese and butter together. Add sugar, mix well, and stir in vanilla. Add pecans. Spread on cake.

Dirt Cake Parfait
8 oz cream cheese, softened at room temperature
1 cup sugar
2 pkg chocolate pudding mix
4 cups whole milk
1 pkg Oreo Cookies
1 lb gummy worms

In a mixing bowl, blend together cream cheese, sugar, milk, and pudding mix. Using a food processor, add cookies 5 or 6 at a time to break into small crumbs. In a parfait cup, place a layer of pudding, then of crumbs and repeat, ending with crumbs. As you fill, add a couple of gummy worms. Allow the head to come out the top and hang over the side of the cup.

Kids love these and can help you make them. Be sure that the cream cheese, sugar, and milk are thoroughly mixed before stirring in the instant pudding mix.

Chocolate Whipped Cream Cake

> 1 2/3 cup whipping cream, chilled
> 3 eggs
> 3 oz unsweetened chocolate, melted
> 1 tsp vanilla
> 2 1/4 cups flour
> 1 ½ cups sugar
> 2 1/4 tsp baking powder
> 1 tsp salt

Beat cream until stiff. Beat eggs until thick and lemon colored. Fold eggs, chocolate, and vanilla into cream. Stir remaining ingredients together and fold into cream mixture until fully blended. Pour into a greased and floured 9x13" pan. Bake in a preheated 350 deg oven about 45 minutes. Cool before serving.

Original Lemon Loaf Cake

Recipes to Remember   Good Samaritan Center   Lenoir City

> 1 pkg yellow cake mix (these folks suggest Duncan Hines)
> 1 pkg lemon Jell-O
> 2/3 cup boiling water
> 1 stick butter
> 5 eggs

Melt butter. Dissolve Jell-O in boiling water and cool slightly. Mix cake mix and melted butter. Add eggs, one at a time, beating well after each addition. Pour dissolved Jell-O into cake mixture while continuing to beat. Beat an additional two minutes. Pour into a heavily sprayed Bundt pan. Bake for 40 to 45 minutes at 350 deg or until cake pulls away from sides. Do not overbake! Keep cake tightly covered to maintain moistness.

White Lily Orange Pecan Pound Cake

Belinda Ellis   White Lily Foods

> 3/4 cup (1 ½ sticks) butter or margarine, softened
> 2 2/3 cups granulated sugar
> 5 large eggs, at room temperature
> 2 TBSP orange juice
> 1 TBSP honey
> 1 tsp almond extract
> 2 ½ cups White Lily All-Purpose Flour
> 1/4 tsp baking soda
> 1 cup sour cream
> 1 TBSP grated orange peel
> 1 cup chopped pecans, toasted*

Honey-Orange Glaze (recipe follows)

Preheat oven to 325°. Generously coat a 10-inch tube pan or 12-cup** Bundt pan with cooking spray; dust with flour. In large mixer bowl, beat butter about 30 seconds or until creamy. Gradually add sugar; beat 7 minutes. Add eggs 1 at a time, beating well after each addition. Add orange juice, honey, and almond extract. In medium bowl, stir together flour and baking soda; add alternately with sour cream. Beat on low speed after each addition, just until combined; do not over mix. Fold in orange peel and pecans. Spoon batter into pan to fill about half full ** Bake 80 to 90 minutes or until wooden pick inserted in center comes out clean. Cool in pan 10 minutes. Remove from pan. Cool completely on wire rack. Drizzle with Honey-Orange Glaze.

Honey-Orange Glaze:
> 1/4 cup (½ stick) butter or margarine
> 1/4 cup packed brown sugar
> 1/4 cup pure clover honey
> 1 teaspoon grated orange peel

In 1-cup glass measure, microwave butter on High for 1 minute or until melted. Stir in brown sugar, honey, and orange peel. Microwave on High for 1 minute longer.

Chocolate Yeast Cake
This is an old cake recipe which we did years ago. We lost it. It was in a recent issue of Grit which our Nashville correspondent Shirley Bridges so kindly gives us.
> 1 tsp dry yeast
> 1/4 cup warm water (105 deg to 115 deg)
> 1 cup shortening
> 2 cups sugar
> 3 eggs
> 3 squares unsweetened chocolate, melted
> 2 3/4 cups all purpose flour
> ½ tsp salt
> 1 cup milk
> 1 ½ tsp vanilla
> 1 tsp baking soda
> 3 TBSP hot water

In a small bowl, dissolve yeast in warm water and set aside. In the large bowl of a large mixer, cream shortening and add sugar. Cream until light and fluffy. Add eggs, one at a time beating well after each addition. Add melted chocolate and beat well. Combine flour and salt and add alternately with milk, starting and ending with flour. Mix well after each addition. Stir in yeast mixture and vanilla. Cover and refrigerate overnight. The next day, heat oven to 350 deg. Grease and flour 3 8" cake pans or 2 9" cake pans. Dissolve soda in hot water and stir into refrigerated batter. Pour batter into cake pans and bake for 25 to 30 minutes or until the cake tests done. Allow to cool about 10 minutes in the pan before turning out to cool completely before icing with chocolate icing.

Chocolate Icing:
>
> 1/4 cup plus 2 TBSP butter
> 1/4 cup plus 2 TBSP milk
> 3 squares unsweetened chocolate
> 1/8 tsp salt
> 1 TBSP vanilla
> 4 ½ to 5 cups confectioner's sugar

Place the butter, milk, and chocolate in a microwave proof bowl and heat, checking often until completely melted. Stir to mix. Allow to cool about 10 minutes before you start to beat in the sugar. Beat in sugar until the mixture reaches spreading consistency. The exact amount of sugar needed will vary. Stir in salt and vanilla. Spread between layers and to cover the sides and top of the cake.

Cream of Coconut Cake
Katherine Bell and Wanda Kahltoff
(our very own cousins)
>
> 1 white cake mix
> 1 large can Baker's coconut
> 1 can sweetened condensed milk
> 1 8.5 oz can cream of coconut
> 1 8 oz carton of whipped topping

Prepare cake according to package directions, including 2/3 cup coconut. Mix well and bake according to package instructions. Take the baked cake from the oven and punch holes in the cake. While warm, pour on the sweetened condensed milk and spread evenly over cake. Allow to cool. Mix whipped topping and cream of coconut and spread on cake. Sprinkle coconut on top and refrigerate until ready to serve.

Tunnel of Fudge Cake
The Tunnel of Fudge Cake, a second-place Pillsbury Bake-Off winner in 1966, was developed by Ella Rita Helfrich of Houston, Texas, who won $5,000. The original recipe used a product called Double Dutch Fudge Buttercream Frosting Mix, which the company has discontinued. However, because of many consumer requests, its test kitchens developed this recipe, which uses scratch ingredients. Nuts are essential to the cake's success.
>
> 3 ½ sticks butter or margarine, softened (1 3/4 cups), plus more for greasing pan
> 2 1/4 cups all-purpose flour, plus more for flouring pan
> 1 3/4 cups granulated sugar
> 6 large eggs
> 2 cups confectioners' sugar
> 3/4 cup unsweetened cocoa powder

134

2 cups chopped walnuts (8 ounces)

Heat the oven to 350*F. Grease a 12-cup Bundt pan or 10-inch angel cake pan. Dust with flour and tap out the excess. In a large bowl, beat the butter and granulated sugar using an electric mixer on medium speed until light and fluffy, for 1 to 2 minutes. Add the eggs, one at a time, beating well after each addition. Gradually add 2 cups confectioners' sugar, beating until well-blended. By hand, stir in 21/4 cups flour, 3/4 cup cocoa and the nuts; mix until well-blended. Spoon the batter into the prepared pan and spread evenly. Bake for 58 to 62 minutes. Let the cake cool upright in the pan on a rack for 1 hour, then invert onto a serving plate and let cool completely.

If you want to glaze the cake, make the glaze in the following way: In a small bowl, combine 3/4 cup confectioners' sugar, 1/4 cup cocoa and 11/2 tablespoons milk. Mix until well blended, adding the remaining ½ tablespoon milk to make a spooning consistency. Spoon the glaze over the top of the cooled cake, allowing some to run down sides. Store the cake tightly covered.
Makes 12 to 14 servings.

Recipe courtesy of The Pillsbury Company.

Mrs. Hunley's Pound Cake
> 1 cup butter
> 2 cups sugar
> 4 eggs, separated
> 1 cup milk
> 3 cups flour
> 2 tsp baking powder
> 2 tsp vanilla

Separate eggs into two bowls. With a whisk or beater beat yolks until thick. Wash the beater before whipping the egg whites until soft peaks form. In a large mixing bowl, cream butter and add sugar and egg yolks and beat to mix. Mix flour with baking powder and add alternately with milk. Add flavoring and fold in beaten egg whites. Bake in a greased and floured large tube pan at 350 deg for about one hour. Allow to cool in the pan about 10 to 15 minutes before turning out.

In case you are interested, Mrs. Hunley was our next door neighbor many years ago when I was young. She gave this recipe to my mother who used it for the rest of her life. I love pound cake and this one has a special place in my heart.

Hot Fudge Pudding Cake with Peanut Butter
> ½ cup flour
> 1/4 cup sugar
> 3/4 tsp baking powder
> 1/3 cup milk

1 TBSP oil
½ tsp vanilla
1/4 cup peanut butter
½ cup sugar
3 TBSP cocoa powder
1 cup boiling water
vanilla ice cream

Combine flour, 1/4 cup sugar, and baking powder. Mix peanut butter, milk, oil, and vanilla until smooth. Stir into flour mixture and pour into greased slow cooker. Mix together ½ cup sugar and cocoa powder. Sprinkle over batter in slow cooker. Pour boiling water over. Do not stir. Cover and cook on high about 2 to 3 hours. Serve with ice cream.

Fourth of July Cupcakes
1 pkg chocolate cake mix
Ingredients to prepare cake as pkg directs
1 can any flavor white cake icing
strawberries and blue berries

Prepare cake mix as directed on pkg. Pour into muffin tins which have been lined with a cupcake cup. Bake. Allow to cool. Spread with icing. While icing is still soft, press half a strawberry and some blueberries into the icing. Serve.

Cola Cake
1 white cake mix (18.25 oz size)
1/4 cup cocoa
1 stick butter, melted
1 cup cola (pick your favorite)
½ cup buttermilk
2 eggs
1 tsp vanilla
1 ½ cups miniature marshmallows

Place all ingredients, except marshmallows, into a large mixer bowl and using the flat paddle, mix about one minute at low speed. Increase speed to medium and mix an additional 2 minutes or until mixture is fully blended. Stir in marshmallows. Pour into a 9x13" dish which has been sprayed with cooking oil spray. Bake at 350 deg about 40 to 45 minutes. Remove from the oven and allow to cool about 15 minutes. You may then ice with cola frosting (recipe follows) if you wish. It is good with our without it.

Cola Icing:
1 stick butter
1/4 cup cocoa powder
1/3 cup cola (use the same one as the cake or it will taste funny)

4 cups confectioners sugar
1 cup finely chopped pecans

Place the butter in a saucepan and start to melt over medium heat. As the butter melts, stir in the cocoa and the cola.   Bring just to a boil. Remove from heat and stir in confectioners sugar. Beat until it is thickened and smooth. Stir in pecans. Pour icing over warm cake and smooth with a spatula. Allow to cool at least another half hour before serving.

Apple Cake
3 eggs
2 cups sugar
1 cup cooking oil
2 cups all purpose flour
2 tsp cinnamon
1 tsp baking soda
½ tsp salt
1 tsp vanilla
1 cup chopped walnuts
4 cups peeled, cored and thinly sliced tart apples (about 5 medium apples)

Beat eggs with a mixer until thick and light. Combine sugar and oil; pour into eggs with mixer on medium speed. Stir together flour, cinnamon, baking soda, and salt; add to egg mixture with vanilla, beat to mix. Stir in walnuts. Spread apples in a 13x9x2 inch pan which has been sprayed with cooking oil spray. Pour batter over apples, spreading to cover. Bake in a 350 degree oven for 1 hour. Remove from oven and cool. If you wish, you may spread with Cream Cheese Icing.

Cream Cheese Icing
6 oz cream cheese, softened
1/4 cup melted butter
2 cups powdered sugar
1 tsp lemon juice

Beat cream cheese until fluffy. Beat in butter; then beat in powdered sugar and lemon juice. Spread over cooled cake. Refrigerate.

Chocolate Chip Orange Coke Cake
A real treat from Cissie Ivey in the Bakery at Dollywood
2 cups all purpose flour
2 cups sugar
1 cup vegetable oil
3 TBSP cocoa
1 cup chocolate chips
1 tsp baking soda

137

1 tsp baking powder
dash of salt
1 cup Coke
2 oz orange zest

Icing
    4 cups sugar
    6 TBSP water
    2 TBSP cocoa
    dash of salt
    1 TBSP cooking oil
    1 cup chocolate chips
    orange slices for garnish

Combine flour and sugar in mixing bowl. Heat 1 cup vegetable oil, 3 TBSP cocoa, 1 cup coke to boiling and pour over flour and sugar. Mix thoroughly. Add baking powder, baking soda, salt, chocolate chips, and orange zest and mix well. Bake in a greased and floured round pan for 40 minutes at 350 deg.

While still hot frost with icing. Combine oil, cocoa, and cola and heat to a boil pour over sugar and mix well. Spread over hot cake. Decorate cake with orange slices.

Joyce's Bundt Cake
The Girls at Joyce's Beauty Shop and several others
    1 pkg yellow cake mix
    4 eggs
    1 cup water
    3/4 cup oil
    1 cup pecans, chopped
    1 can coconut pecan frosting

Mix all together. Bake in a greased and floured bundt pan from 45 to 60 minutes at 350 degrees. Allow to cool before turning out.

Cream of Coconut Cake
    1 (18.25-ounce) pkg white cake mix
    3 eggs
    1/4 cup vegetable oil
    1 (8-ounce) can cream of coconut
    1 cup sour cream

Preheat oven to 350 deg. Grease and flour a 9 x 13 pan. Combine in large mixing bowl, cake mix, eggs, vegetable oil, cream of coconut, and sour cream; beat with electric mixer for 4 minutes. Pour batter into prepared pan. Bake for 35 to 40 minutes, or until wooden pick inserted in center comes out clean. Cool cake completely before frosting. I like the following cream cheese frosting for this cake. It is far easier than the traditional 7 minute frosting and looks just as pretty when covered with coconut.

<u>Cream Cheese Frosting</u>
>   1 (8-ounce) pkg cream cheese, softened
>   1 tsp vanilla extract
>   2 TBSP milk
>   4 cups powdered sugar
>   Flaked coconut

Combine cream cheese, vanilla, milk, and powdered sugar and beat with electric mixer until smooth. If thinner consistency is desired, add more milk, a teaspoon at a time until you reach the desired consistency. Frost cake and sprinkle the top generously with coconut.

Can This Be for Real Fudge Cake
>   2/3 cup butter
>   1 ½ cups sugar
>   3 eggs
>   1 tsp vanilla
>   ½ cup cocoa
>   2 1/4 cups plain flour
>   1 tsp each baking powder and soda
>   1/4 tsp salt
>   1 cup beer (not light)
>   2/3 cup chopped kraut, rinsed and drained

Cream butter and sugar. Add eggs. Mix all dry ingredients together thoroughly. Alternately add the dry ingredients with the beer. Stir in the kraut. You may bake this in two greased and floured 9" cake pans or in a greased and floured 9x13 baking pan. The layer pans will need to bake in a 350 deg oven about 35 minutes. The 9x13" pan will need about 40 minutes. Test either to be sure they are done. Allow to cool at least 10 minutes if you used round cake pans before you turn out.

Here is an easy fudge frosting which can be used either with layers or with the sheet cake.
<u>Easy Fudge Frosting</u>
>   2 4 oz bars Baker's sweet cooking chocolate
>   2 3 oz pkgs cream cheese
>   2 TBSP cream
>   2 cups sifted confectioners sugar
>   1/4 tsp salt
>   1 tsp vanilla

Melt the chocolate according to pkg directions. Blend in the cream, vanilla, and the cream cheese. Beat in the powdered sugar. Spread on either cake after it has cooled completely.

Quick Red, White, and Blue Cake
    1 pkg white cake mix
    Ingredients to prepare cake according to pkg directions
    1 small pkg blue gelatin
    1 small pkg red gelatin

Prepare cake mix according to pkg directions. Spoon out about 1 cup of batter into each of the two bowls. Add blue gelatin to one bowl and red to the other. Stir to mix. Pour about half the white cake mix into a prepared bundt cake pan. Spoon large globs of red and blue cake mix onto it using about half of each. Pour on rest of white batter and put the rest of the colored mix on top. Cut through batter in an "S" shaped manner to swirl color. Bake according to pkg directions. Turn out onto a plate and allow to cool. Sprinkle with powdered sugar. By the way, sugar free gelatin works fine in this if you can find sugar free blue.

Glazed Irish Tea Cake
    1 1/4 tsp baking powder
    3/4 cup butter, softened
    1/4 tsp salt
    1 cup sugar
    1 cup dried currants
    2 tsp vanilla
    2/3 cup buttermilk
    2 eggs
    3 oz cream cheese, softened
    1 3/4 cups plain flour

Glaze
    ½ cup confectioners' sugar
    2 tsp lemon juice

Generously grease a 9-inch (7-cup capacity) loaf pan. Dust with flour; tap pan over sink to discard excess flour. Cut piece of parchment paper or waxed paper to fit bottom of pan. Set aside. Use mixer to cream butter, sugar, and vanilla until fluffy. Add eggs, 1 at a time, beating each until fluffy. Add cream cheese. Mix until well combined. Mix flour, baking powder, and salt together. Put currants in small bowl. Add 1/4 cup of flour mixture to currants. Stir currants until well coated. Add remaining flour to batter, alternating with buttermilk. Mix until smooth. Use wooden spoon to stir in currants and the remaining flour. Stir until well combined. Transfer batter to prepared pan. Smooth surface with spatula. Bake at 325 deg until well-browned and toothpick inserted into center comes out clean, about 1 hour and 25 minutes. Cake will crack on top. Let cake rest in pan for 10 minutes. Use flexible metal spatula to separate cake from sides of pan. Carefully remove cake from pan to cooling rack. Peel off waxed paper. Make glaze by mixing lemon juice with confectioner's sugar. Spread glaze on warm cake. Let cake cool completely. Cake can be stored 3 days at room temperature in foil. Cake can also be frozen up to 3 months, wrapped airtight.

Lady Vols Big Orange Velvet Pound Cake.
    1 cup butter
    ½ cup shortening
    3 cups sugar
    7 eggs
    2 tsp orange extract
    1 oz orange food color (or ½ oz yellow and ½ oz red)
    3 cups plain flour
    1/4 tsp salt
    1 cup milk

Cream butter, sugar, and shortening. Add eggs, one at a time, beating after each addition. Add flavoring and food color. Mix salt with flour and add alternately with milk. Turn into a large tube pan which has been greased and floured. Bake at 325 deg for 1 hour and 20 minutes or until it tests done. Allow to cool and frost with cream cheese frosting.

Jenny Janeway's Carrot Cake
Jennie Janeway   Baptist Hospital
    2 cups all-purpose flour
    2 tsp baking soda
    3 tsp ground cinnamon
    1/2 tsp salt
    3 large eggs
    2 cups sugar
    3/4 cup vegetable oil
    3/4 cup buttermilk
    2 tsp vanilla extract
    2 cups grated carrots
    1 (8 ounce) can crushed pineapple drained
    1 (3 1/2 ounce) can sweetened flaked coconut
    1 cup pecans
    buttermilk glaze
    cream cheese frosting

Stir together first 4 ingredients. Beat eggs and next four ingredients at medium speed with an electric mixer until smooth. Add flour mixture, beating at low speed until blended. Fold in carrots and next 3 ingredient. Pour batter into a greased and floured 13x9 inch pan. Bake at 350 deg for 30 minutes, cover pan loosely with aluminum foil to prevent excessive browning, and bake 13 more minutes or until a wooden pick inserted into center comes out clean. Drizzle Buttermilk Glaze evenly over cake after you have pierced it may times with the handle of a wooden spoon. Spread Cream Cheese Frosting evenly over cake.

Buttermilk Glaze:
     2 cups sugar
     3 tsp baking soda
     1 cup butter
     1 cup buttermilk
     2 TBSP light corn syrup
     2 TBSP vanilla extract

Bring sugar, baking soda, butter, buttermilk, and corn syrup to a boil in a Dutch oven over medium heat. Boil, stirring often, 4 minutes or until mixture is golden brown. Remove from heat, and stir in vanilla extract.

Cream Cheese Frosting :
     1 cup butter softened
     3 (8 Ounce) packages cream cheese
     2 (16 ounce)packages powdered sugar
     3 tsp vanilla extract
Beat butter and cream cheese at medium speed with an electric mixer until creamy. Add powdered sugar and vanilla; beat at high speed 10 seconds or until smooth

Slow Cooker Hot Fudge Cake
     1 cup plain flour
     ½ cup sugar
     2 TBSP baking cocoa
     2 tsp baking soda
     ½ tsp salt
     ½ cup milk
     2 TBSP vegetable oil
     1 tsp vanilla
     ½ cup chopped nuts
     ½ cup brown sugar, packed
     1/4 cup baking cocoa
     1 ½ cups hot water

Spray inside of slow cooker with cooking oil spray. Mix flour, sugar, 2 TBSP cocoa, baking soda, and salt. Stir in milk, oil, and vanilla until smooth. Stir in nuts and spread batter in slow cooker. Mix brown sugar and 1/4 cup cocoa. Stir in hot water until smooth and pour evenly over batter in cooker. Cover and cook on low about 2 to 2 ½ hours. Turn off cooker and uncover. Allow to cool about 30 minutes before serving the warm cake with the sauce which will have formed spooned over it. Some ice cream would not hurt.

Macaroon Cake

Originally given to us by Zelma Cate about 5 or 6 years ago   Note: This cake does not have coconut in it.

> 2 cups each, sugar and flour
> 1 cup wesson oil
> 6 eggs
> 1 tsp vanilla flavoring
> 2 tsp lemon flavoring

Mix together sugar, flour, and oil. Add eggs one at a time, beating after each. Add flavorings. Spray a tube pan with cooking oil spray and line the bottom with waxed paper. Do not flour. Turn batter into pan and bake at 300 deg for 45 minutes and then 325 deg for 15 minutes. Allow cool 10 to 15 minutes in pan before turning out.

Ginger Marble Cake

> 1 pkg pound cake mix
> 1 pkg gingerbread mix
> confectioners sugar

Prepare pound cake mix as instructed on the package using 3/4 cup water. Prepare gingerbread mix as instructed on the package using 3/4 cup water. Spoon white and brown batters alternately into a bundt or 10" tube pan which has been greased and floured. Move a table knife through the batter in an "s" pattern to form a marbled effect. Bake one hour at 325 deg or until cake tests done. Cool 15 minutes on a rack before turning out onto a rack to cool completely.   When ready to cut the cake, dust with confectioner's sugar.

Fresh Peach Cake

> 1 ½ cups brown sugar
> ½ cup butter
> 1 egg, well beaten
> 2 cups flour
> 1 tsp baking soda
> 1 cup buttermilk
> 2 cups diced fresh peaches

Topping:

> 1/4 cup sugar
> 1 tsp nutmeg (you may use cinnamon if you like)

Cream together the brown sugar and butter. Add egg. Sift together four and baking soda. Add to creamed mixture alternately with buttermilk. Lightly fold in peaches. Pour batter into a 9x13" pan which has been sprayed with cooking oil spray. Combine sugar and nutmeg and sprinkle over the batter. Bake at 350 deg for about 35 minutes or until cake tests done.

Peach Upside Down Cake
> 2 lbs fresh peaches (freestone works best for this)
> ½ cup light brown sugar
> 5 TBSP butter
> 2 1/4 cups flour
> 1 ½ tsp baking soda
> 1/4 tsp salt
> ½ tsp each cinnamon, ginger, and nutmeg
> 1 cup granulated sugar
> 1 stick butter
> 1 egg
> 1 tsp vanilla
> 1 ½ cups sour cream

Peel and halve the peaches. Melt 5 TBSP butter in a skillet which can be placed into the oven (cast iron is great) and stir in brown sugar. Cook until sugar is dissolved. Remove from heat and place the peach halves into the skillet with the cut side up. Mix flour, salt, baking soda, and spices. Cream stick of butter with granulated sugar and beat in egg and vanilla. Add the flour mixture alternately with the sour cream, starting and ending with flour. Spread batter over peaches and place in a 350 deg oven. Bake about 50 to 55 minutes or until cake tests down. Remove from oven and allow to stand a couple of minutes. Turn out onto a plate large enough to catch the caramel which will have formed. Serve warm or cold with some vanilla ice cream.

Chocolate Macaroon Bundt Cake
> 1 (18.25 ounce) package chocolate cake mix
> 3/4 cup cold coffee
> 1/4 cup vegetable oil
> 3 eggs
> 2/3 cup chopped nuts
> 1 egg
> 1/8 tsp salt
> 1 cup flaked coconut
> 1 tsp vanilla
> 1/3 cup sugar
> 1 (8 oz.) pkg cream cheese, softened

Mix the cake mix with the coffee, oil, and 3 eggs. Beat until smooth. Turn into a bundt pan which has been sprayed with cooking oil spray. Sprinkle nuts over top. Beat together the egg and the salt until light. Stir into cream cheese until blended. Stir in sugar, vanilla, and coconut. Drop coconut mixture onto cake keeping it away from the edges of the pan. Bake at 350 deg about 45 minutes or until it tests done. Allow to cool about 10 minutes in the pan before turning out.

If you wish, you can make a glaze for this cake by heating ½ cup heavy cream in a heavy saucepan until it almost boils. Stir in ½ cup chocolate chips and stir until chocolate is melted. Drizzle over cooled cake.

King's Cake

This is merely one version of this popular treat. This comes from an old New Orleans cookbook although the standard King's Cake is like a yeast raised coffee cake. I like this better.

    3 ½ cups flour
    1 ½ cups sugar
    1 cup water
    2/3 cup vegetable oil
    1/3 cup nonfat dry milk
    3 teaspoons baking powder
    1 teaspoon vanilla
    ½ teaspoon salt
    8 egg whites
    Light Lemon Glaze (recipe follows)
    Colored sugar crystals
    Small china or plastic baby doll*

Preheat oven to 375 deg. Grease and flour a 10-inch fancy tube pan. Combine flour with sugar, water, oil, dry milk, baking powder, vanilla, and salt in a bowl. Mix until smooth. Whip the egg whites until stiff. Fold whipped egg whites into the batter until evenly blended. Spoon batter into the prepared pan. Bake 40 to 50 minutes until cake bounces back when gently touched in the center. Turn out of pan onto cake rack; cool thoroughly. Drizzle with Light Lemon Glaze and decorate with purple, green, and yellow crystal sugar.

Light Lemon Glaze:
Mix 1 cup sifted powdered sugar with 1 tablespoon fresh lemon juice, ½ teaspoon grated lemon rind, a dash of salt, and 2 to 3 tablespoons hot water until mixture is smooth and can be drizzled onto the cake.

If you do not happen to have colored crystal sugar, you can divide the glaze into three bowls and color it with food color before drizzling on the cake. This will work better if you leave the glaze fairly thick.

7-UP Cake

Serena Brady   Morristown, Tn
        3 sticks butter
        3 cups sugar
        5 eggs
        3 cups plain flour
        2 TBSP lemon extract
        3/4 cup 7-UP

Cream sugar and butter until fluffy. Beat in eggs, one at a time, beating with each addition. Add flour and lemon extract. Fold in 7-UP. Pour into a well greased 12 cup Bundt pan and bake in a 325 deg oven about 1 hour and 15 minutes. Allow to cool in the pan a few minutes before turning out.

Sweet Potato Cake
    1 box yellow cake mix
    3 eggs beaten
    1 29 oz can sweet potatoes
    ½ cup white sugar
    1/3 cup cooking oil
    ½ cup brown sugar
    ½ cup chopped pecans

Heat oven to 350°. Grease and flour Bundt pan. Into prepared pan sprinkle mixture of brown sugar and chopped pecans. Mash sweet potatoes (do not drain) with white sugar and cooking oil. In electric mixer, mix dry cake mix with beaten eggs and the sweet potato mixture. Pour into Bundt pan and bake at 325 for about 1 hour. Test for doneness with cake tester or toothpick. When done, let sit for 10-15 minutes on wire rack in pan, then invert onto a 10" plate. No frosting is needed because it has its own crunchy brown sugar/pecan topping.

Traditional Bunny Cake
    1 pkg white cake mix
    ingredients to make cake according to pkg directions
    cream cheese icing (see below)
    coconut
    candy for decoration

Bake the cake according to package directions in 2 9" layers. Cool. Place one layer about 2/3 way down a large platter. From the second layer, cut an oval from each side of the layer to make the ears. Use the remaining piece for a bow tie. Trim the end from one end of each "ear" piece and place near the top of the cake layer so they are "ear looking". Place the bowtie piece at the bottom of the center piece. Ice with cream cheese icing. Cover "face" generously with coconut. Place round candies for eyes, nose, and mouth. Licorice strings make nice whiskers. Be creative. Add some flat candies to the tie for polka dots. Smile when you serve it.

Cream Cheese Frosting
    1 (8-ounce) pkg cream cheese, softened
    1 tsp vanilla extract
    2 TBSP milk
    4 cups powdered sugar
    Flaked coconut

Combine cream cheese, vanilla, milk, and powdered sugar and beat with electric mixer until smooth. If thinner consistency is desired, add more milk, a teaspoon at a time until you reach the desired consistency.

Double Lemon Streusel Cake
    1 pkg lemon cake mix
    ½ cup cold butter
    ½ cup walnuts, chopped
    2 eggs
    3/4 cup milk
    1 pkg (8 oz) cream cheese, softened
    1/4 cup sugar
    1 TBSP lemon juice
    1 tsp lemon peel

Heat oven to 350°. Grease 9 x 13 inch pan. Cut butter into cake mix, reserving 1 cup. Set reserved mix aside for topping. Add eggs and milk to cake mix, beating on high for 2 minutes. Pour into pan. In separate bowl, beat cream cheese, sugar, lemon juice, and peel until smooth. Spoon over batter, spreading to edges of pan. Add chopped nuts to reserved cake mix. Sprinkle over cream cheese mixture. Bake 30-35 minutes.

This cake is a little more trouble than we usually do, but it is SO good.

Lemonade Pound Cake
    1 pkg white cake mix
    1 cup sour cream
    1 6 oz container frozen lemonade concentrate, thawed
    3 oz cream cheese, softened
    3 eggs

Lightly spray a 12 cup bundt pan with cooking oil spray. Place the cake mix, sour cream, lemonade concentrate, cream cheese, and eggs in the large bowl of an electric mixer. Beat on low about 1 minute to mix, scraping the bowl if necessary. Increase speed to medium and beat about 2 minutes more. Scrape batter into prepared bundt pan and bake about 40 to 45 minutes in a preheated 350 deg oven. Allow the cake to cool about 10 minutes before turning out onto a plate. If you feel that a cake must be glazed to be acceptable, you can make an easy glaze of mixing 3 TBSP lemon juice with 1 cup confectioners sugar. You may add a little grated lemon zest if you want to increase the flavor. Drizzle this glaze over the warm cake for maximum effect.

Banana Bundt Cake
    3 cups plain flour
    2 cups sugar
    1 tsp baking soda

1 tsp cinnamon
3 eggs, lightly beaten
1 cup vegetable oil
2 cups finely chopped ripe bananas (about 3 medium sized bananas)
1 8 oz can crushed pineapple, undrained
½ cup flaked coconut
1 ½ tsp vanilla
1 cup chopped nuts

In a large bowl, combine the flour, sugar, baking soda, and cinnamon. Add the eggs, oil, bananas, pineapple, and vanilla. Stir together until just mixed. Fold in coconut and nuts. Pour into a greased bundt pan and bake at 350 deg about 60 to 70 minutes or until it tests done. Cool for 10 minutes before removing cake from pan to a wire rack to cool completely.

Black Forest Pudding Cake
2 21 oz cans cherry pie filling
1 12 oz pkg semi sweet chocolate chips
1 cup pecans, chopped
1 18.25 oz pkg chocolate cake mix
3/4 cup butter, melted

Spread pie filling on the bottom of a 9x13" baking pan which has been sprayed with cooking oil spray. Sprinkle with half the pecans and half the chocolate chips. Sprinkle dry cake mix evenly over pecans. Sprinkle with remaining chocolate chips and pecans. Drizzle with melted butter. Bake at 350 deg about 50 minutes or until bubbly. Serve warm with whipped cream or ice cream.

Sweet Chocolate Pound Cake
1 12 oz pkg milk chocolate chips
½ cup butter, softened
2 cups sugar
4 eggs
2 tsp vanilla
1 cup buttermilk
2 TBSP water
2 ½ cups plain flour
½ tsp salt
1/4 tsp baking soda

Place the chips in a bowl and melt in the microwave by heating about 45 seconds, then stirring and continuing to heat in 15 second intervals until melted. Set aside. In a mixing bowl, cream butter and sugar until light and fluffy. Add eggs, one at a time, beating well after each addition. Blend in melted chocolate and vanilla. Combine buttermilk and water. Combine flour, salt, and soda. Add liquid and flour mixture alternately with the buttermilk mixture, beginning and ending with flour. Pour into a greased and floured tube pan or bundt pan. Bake at 325 deg about 1 ½ hours or until it tests done. Cool for 10 minutes in the pan before turning out onto a rack to cool. If you wish, you may dust the cake with confectioners' sugar.

Pina Colada Cake
> 1 yellow cake mix (with ingredients to prepare according to box directions)
> 1 15 oz can Coco Lopez Cream of Coconut
> ½ 20 can crushed pineapple, drained (or use an 8 oz can if you can find one)
> 2 to 3 cups whipped topping
> toasted coconut

Bake cake according to package directions in a well greased 9x13" pan. Allow to cool. Pierce the cake with a fork all over top. Spread on the Cream of Coconut. Spread the drained pineapple over that. Ice the top with whipped topping.   Sprinkle with toasted coconut. You should chill the cake until you are ready to serve and store in the refrigerator until you have finished it.

War Cake
> 1 cup brown sugar
> 1 cup water
> 1 cup raisins
> 2 TBSP butter (or margarine)
> 1 tsp cinnamon
> ½ tsp cloves, ground
> 1 ½ cups flour
> ½ tsp salt
> ½ tsp baking powder
> ½ tsp soda
> ½ cup chopped walnuts

Preheat oven to 350 deg. Grease and flour an 8x4" baking pan. Place brown sugar, water, raisins, butter, cinnamon, and cloves in a heavy saucepan and bring to a boil. Turn down heat and cook gently for 5 minutes. Remove from heat and let cool until the mixture is lukewarm. Mix the flour, salt, baking powder, and baking soda. Add flour mixture to the cooled sugar mixture, beating until the batter is smooth. Stir in the walnuts. Spread evenly in the baking pan and bake for 25 to 30 minutes or until a toothpick inserted in the center of the cake comes out clean. Let cool in the pan 10 minutes, then turn onto a rack to cool completely.

Sour Cream Pound Cake
Judy Armstrong   From Recipes to Raise the Roof
> 1 Box Duncan Hines Butter Yellow Cake mix
> ½ pt (1 cup) sour cream

1 tsp vanilla
1 cup pecans, chopped
½ cup sugar
4 eggs
3/4 cup oil
3 TBSP brown sugar
1 ½ tsp cinnamon

Mix together all ingredients except brown sugar and cinnamon. Pour half cake batter into a bundt pan. Sprinkle with cinnamon and brown sugar. Then pour rest of batter on top. Bake at 350 deg for 1 hour or until done.

Pies

Sour Cream Apple Pie
2 TBSP all-purpose flour
1/4 teaspoon salt
3/4 cup white sugar
1/4 tsp cinnamon
1 egg
1 cup sour cream
1 teaspoon vanilla extract
3 cups apples, peeled and sliced
1 9 inch deep dish pie shell, uncooked
1/3 cup white sugar
1/3 cup all-purpose flour
1 tsp ground cinnamon
2 TBSP butter

Stir together 2 tablespoons flour, salt, 3/4 cup sugar, and nutmeg in bowl. Combine egg, sour cream, and vanilla in another bowl; mix well. Add egg mixture to dry ingredients; mix well. Stir in apples, and spoon mixture into unbaked pie shell. Bake in a preheated 400˚ oven 15 minutes. Reduce temperature to 350˚ and bake 30 minutes more. Remove pie from oven. Combine 1/3 cup sugar 1/3, cup flour, and 1 teaspoon ground cinnamon in bowl. Cut in 2 tablespoons butter or regular margarine until crumbly, using a pastry blender. Sprinkle cinnamon mixture over pie. Return to oven and bake 10 minutes more or until topping is brown. Cool on rack. This is good warm or cold.

Honey Pecan Pumpkin Pie
2 cans solid pack pumpkin
3/4 cup honey
1 1/4 tsp ground cinnamon
1 tsp ground ginger
½ tsp ground nutmeg

½ tsp salt
2 cups heavy cream
3 eggs, beaten
2 (9 inch) unbaked deep dish pie crusts
3/4 cup chopped pecans

Preheat oven to 350 deg.   In a medium bowl, mix pumpkin, honey, cinnamon, ginger, nutmeg, and salt. Gradually blend in heavy cream and eggs. Pour into crusts, and top with pecans. Bake pies in the preheated oven about 50 minutes, or until a knife inserted in the center comes out clean.

Maryland White Potato Pie
Trish Hensley of Enoree, S.C. gave this to me after we talked about it at Homecoming at the Museum of Appalachia. It is weird, but it is good.
2 medium potatoes, peeled, cooked, and mashed
2/3 cup butter
1 cup sugar
½ tsp baking powder
pinch of salt
½ cup whipping cream
½ cup milk
2 tsp lemon rind, grated
2 TBSP lemon juice
1 tsp vanilla extract
1/8 tsp nutmeg
4 eggs, beaten
9" unbaked deep dish pie shell

Combine potatoes, butter, sugar, baking powder, and salt in a mixing bowl and mix well. Gradually add whipping cream and milk stirring well until blended. Stir in lemon rind, juice, vanilla, and nutmeg. Add eggs and mix well. Pour mixture into pastry shell and bake at 350 deg for 55 minutes or until a knife inserted in center comes out clean. Cool before serving.

Milk Chocolate Mousse Pie
1 3 oz pkg cream cheese, softened
1/3 cup hot fudge ice cream topping
1 9" chocolate crumb crust
2 pkg Nestle Milk Chocolate Mousse Mix
1 cup whipped topping
additional whipped topping for garnish is desired

In a small mixing bowl, beat cream cheese and hot fudge topping until mixed. Drop by TBSPfuls onto bottom of pie crust. Spread carefully. Prepare mousse mix according to package directions and fold whipped topping into it. Spread over cream cheese mixture in pie crust. Chill for at least 30 minutes. When ready to serve, you may either decorate the top of the pie with additional whipped topping or add a dollop to each piece of pie.

Basic Lemon Meringue Pie
    ½ cup granulated sugar
    3 TBSP cornstarch
    1/4 tsp salt
    1 cup water
    3 large eggs, separated
    1 TBSP butter
    1/4 cup lemon juice
    1 (9-inch) baked pie shell
    1/8 tsp cream of tartar
    2 TBSP granulated sugar

Pie Filling:
Place about 2 inches of water in the bottom of a double boiler, cover, and place on heat. Before placing over bottom of double boiler, combine sugar, cornstarch, and salt in the double boiler top. Gradually add water, stirring to make sure no lumps form. Whisk in the egg yolks. Place on top of double boiler bottom and stir until thickened. Remove from heat. Stir in the butter, and lemon juice. Pour into the pie shell. Refrigerate until thoroughly chilled.

Meringue:
Before starting to make the meringue, preheat the oven to 400°F. Beat the room temperature egg whites with the cream of tartar until soft peaks form. Beat in sugar until stiff peaks form. Cover the top of the pie with the meringue, using a spatula. Be sure that the meringue is sealed to the pie shell all around.   Place in the oven for about five minutes, or until the meringue browns. Remove from oven and serve or return to refrigerator to chill before serving.

Basic Pastry:
    1 1/3 cup all-purpose flour
    ½ cup Crisco shortening
    ½ tsp salt
    3 TBSP ice water (approx)

Mix flour and salt in mixing bowl. Cut shortening into the flour with a pastry cutter, until mixture resembles coarse corn meal. Do not use your hands to try and mix it, the heat from you hands will melt the shortening, causing the pastry to be "heavy", not light and flaky. Once mixture is the right texture, add the ice water and combine with a fork. It may appear as if it needs more water, it does not. Quickly gather the dough into a ball and flatten into a 4-inch-wide disk. Wrap in plastic, and refrigerate at least 30 minutes. Makes 1 (9-inch) pie crust.

<u>To Roll-Out Dough:</u>
Remove dough disk from refrigerator. If stiff and very cold, let stand until dough is cool but malleable. Using a floured rolling pin, roll dough disk on a lightly floured surface from the center out in each direction, forming a 12-inch circle. To transfer dough, carefully roll it around the rolling pin, lift and unroll dough, centering it in an ungreased 9-inch regular or deep-dish pie plate. (Or you can fold dough in quarters, then place dough point in center of pie pan and unfold dough, whatever is easiest for you.)

<u>To bake empty pie shell</u>:
Place the pie shell in the dish and flute edges as you please. Place a sheet of waxed paper in the pie shell and add a couple of cups of rice or dry beans. Place into a 400 deg oven about 5 minutes. Remove the paper and beans or rice and replace in the oven until brown. If the pie shell puffs up, pierce it and press down lightly while still hot.

Green Tomato Pie
Brenda Cooper   Maryville, Tn
        3 1/4 to 4 cups chopped and peeled green tomatoes
        1/8 cup lemon juice
        1/4 cup corn starch
        1/4 cup melted butter
        1 ½ to 1 3/4 cups sugar
        1 tsp cinnamon
        pastry for a double crust pie

Soak tomatoes for 10 minutes in lemon juice. Mix in corn starch, butter, cinnamon, and sugar. Mix well. Cook in microwave on high for 10 minutes. Turn into prepared crust and cover to make a two crust pie. Bake at 350 for 45 minutes to an hour.

Chocolate Chess Pie
        1 cup sugar
        1/4 cup cocoa
        6 TBSP butter, melted and cooled
        2 TBSP flour
        2 TBSP cornmeal
        3 eggs
        1 cup milk
        1 tsp vanilla

Mix together sugar, cocoa, flour, and cornmeal. Beat in the eggs and butter. Slowly stir in the milk until it is fully blended. Stir in the vanilla. Pour into an unbaked 9" pastry shell and bake for about 40 minutes in a preheated 350 deg oven.

Lemon Chess Pie
        3 large eggs
        1 cup white sugar

Juice of 2 lemons
Zest of 1 lemon
2 tablespoons butter, melted
1 tablespoon plain yellow cornmeal
9" unbaked pie shell

Place a baking sheet in the oven and preheat the oven to 325 deg. Beat eggs until light. Beat the sugar into the eggs a little at a time, trying to dissolve the sugar as you go. Add lemon juice, lemon zest, cornmeal, and melted butter and mix thoroughly. Pour into pie shell. Place on the baking sheet in the preheated oven and bake 40 to 45 minutes, until pie is lightly browned and set. Remove to a rack and let cool completely.

Lemon Chess Pie
Favorite Recipes Home Style   Debbie Cummings
    1/4 cup butter
    1 ½ cups sugar
    4 eggs
    1 scant TBSP white cornmeal
    juice of 2 lemons

Cream together butter, sugar, and eggs, one at a time. Stir until well mixed, but don't beat. Add cornmeal and lemon juice. Pour in unbaked pie shell and bake in slow (325 deg) oven for 30 minutes.

Key Lime Pie
Shirley McCarroll   Roane Medical Center Diabetic Support Group Cookbook
    1 reduced fat graham cracker pie crust
    14 oz fat-free sweetened condensed milk
    8 oz fat free egg substitute
    ½ cup lime juice (fresh is best)
    8 oz whipped topping

Preheat oven to 325 deg. Place graham cracker pie crust on a baking sheet and set aside. Whisk together condensed milk, egg substitute and lime juice. Pour mixture into crust and bake until center looks set but still slightly giving, like gelatin (about 15 minutes). Cool completely on a wire rack. Transfer to refrigerator and chill completely (about 1 to 2 hours). Spread whipped topping over pie. Cut into 10 servings and serve.

Key Lime Pie
A weight watcher recipe which is great for diabetics
    1 reduced-fat graham cracker Pie crust
    1 pkg (4 serving size) sugar-free lime-flavored gelatin
    1/4 cup boiling water
    2 6-oz. containers key lime pie flavor light yogurt

1 8-oz container of fat-free whipped topping, thawed

In large heat-resistant bowl, dissolve gelatin in boiling water. Stir in
yogurt with wire whisk. Fold in whipped topping with wooden spoon. Spread
in crust and refrigerate at least 2 hours.

Kiwi-Lime Pie
Pillsbury Refrigerated Pie Crust Championship
Jennifer Hughes of Mascot, 1st Place
Won $200 + chance to win $1000 grand prize.
>   1 pkg Pillsbury refrigerated pie crusts
>   ½ cup lightly salted macadamia nuts, chopped
>   1 tsp unflavored gelatin
>   2 TBSP very warm water
>   1 (8 oz) pkg cream cheese, softened
>   1 (10 oz.) jar lime curd*, divided (2/3 c. & 1/3 c.)
>   5 kiwi sliced

Glaze:
>   2 TBSP lime juice
>   2 TBSP water
>   3 TBSP +1 tsp sugar
>   1 tsp cornstarch

Heat oven to 450F. Unroll one pie dough onto pie plate and crimp edges. Prick bottom
and sides with fork. Bake in oven for 11-12 min. or until golden on edge and bottom.
Spread on bottom of crust: ½ cup lightly salted macadamia nuts, chopped. Combine 1
tsp unflavored gelatin and 2 TBSP very warm water. Mix with cream cheese. Add 2/3
cup lime curd and mix until smooth. Spoon filling over macadamia nuts. Chill 1 hr.
Cut out a circle the diameter of the inside of the pie + ½ inch with the other pie crust.
Bake 8 min. or until golden at 450F. Cool. Place on top of pie. Spread remaining 1/3 c.
lime curd on top of crust.
Arrange kiwi in circular pattern on top of curd. Mix glaze ingredients and heat in
microwave 1 minute, stirring 2-3 times until bubbly and thick. Brush on top of kiwi. Chill
at least 1 hr more. Garnish with a wedge of lime in the center of the pie, if desired.

Peaches and Cream Pie
>   6 to 8 large peaches, peeled, pitted, and sliced
>   1 9" deep dish pie shell, unbaked
>   1 cup whipping cream
>   1 cup sugar
>   3 TBSP plain flour
>   nutmeg

Place fresh peach slices in the pie shell. Thoroughly mix the sugar and flour. Stir into

unwhipped cream. Pour over peaches. Sprinkle with nutmeg (cinnamon will work).
Bake at 350 deg about 60 minutes or until thick and brown. Allow to cool before
serving.

Krystal Chocolate Pie
Published in the Knoxville News-Sentinel as originally published in the Jacksonville Fl.
Journal. (Undated)
>   2 cups sweet milk
>   7 TBSP cornstarch
>   1 1/4 cups sugar
>   1/4 cup cocoa
>   1 egg plus 1 yolk
>   dash salt
>   1/4 tsp vanilla

Heat milk in the top of double boiler (over hot water) until hot, but not boiling. Mix sugar,
cornstarch, cocoa, and salt in mixer. Add the hot milk. Mix for 1 minute or until smooth.
Add egg and yolk and mix well. Pour mixture back in top of double boiler. Stir
occasionally until mixture begins to coat the sides of pan, then stir constantly until thick
to prevent lumping. Place mixture in mixer, add vanilla, and beat on "second speed"
until cool. Pour into prepared pie crust.   The instructions say to allow the filling to cool
overnight in refrigerator if you can. Pour it into the prepared pie shell and smooth the
top. Spread with whipped cream or whipped topping and smooth that as well. Garnish
with chocolate curls if you wish.

Easter Egg Hunt Pie
>   1 prepared graham cracker pie crust
>   1 8 oz pkg cream cheese, softened
>   1 14 oz can sweetened condensed milk
>   3/4 cup water
>   1 4 serving size pkg instant vanilla pudding mix
>   1 ½ cups whipped topping
>   16 (more or less) miniature chocolate Easter eggs

In a large mixer bowl, beat cream cheese until fluffy. Gradually beat in condensed milk
until smooth. Add water and pudding mix. Beat on low speed until smooth. Gently fold
in whipped topping. Spoon half of pie filling into crust. Sprinkle chocolate eggs over
filling. Cover with remaining filling. Chill before serving.

Poor Man's Pecan Pie (Oatmeal Pie)
Arie Hatmaker of LaFollette, Tn. gave us this recipe
>   1 cup oatmeal
>   2/3 cup each, sugar and maple flavored syrup
>   1 stick butter, melted

1 tsp vanilla
2 eggs
1 9" deep dish pie shell, unbaked

Mix the oatmeal and sugar. In the bowl of a mixer, mix the melted butter, syrup, flavoring, and eggs until fluffy. Beat in the oatmeal mixture and turn into the pie shell. Bake in a preheated 350 deg oven for 45 minutes or until barely set in the middle. Cool before serving.

Butterscotch Pecan Pie
4 TBSP butter, melted
1 cup brown sugar
1/4 cup light corn syrup
3 eggs
½ tsp vanilla
1 cup pecans
1 cup butterscotch chips
1 9" deep dish pie shell, unbaked

Beat the melted butter into the brown sugar, corn syrup, eggs, vanilla, and salt. When thoroughly blended, stir in the pecans and the butterscotch chips. Pour into the unbaked pie shell and bake at 350 deg for about 40 to 45 minutes. All to cool before serving.

Easy Apple Pie
4 cups cooking apples, peeled and sliced
3/4 cup sugar
½ stick butter
1/4 cup water
2 tsp ground cinnamon
1 cup self rising flour
1 cup sugar
1 cup milk

In a heavy saucepan, place the apples, sugar, water, and butter over medium heat. Allow to come slowly to a boil. Cook about 2 or 3 minutes. Pour into a 9x13" pan which has been sprayed with cooking oil spray. Mix flour, sugar, and milk and pour evenly over the apple mixture. Bake at 350 deg about 45 minutes or until topping is brown and the juices are thick and bubbly. Serve warm with a slice of Sweetwater Valley Cheese (Or Cabot or your favorite variety)

Nieman Marcus Pie
Diane Goes
1 Box German Chocolate cake mix

1 stick butter (softened)
2 eggs
1 box powdered sugar
1 8 oz package cream cheese
2 eggs
1 cup coarsely chopped pecans

Heat oven to 350 deg. Grease and lightly flour 9x13" pan. Combine dry cake mix, butter, and eggs. Mix thoroughly and spread into pan. Sprinkle nuts over mixture, pressing into batter. Combine powdered sugar, cream cheese, and eggs. Mix thoroughly and pour over chocolate mixture and nuts. Bake 30 - 40 minutes. Cool on rack and cut into squares.

Old Fashioned Raisin Pie
2 cups raisins
2 cups water
3/4 cup sugar
2 TBSP cornstarch
½ tsp cinnamon
1/4 tsp salt
1 TBSP vinegar
1 butter
Pastry for double crust

Combine raisins and water; boil 5 minutes. Thoroughly blend sugar, cornstarch, cinnamon, and salt. Add to raisin and cook, stirring until clear. Remove from heat. Stir in vinegar and butter; cool slightly. Turn into pastry lined 9" pan. Cover with top crust. Cut slits into top crust to allow steam to escape. A decorative pattern is nice. Bake at 375 degrees for about 30 to 40 minutes or until golden brown.

Sherry's White Chocolate Banana Cream Pie
Sherry Estes   Powell, TN
1 frozen pie crust, thawed (I use Mrs. Smith's 9" Deep Dish Shortbread Crust)
2 1 oz packages fat-free, sugar-free, instant white chocolate pudding
2¾ cups cold fat-free milk
2-3 bananas, sliced thin on an angle
1 8 oz tub lite or fat-free Cool Whip

Preheat oven to 375 deg. Carefully line thawed pie crust with foil and fill with dry beans or rice. Bake on middle oven rack for 15 minutes. Discard foil and dry beans or rice. Cool crust completely. Beat pudding mix into milk in bowl with wire whisk for 2 minutes. Fold in ½ tub of Cool Whip. Line the baked and cooled pie shell with ½ the prepared pudding. Add a layer of bananas. Repeat layers with remaining pudding and bananas. Top with remaining Cool Whip. Refrigerate at least 3 hours, until set.

Coconut Pie

Lynda Wright   Corryton, Tn. (My hometown)
>   2 cups milk
>   3/4 cup sugar
>   ½ cup biscuit mix
>   4 eggs
>   1/4 cup butter
>   1 ½ teaspoons vanilla
>   1 cup Bakers Angel Flake coconut

Combine milk, sugar, biscuit mix, eggs, margarine, and vanilla in electric blender container. Cover and blend on low speed for 3 minutes. Pour into greased pie pan. Let stand about 5 minutes, then sprinkle with coconut. Bake at 350 degrees for 40 minutes. Serve warm or cool.

Guilt Free Lemon Pie

>   1 regular size pkg instant vanilla sugar free pudding mix
>   2 cups skim milk
>   1 pkg Crystal-Lite Lemonade Powder
>   1 8 oz pkg frozen whipped topping
>   graham cracker pie shell

Pour cold milk into mixing bowl and add pudding mix. Whisk until mixture starts to thicken. Beat in Crystal-Lite powder. Fold in about 3/4 of whipped topping. Turn into a graham cracker pie crust. Decorate top with whipped topping. Chill before serving.

Pineapple Lemon Pie

Jean Millis
>   1 pre-made graham cracker crust
>   1 small can crushed pineapple with juice
>   juice of 1 fresh lemon
>   1 small lemon instant pudding
>   1 cup whipped topping

Mix all ingredients, except crust, together and turn into pie shell. Chill before serving.

Cappuccino Pie

>   1 chocolate crumb pie shell
>   1 instant vanilla pudding
>   3 TBSP instant cappuccino powder
>   1 cup milk
>   whipped topping

Combine the pudding with the coffee powder. Stir in the milk. Stir in about 2 cups whipped topping. Turn into pie shell and chill. Serve with remaining whipped topping.

Sylvia Ford's Winning Apple Pie

6-8 unpeeled apples, chopped. Place apples in a pie pan.

Mix together:

- 1 c sugar
- 1 c all-purpose flour
- 1 tsp salt
- 1 tsp baking powder
- 1 tsp cinnamon
- 1 egg
- 1 stick butter
- 1 cup pecans, chopped

Beat 1 egg well and add to above dry ingredients. Melt 1 of stick butter (not margarine) and add to mixture. Stir in 1 cup of chopped pecans and mix well until crumbly. Place on top of apples. Bake in 350-degree oven for 45 minutes.

Caramel Sauce:

- 6 TBSP butter (not margarine)
- 1 ¼ cup packed dark brown sugar
- 1 cup cream

Cook over low until it boils, then boil for 2 minutes on low, stirring constantly. Remove from heat and stir in 1 tsp vanilla extract.

Whipped Cream:

Beat together 1 small carton whipping cream and powdered sugar to taste.

Serve apple pie with warm caramel sauce topped with whipped cream. Enjoy!!!

Apple Cranberry Crisp

- 5 medium apples, peeled and sliced thin
- 2 cups fresh cranberries
- 3/4 cup sugar
- 2 TBSP flour

Topping:

- 2/3 cup flour
- 1 cup quick cooking oats
- 3/4 cup brown sugar, packed
- ½ tsp cinnamon
- ½ cup butter, cut into pieces

Mix sugar and 2 TBSP flour and toss with fruit. Spread in a 2 quart baking dish. In a medium bowl, mix flour, oats, sugar, and cinnamon. With a pastry blender or a fork, work in butter until mixture resembles fine crumbs. Sprinkle over fruit. Bake at 375 deg about 35 to 40 minutes or until bubbly and brown.

Note: For a festive treat, serve this warm with chilled egg nog to pour over it.

Now here is a simpler version of this old favorite:

Cranberry Apple Crisp
> 6 cups cooking apples, peeled, cored, and sliced thin
> 12 oz pkg fresh cranberries
> 1 ½ cup sugar, divided
> 1 ½ sticks butter, sliced
> 3/4 cup flour
> 2 cups oatmeal

Toss the apples, cranberries, and 1 cup sugar. Spread evenly in a 9x13" pan which has been sprayed with cooking oil spray. Mix the remaining ½ cup sugar with the flour and oatmeal. Cut in the butter until crumbs form. Sprinkle mixture evenly over apples. Bake in a 350 deg oven about an hour or until bubbly and browned. Serve warm.

Rhubarb-Strawberry Cobbler
> 1 1/4 cup sugar
> 3 TBSP plain flour
> 1 ½ tsp cinnamon
> 1 ½ tsp orange zest
> 6 cups rhubarb, coarsely chopped
> 3 cups strawberries, sliced
> 6 White Lily frozen "Taste of Butter" biscuits

Mix strawberries and rhubarb with sugar, flour, zest, and cinnamon. Spread mixture in 13 x 9 inch baking dish.   Bake in 400 deg oven 15 minutes. Cut still frozen biscuits in quarters and arrange evenly over top of hot fruit. Sprinkle lightly with sugar. Return to oven. Reduce heat to 375 and bake an additional 20 to 25 minutes or until biscuits are brown and juice is thickened. Serve hot, warm, or cold and some vanilla ice cream would not be bad on it.

If you prefer to make your own topping instead of using the biscuits, here is a recipe.
> 1 ½ cup plain flour
> 3 TBSP sugar
> 1 ½ tsp baking powder
> ½ tsp baking soda
> 1/4 tsp salt
> 3 TBSP butter, chilled
> 1 cup buttermilk

In large bowl, combine flour, sugar, baking powder, baking soda, and salt. Using fingers or two knives, cut in butter until mixture resembles small peas. With fork, stir in buttermilk just until soft dough forms. Drop by TBSPfuls in 12 mounds on top of hot fruit filling.   Bake in 400 deg oven 25 minutes or until topping is golden brown

Peanut Butter Chocolate Cheesecake Pie
Winner in the Pie Category
Betty Farrar Baptist Health System
Human Resources Department

- 1 prepared 9 inch chocolate crumb crust (I make my own. See recipe below)
- 1/4 cup plus 2 TBSP chopped peanuts
- 2 TBSP caramel ice cream topping, divided
- 1 2/3 cups (11 oz.) peanut butter & milk chocolate morsels (Nestle')
- 1/4 cup milk
- 1 (8 oz.) cream cheese, softened
- 1/4 cup powdered sugar
- 1 ½ cups frozen non-dairy whipped topping, thawed

Sprinkle 1/4 chopped peanuts onto bottom of crust. Drizzle with 1 TBSP caramel topping. Combine morsels and milk in uncovered microwave-safe bowl.   Microwave on Medium High for 45 seconds. If necessary, microwave at additional 10 second intervals, stirring just until melted. Beat cream cheese and sugar in large bowl until creamy. Beat in chocolate mixture. Add whipped topping and stir until smooth. Spoon into prepared crust. Sprinkle with peanuts, and drizzle with remaining caramel topping. Cover and refrigerate at least one hour.

Recipe for crust:

- 1 stack pack chocolate graham crackers, crushed
- 2 tablespoons brown sugar
- 1/3 cup butter, melted.

Stir together and press into pie plate, using the back of a spoon.

Sweet Potato Crunch Pie
Marie Worley   Dandridge, Tennessee

- 1 (15 ounce) can sweet potatoes, mashed
- 1 (12 ounce) can evaporated milk
- 3 eggs
- 1 ½ cups sugar
- 4 tsp pumpkin pie spice
- ½ tsp salt
- 1 package Duncan Hines Moist Deluxe Yellow Cake Mix
- 1 cup chopped pecans
- 1 cup melted butter
- whipped topping

Preheat oven to 350 degrees. Grease bottom of 9x13 inch pan. Combine sweet potato, evaporated milk, eggs, sugar, spice, and salt in a large bowl. Pour into pan. Sprinkle dry cake mix evenly over the sweet potato mixture. Top with the pecans. Drizzle with the melted butter. Bake at 350 deg for 50 to 55 minutes or until golden brown. Cool completely. Serve with whipped topping. Refrigerate leftovers.

Upside Down Pumpkin Pie
Katherine Bell
        1 (20 oz) can pumpkin
        1 3/4 cups sugar
        2 tsp cinnamon
        ½ tsp ginger
        1 box yellow cake mix
        1 (13 oz) can evaporated milk
        3 eggs, well beaten
        1 tsp nutmeg
        1 cup nuts, chopped
        1 cup butter, melted

Combine all ingredients except the cake mix, nuts, and butter. Mix well and pour into a 9x13" baking dish. Sprinkle cake mix evenly over the top, top with the nuts and drizzle butter over all. Bake at 350 deg for 1 hour. Cool and serve with whipped cream.

Pumpkin Crunch
Carolyn D. Sellers   Knoxville, Tn.
        1 15 oz can pumpkin
        ½ tsp pumpkin pie spice
        2 eggs
        1 cup sugar
        1 large can evaporated milk
        1 box yellow cake mix   (Food Club, of course)
        1 ½ stick butter
        2 cups nuts, chopped   (I used pecans)

Mix the first 5 ingredients in a mixing bowl. Pour into a 9x13" pan. Sprinkle dry cake mix over top of pumpkin mixture. Spread nuts over dry cake mix. Slice butter and lay on top of nuts. Bake at 350 deg for 1 hour.

You will note a great similarity in these last three recipes. I have included all three to show how a good idea gets adapted to personal tastes. This is especially true if you have good cooks working on them.

Lemon Raspberry Tart
Pillsbury Refrigerated Pie Crust Championship
Karen Shankles   1st place

1 2 crust pkg Pillsbury Pie Crusts
1/4 cup confectioners sugar
6 TBSP red raspberry preserves

Filling:
    4 oz cream cheese, softened
    ½ cup plus 2 TBSP sweetened condensed milk
    2 TBSP fresh lemon juice
    ½ tsp freshly grated lemon rind
    1 cup or a 10 oz jar lemon curd
    lemon slices, fresh raspberries, and fresh mint leaves for garnish

Preheat oven to 425 deg. Butter the bottom and rim of a 10 inch tart pan with removable bottom. Remove refrigerated pie crusts from box and let stand at room temperature for 15 minutes.   Sprinkle a 12x12 inch piece of wax paper with 1 TBSP powdered sugar. Place one of the pie crusts on the sugar and sprinkle top with another TBSP of powdered sugar. Press out fold lines and gently roll from the center outward to 11 ½ inch circle. Repeat with remaining pie crust. Spoon the raspberry preserves in the center of one of the crusts and spread outward to within ½ inch of the edge. Dip finger in water and dampen outer edge of raspberry topped crust. Place the other crust on top and press outer edge to seal. Place tart pan on a baking sheet for stability and fit filled crust into pan and press to fit. Prick through upper crust layer with the tines of a fork and place in a preheated oven. Bake for 14 to 16 minutes or until crust is golden brown. Remove from oven and press bottom crust down with the back of a spoon to press out air bubbles. Set aside to cool. In a large bowl, combine cream cheese, sweetened condensed milk, lemon juice, and lemon rind. Beat until smooth. When crust is completely cooled, spread filling evenly into crust. Cover with plastic wrap and refrigerate until set, 20 to 3 hours. When filling is set, stir lemon curd until smooth and spread over cream cheese layer. Cover and refrigerate until ready to serve. To serve, uncover and garnish with lemon slices, fresh raspberries, and mint leaves as desired. Yield 6 to 8 servings.

Cookies:

The Best Peanut Butter Cookies
    1 cup each, shortening and peanut butter (either smooth or crunchy)
    1 cup each, sugar and brown sugar
    2 eggs
    1 tsp vanilla
    3 cups self-rising flour

Cream shortening, peanut butter, and sugar until smooth. Add eggs and vanilla and blend completely. Add flour gradually and mix well. Shape into about 1" balls and place on an ungreased cookie sheet. Press with a fork to form a cris-cross pattern. Bake about 10 minutes at 350 deg. Cool slightly on the pan before moving to a rack to cool completely. Makes about 5 dozen. They will freeze.

Giant Cowboy Cookies
> 1 ½ cups all-purpose flour
> 1 tsp baking powder
> ½ tsp baking soda
> 1/4 tsp salt
> 1 cup butter, at room temperature
> 3/4 cup brown sugar
> ½ cup granulated sugar
> 2 eggs
> 1 tsp vanilla extract
> 2 cups rolled oats
> 2 ½ cups total mix-ins: semisweet chocolate chips, M&M's, chopped walnuts or
> other nuts, and/or raisins or other dried fruit

Heat the oven to 350 deg. In a large bowl, mix together flour, baking powder, baking soda, and salt. In a separate bowl, cream together butter and both sugars, then beat in the eggs. Stir in vanilla extract. Finally, stir in flour mixture. Fold in the rolled oats until thoroughly combined. Measure 2 ½ cups total of the several mix-ins suggested and fold your choices into the dough. Use a 1/4-cup measuring cup to transfer the cookie dough onto an ungreased baking sheet (you'll be able to fit about 6 on a sheet). Wet the bottom of a wide glass and press it onto each cookie to flatten it (alternatively, you can flour the bottom of the glass). Bake for 13 to 15 minutes or until lightly brown. Transfer the cookies to a cooling rack and let cool. Makes approximately 22 cookies.

Almond-Ginger Sandwich Cookies with Orange Filling
Winner in the cookie category Chris Gaskill   Baptist Hospital, PRN
> 1-2/3 cups self-rising flour (low protein flour such as White Lily)
> 1-1/2 tablespoons cornstarch
> 1 teaspoon ginger
> 1 teaspoon cinnamon
> 3/4 cup firmly packed brown sugar
> 1/4 cup white sugar
> 1/4 cup vegetable oil
> 1/4 cup almond butter*
> 1/4 cup finely minced crystallized ginger*
> 1-1/2 tablespoons light-colored corn syrup
> 1 teaspoon almond extract
> 1-1/2 teaspoons vanilla extract
> 1 egg
> orange marmalade

*available at specialty food stores or health food stores

Preheat oven to 375 deg. Sift or whisk together first 4 ingredients in a bowl and set aside. Beat together remaining ingredients except the marmalade with a whisk or electric mixer in a separate bowl until smooth. Stir in flour mixture gradually just until incorporated. Shape dough into (1-inch) balls with lightly greased hands or scoop with a small spring-loaded scoop to keep cookies uniform in size. Place 2 inches apart on baking sheets coated with cooking spray. Flatten balls slightly with the bottom of a glass. Bake at 375 degrees for 7 minutes or until JUST beginning to brown. DO NOT OVERBAKE. Cookies should be cracked on top but not appear done. Cool on pans for 5 minutes then transfer to wire racks to cool completely. Spread bottom of one cookie with marmalade and sandwich with the bottom of another cookie. Makes approximately 2 dozen sandwich cookies.

Quick Lemon Cookies
    1 pkg lemon cake mix
    2 cups whipped topping, thawed
    1 egg

Blend all ingredients thoroughly and drop by full teaspoonfuls onto a lightly greased cookie sheet. Bake at 350 deg for 12 to 15 minutes until puffed and lightly browned. Allow to cool on the pan for a couple of minutes before removing to a wire rack to cool.

Ice Cream Brownie
    your favorite brownie recipe (or brownie mix)
    sugar ice cream Ccnes (the sort with a flat bottom)
    Cool Whip or canned cake icing
    decorations

Make your favorite brownie recipe. Use the brownie mixture to fill the cones about 2/3 full. Stand in a muffin tin. Place in a 350 deg oven and bake about 25 to 30 minute. Remove from oven and allow to cool completely. Once cooled, top with cool whip or icing and decorate with your favorite topping.

Fried Oreo Cookies
    1 large pkg Oreo cookies
    2 cups pancake mix
    1 ½ cups milk
    2 eggs
    4 tsp oil

Preheat deep fryer to 375 deg. Combine pancake mix, milk, eggs, and oil. Mix until there are no lumps. Dip Oreos into batter, make sure both sides are covered and put the Oreos into the deep fryer. The cookie will float so that both sides are golden brown. The cookies will cook fast so watch them so they will not burn. Remove with slotted spoon and let drain for a minute on paper towels. Be careful. The inside of these can be very hot, so allow to cool before eating.

Cranberry Nut Bars

    3 eggs
    1 ½ cup sugar
    1 ½ cup flour
    ½ cup butter, melted
    1 3/4 cups fresh cranberries
    3/4 cup chopped walnuts

Beat eggs until thick. Gradually add sugar, beating until well blended. Stir in flour and melted butter. Fold in cranberries and walnuts. Spread evenly in a greased 9x13 inch baking pan. Bake at 350 deg about 40 to 45 minutes or until brown and tests done. Cool and cut into bars.

S'more Brownies

    15 squares honey graham crackers
    3/4 cup (1-1/2 sticks) butter
    4 squares unsweetened baking chocolate
    2 cups sugar
    3 eggs
    1 tsp. vanilla
    1 cup flour
    2-1/2 cups miniature marshmallows
    1 cup semi-sweet chocolate chunks

Preheat oven to 350 deg. Line 13x9-inch baking pan with foil, with ends of foil extending beyond sides of pan; grease foil. Place the 15 graham cracker squares in bottom of pan, overlapping slightly. Place butter and chocolate in large microwavable bowl. Microwave on HIGH 2 minutes or until butter is melted. Stir until chocolate is completely melted. Stir in sugar. Add eggs and vanilla; mix well. Stir in flour until well blended. Spread over graham squares in pan. Bake 30 to 32 minutes or until toothpick inserted in center comes out with fudgy crumbs. (Do not overbake.) Sprinkle evenly with marshmallows and chocolate chunks. Bake an additional 3 to 5 minutes or until marshmallows begin to puff. Cool in pan on wire rack. Lift out of pan onto cutting board using foil handles. Cut into 36 bars.

Easy Nut Bars

    1 roll (or package) chocolate chip cookie dough
    1 ½ cups chopped nuts (pecans or walnuts work nicely)
    ½ cup each, chocolate chips and butterscotch chips

Spray a 9x13" pan lightly with cooking oil spray. Press cookie dough into pan to cover the bottom evenly. Sprinkle nuts over cookie dough and press in lightly. Bake in a 350 deg oven about 15 minutes or until lightly browned. Remove from oven and immediately sprinkle chocolate and butterscotch chips over top of cookies. Return to oven a couple of minutes to melt chips. Spread lightly over top of cookies. Allow to cool completely before cutting into bars.

White Lily Pecan Old-Fashioned Thumbprint Cookies
White Lily Flour makes softer cookies that keep well.
Belinda Ellis   White Lily Foods

      1 cup butter, softened
      ½ cup confectioners' sugar
      ¼ tsp salt
      1 TBSP vanilla extract
      2 cups White Lily All-Purpose Flour
      1 cup finely chopped pecans

Filling: Pumpkin butter or your favorite flavor jam.

Cream butter and sugar until smooth. Add salt and vanilla. Combine flour and pecans and add to sugar mixture. Cover and refrigerate for at least an hour or up to three days. Preheat oven to 350 deg. Shape dough into 1 heaping teaspoon size balls. Place three inches apart on baking pan lined with parchment paper or ungreased.   Place thumb in the center of each to make an indentation. Bake 15 minutes or until lightly browned and set. Cool completely. Fill each cookie with pumpkin butter or use your favorite jam. Makes 60 cookies.

Crisp Fruit Cake Cookies
      1 cup butter, softened
      2 cups sugar
      3 eggs
      3 cups self rising flour
      1 tsp soda
      1 tsp vanilla
      ½ lb candied cherries
      ½ lb candied pineapple
      2 cups finely chopped pecans

Cream butter and sugar completely. Add eggs one at a time, beating well after each egg. Beat in vanilla. Stir soda into flour and add to butter mixture until it is completely blended. Chop the pineapple and cherries as fine as you like. I chop them pretty fine in the Cuisineart. Stir in candied fruit and pecans. Drop by teaspoonful onto an ungreased cookie sheet allowing at least 2 inches between cookies. These cookies will spread (a lot). Bake at 350 deg about 12 minutes or until lightly browned. Allow to cool about 2 minutes on pan before CAREFULLY lifting them off onto a rack to cool. As the cookies bake, they will rise and then fall. As they cool they will become crisp around the edges and chewy in the center.

Raspberry Truffle Brownies

Glenmore Victorian Mansion   Sharon Redden
        1/2 cup butter
        1 1/4 cups semi sweet chocolate chips
        2 eggs
        3/4 cup brown sugar, packed
        1 tsp instant coffee crystals
        2 TBSP water
        1/2 tsp baking powder
        3/4 cup plain flour

Filling:
        1 cup semi sweet chocolate chips
        1 8 oz pkg cream cheese
        1/4 cup confectioners sugar
        1/3 cup seedless raspberry jam

Glaze:
        1/4 cup semi sweet chocolate chips
        1 tsp shortening

Brownies:
Melt butter and chocolate chips, and allow to cool slightly. Beat eggs and brown sugar in large bowl. Dissolve coffee in water. Add to egg mixture with melted chocolate. Mix well. Combine baking powder and flour and stir into chocolate mixture. Spread in greased 9" baking pan. Bake at 350 deg about 30 minutes or until brownies test done. Allow to cool.

Filling:
Melt chocolate chips and allow to cool. Beat cream cheese until fluffy and add sugar and jam. Stir in chocolate and spread over brownies.

Glaze:
Melt chocolate chips and stir in shortening. Drizzle over brownies.

Cut into very small squares.

My Favorite Cookies in All the World (Sometimes called REESE'S Chewy Chocolate Cookies)
        2 cups all purpose flour
        3/4 cup cocoa
        1 tsp baking soda
        ½ tsp salt
        1 1/4 cups (2 ½ sticks) butter, softened
        2 cups sugar
        2 eggs

2 tsp vanilla
1 10 oz pkg REESE'S Peanut Butter Chips

Heat oven to 350 deg. Stir together flour, cocoa, baking soda, and salt. Beat butter and sugar in large bowl with mixer until fluffy. Add eggs and vanilla. Gradually add flour mixture, beating well. Stir in peanut butter chips. Drop by rounded teaspoons onto ungreased cookie sheet. Bake 8 to 9 minutes (Do not overbake. Cookies will be soft. They will puff while baking and flatten while cooling). Cool slightly. Remove from cookie sheet to a rack and cool completely.

Gooey Chocolate Nut Bars
Crust:
>   1 ½ cups flour
>   ½ cup butter, softened
>   1/4 cup brown sugar, firmly packed

Topping:
>   1 ½ cups salted nuts, coarsely chopped (either peanuts or cashews are nice)
>   1 ½ cups semi-sweet chocolate chips
>   3/4 cup sugar
>   3/4 cup dark corn syrup
>   3 eggs, beaten
>   3 TBSP butter, melted
>   2 tsp vanilla

Combine all crust ingredients and beat until the mixture resembles coarse crumbs. Press onto bottom of an ungreased 9x13" pan. Bake at 350 deg about 15 minutes or just until edges start to brown. While the crust is baking, mix all topping ingredients. Spread topping over hot crust. Continue baking about 30 to 35 minutes or until top is set. Cool completely before cutting into bars. Store covered in the refrigerator.

Peanut Butter Bars
Jeff Crumpley   Seymour Tn
>   ½ cup peanut butter
>   ½ cup butter
>   1 ½ cups sugar
>   2 eggs
>   1 TBSP vanilla
>   1 cup flour

Heat oven to 350 deg. Flour and grease 13x9 pan. Melt peanut butter and butter together. Add remaining ingredients and stir until blended. Pour into prepared pan and bake 25 to 30 minutes. Allow to cool and cut into bars.

No-Bake Chocolate Oatmeal cookies

2 cups sugar
1/4 cup cocoa
½ cup milk
1/4 cup butter
2 ½ cups regular oats, uncooked
3/4 cup creamy peanut butter
2 tsp vanilla

Combine sugar, cocoa, milk, and butter in a large, heavy saucepan. Cook over medium heat, stirring occasionally until mixture boils. Boil for one minute and remove from heat. Stir in all other ingredients and blend completely. Drop by teaspoonfuls onto waxed paper and allow to cool completely. Store in an airtight container.

Crispy Lemon Cookies
1 18.25 ounce pkg lemon cake mix
1 cup crisp rice cereal
½ cup butter, melted
1 egg

Preheat oven to 350 deg. In a medium bowl, combine the cake mix and crispy rice cereal. Stir in the egg and melted butter until everything comes together. Roll into firm 1 inch balls and place them 2 inches apart on an ungreased cookie sheet. Bake for 10 to 12 minutes in the preheated oven. Cool for 1 minute on the baking sheets before removing to cool completely on wire racks.

Pumpkin Bars
2 cups plain flour
2 tsp baking powder
1 tsp baking soda
½ tsp each, ginger, nutmeg, and cinnamon
1 tsp salt
4 eggs
1 15 oz can pumpkin
1 ½ cups sugar
1 cup cooking oil
½ cup walnuts, chopped

In the cusineart or a heavy mixer, combine eggs, pumpkin, sugar, and cooking oil. Beat until blended. Mix together the flour, baking powder, soda, salt, and spices. Add to the pumpkin mixture and blend completely. Stir in the walnuts. Spread evenly in a 9x13" ungreased pan. Bake in a preheated 350 deg oven about 30 minutes. Allow to cool. Cut into squares.

If you would like, you can ice these bars with the following icing.

Cream Cheese Frosting
>6 oz cream cheese, softened
>1/3 cup butter, softened
>4 ½ cups powdered sugar
>2 tsp vanilla

With a heavy mixer, cream together the butter and cream cheese. Beat in the powdered sugar a little at a time. Beat in vanilla and continue to beat until the icing is very thick and fluffy. Spread onto the cooled pumpkin bars.

Pumpkin Cheesecake Squares
>1 pkg spice cake mix
>½ stick butter
>4 eggs, divided
>2 8 oz pkgs cream cheese
>1 can sweetened condensed milk
>1 cup canned pumpkin
>½ cup light brown sugar, packed
>½ tsp each, cinnamon, nutmeg, and ginger

Topping:
>1 cup sour cream
>1/4 cup light brown sugar, packed

Reserve ½ cup of cake mix for the filling. Place remaining cake mix in a heavy mixer bowl and add melted butter and one egg. Mix until mixture forms a ball. Using fingers, press into a 9x13" pan which has been sprayed with cooking oil spray. Cover the bottom of the pan and press the mixture about 1" up the sides. Blend the cream cheese until it is smooth. Add milk, ½ cup cake mix, remaining 3 eggs, pumpkin, brown sugar, and spices and continue to beat until the mixture is smooth. Pour over the cake mixture. Place in a 325 deg oven and bake about 40 to 45 minutes. The center of the cake should be set. While the cake is baking, mix the sour cream and sugar for the topping. When the cake is done, remove from the oven and spread the topping over it. Return to the oven about 7 to 10 minutes or until the topping is set. Remove from oven and cool. Cover and chill overnight before serving.

Chocolate Walnut Brownies
>1 pkg devil's food cake mix w/pudding
>5 TBSP butter, melted
>1/3 cup milk
>1 large egg
>1 tsp vanilla
>1 cup chocolate chips
>3/4 cup walnuts, chopped (black walnuts are particularly nice)

Place the cake mix, butter, milk, egg, and vanilla in a large bowl and mix with a mixer about 1 to 2 minutes or until completely mixed. Stir in the chips and walnuts. Turn into a greased and floured 9x13" pan and spread evenly over the pan. You may have to use a fork or your fingers to get the fairly stiff dough spread. It will barely cover the pan. Bake in a 350 deg oven about 20 to 25 minutes. Allow the brownies to cool in the pan before cutting them out. They will be thin and chewy.

Crispy Chocolate Heart Cookies
>   1 cup semisweet chocolate pieces
>   1/4 cup light-colored corn syrup
>   2 TBSP butter or margarine
>   3 cups crisp rice cereal
>   Frosting (optional)
>   ½ tsp butter

Line a cookie sheet with waxed paper. Grease the waxed paper with the ½ teaspoon butter or margarine. Set aside. Put the chocolate pieces, corn syrup, and the 2 tablespoons butter in a heavy medium saucepan. Put pan on low heat. Cook until chocolate and butter are melted, stirring all the time with a wooden spoon. Add the rice cereal to the melted chocolate mixture. Stir with a wooden spoon until the cereal is evenly coated with chocolate. Turn the chocolate-coated cereal out onto the prepared cookie sheet. Pat it into a 12x6-inch rectangle. Chill about 20 minutes or until slightly firm. Cut cereal mixture into heart shapes with a heart-shaped cookie cutter. Decorate with frosting, if you like. Chill until firm; wrap each heart in plastic wrap. Chill until serving time.

If you prefer, you may put the chocolate, butter, and corn syrup into a microwave dish and heat until the chocolate is melted. This will take about 1 minute. Stir once during cooking.

Easy Sugar Cookies
>   1 cup white sugar
>   1 cup butter
>   2 eggs
>   3 ½ cups sifted all-purpose flour
>   2 teaspoons baking powder
>   2 teaspoons vanilla extract

Melt the butter in the microwave or over low heat. Mix together the sugar, butter, and the eggs. Beat well. Stir in the flour and the baking powder. Mix in the vanilla. Drop by teaspoon onto cookie sheets. You may either leave these as you drop them for little balls of cookies, press down with your fingers for irregular cookies, or dip the bottom of a smooth glass in sugar and press down. Bake for 10-15 minutes or until golden brown at 375 deg.

Layered Bars

    1 8 oz can refrigerated crescent dinner rolls
    1 cup white vanilla chips
    1 cup semi-sweet chocolate chips
    1 cup slivered almonds
    1 cup cashew halves and pieces
    1 14 oz can sweetened condensed milk

Line a 9x13" pan with foil using pieces long enough to stick up over the sides. Grease and flour the foil and spray with cooking oil spray. Open and unroll rolls into 2 long rectangles. Press these into the foil lined pan to cover the bottom and about ½" up the sides. Bake in a 375 deg oven about 5 minutes. Remove partially baked crust from oven. Sprinkle with the vanilla chips, the semi-sweet chips, almonds, and cashews. Drizzle sweetened condensed milk evenly over the top. Return to oven and bake and additional 20 to 25 minutes or until lightly browned. Remove from oven. Allow to cool completely. Use foil to lift out of the pan, and cut into bars.

Lemon Squares

    1 ½ cups all-purpose flour
    2/3 cup confectioners' sugar
    3/4 cup butter or margarine, softened
    3 eggs
    1 ½ cups white sugar
    3 TBSP all-purpose flour
    1/4 cup lemon juice
    1/3 cup confectioners' sugar for decoration

Preheat the oven to 375 deg. Grease a 9x13 inch baking pan (or spray with cooking oil spray). Combine the flour, 2/3 cup confectioners' sugar, and butter. Pat dough into prepared pan. Bake for 20 minutes in the preheated oven, until slightly golden. While the crust is baking, whisk together eggs, white sugar, flour, and lemon juice until frothy. Pour this lemon mixture over the hot crust. Return to the preheated oven for an additional 20 to 25 minutes, or until light golden brown. Cool on a wire rack. Dust the top with confectioners' sugar. Cut into squares.

Soft and Chewy Peanut Butter Cookies

    2 cups plain flour
    ½ tsp baking soda
    1/4 tsp salt
    1 1/4 cups packed brown sugar
    1 1/4 cups white sugar
    1 cup butter, softened
    3 eggs
    1 cup creamy peanut butter
    2 teaspoons vanilla extract

Preheat oven to 300 deg. In a medium bowl, combine flour, soda, and salt. Mix well with a wire whisk set aside. In a large bowl, blend sugars, using an electric mixer set at medium speed. Add butter, and mix to form a grainy paste, scraping the sides of the bowl. Add eggs, peanut butter, and vanilla and mix at medium speed until light and fluffy. Add the flour mixture and mix at low speed until just mixed. Drop by rounded spoonfuls onto an ungreased cookie sheet. With a wet fork gently press cookies in a crisscrossed pattern. Bake for 18-22 minutes or until slightly brown along edges.

Resurrection Cookies

        1 cup pecan halves
        1 tsp vinegar
        3 egg whites
        pinch salt
        1 cup sugar
        zipper baggie
        wooden spoon
        tape
        Bible

Preheat oven to 300 F. Place pecans in zipper baggie and let children beat them with the wooden spoon to break into small pieces. Explain that after Jesus was arrested he was beaten by the Roman soldiers. Read John 19:1-3. Let each child smell the vinegar. Put 1 tsp. vinegar into mixing bowl. Explain that when Jesus was thirsty on the cross he was given vinegar to drink. Read John 19:28-30.
Add egg whites to vinegar. Eggs represent life. Explain that Jesus gave His life to give us life. Read John 10:10-11. Sprinkle a little salt into each child's hand. Let them taste it and brush the rest into the bowl. Explain that this represents the salty tears shed by Jesus' followers, and the bitterness of our own sin. Read Luke 23:27.
So far, the ingredients are not very appetizing. Add 1 c. sugar. Explain that the sweetest part of the story is that Jesus died because He loves us. He wants us to know and belong to Him. Read PS. 34:8 and John 3:16.
Beat with a mixer on high speed for 12 to 15 minutes until stiff peaks are formed. Explain that the color white represents the purity in God's eyes of those whose sins have been cleansed by Jesus. Read Isa.1:18 and John 3:1-3. Fold in broken nuts. Drop by teaspoons onto wax paper covered cookie sheet. Explain that each mound represents the rocky tomb where Jesus' body was laid. Read Matt. 27:57-60.
Put the cookie sheet in the oven, close the door and turn the oven OFF. Give each child a piece of tape and seal the oven door. Explain that Jesus' tomb was sealed. Read Matt. 27:65-66.
GO TO BED! Explain that they may feel sad to leave the cookies in the oven overnight. Jesus' followers were in despair when the tomb was sealed. Read John 16:20 and 22.
On Resurrection morning, open the oven and give everyone a cookie. Notice the cracked surface and take a bite. The cookies are hollow! On the first Resurrection day Jesus' followers were amazed to find the tomb open and empty. Read Matt. 28:1-9.
HE HAS RISEN!

Special Peanut Butter Cookies
      1 cup peanut butter (smooth or chunky)
      1 cup sugar
      1 egg
      1 tsp soda

Mix all ingredients. Rolling into balls about 1" across. Place on a lightly greased cookie sheet and press down with a fork. Bake at 350 deg about 10 to 12 minutes or until just barely brown. Allow to cool on pan about 5 minutes before lifting them onto a rack with a spatula to allow to cool completely.

These are great to make with kids. Since there is no flour, there is little mess. Please note that these come out of the oven very, very soft. They firm up as they cool to make wonderful crunchy cookies.

Skillet Cookies
      1 egg, beaten
      1 cup sugar
      1 stick butter
      ½ lb chopped dates
      ½ cup pecans, chopped
      2 cups crisp rice cereal
      2 cups coconut (approx)

Melt butter and beat in sugar, egg, and dates. Cook over medium heat, stirring constantly, about 10 minutes or until thick. Remove from heat and allow to cool slightly. Stir in rice cereal and pecans. While still warm, shape into 1 inch balls and roll in coconut.

Cream Cheese Cookies
      3/4 cup butter
      8 oz cream cheese, softened
      1 cup sugar
      3/4 tsp salt
      1 tsp vanilla
      1 egg
      2 TBSP milk
      2 cups flour
      ½ cup coconut (optional)

Cream together butter, cream cheese, sugar, salt, and vanilla. Add egg and milk, beat well. Add flour and stir in coconut (if you are using). Drop from tsp onto ungreased cookie sheet. Bake at 325 deg for 20 minutes

Good Old Brownies
        1 cup butter
        1 12 oz pkg semi sweet chocolate chips
        2 cups sugar
        4 large eggs
        1 TBSP vanilla
        1 cup all purpose flour
        1 ½ cups chopped nuts, toasted (I like either pecans or walnuts)
        pinch of salt

In a 2 quart microwave proof bowl, melt the butter and one cup of the chocolate chips about 1 ½ minutes or chocolate is melted when the mixture is stirred. Whisk in sugar, vanilla, and then the eggs. Toss nuts, remaining chips and 1 TBSP flour. Stir remaining flour into butter mixture and then stir in the nut mixture. Spread mixture in a greased 9x13" pan and bake at 350 deg for about 35 minutes. Cool on a wire rack before cutting out the brownies.

Almond Toffee Brownies
Another Martha White Recipe
        1 (22.5 oz) pkg Martha White Chewy Fudge Brownie Mix
        ½ cup butter, melted and cooled
        1/3 cup water
        2 eggs
        1 (10 to 12 oz) pkg almond toffee bits
        1/3 cup slivered almonds

In a large bowl, combine brownie mix, butter, water, and eggs. Using a spoon beat 50 strokes or until batter is well blended. Stir in ½ cup almond toffee bits. Spread in a 9x13" pan which has been greased or sprayed with cooking oil spray. Sprinkle remaining bits over batter. Sprinkle evenly with almonds. Bake at 350 deg about 30 to 35 minutes. DO NOT OVERBAKE.

Other Desserts:

Peach and Blueberry Cream Cobbler
        5 peaches, peeled, pitted, and sliced
        1 cup blueberries, washed and picked over
        1 cup sour cream
        1 cup brown sugar
        2 TBSP flour
        One predone pastry sheet
        sugar

Stir flour into brown sugar and mix in sour cream. Stir sour cream mixture into fruit. Turn into an 8" round casserole or a 5x7" dish which has been sprayed with cooking oil spray. Cut pastry into irregular pieces and arrange over top of fruit. Brush with water and sprinkle with sugar. Bake at 350 deg for about one hour or until bubbly and the pastry is brown. Serve warm with sour cream or whipped cream.

White Chocolate Cheesecake with Raspberry Swirl and Macadamia Nut Crust
Grand Prize Winner in the Baptist Hospital Dessert Bake-Off
Minerva Ridner   Baptist Homecare
Crust:

>1 pkg Pepperidge Farm white chocolate and macadamia nut cookies
>½ stick melted butter

Place cookies into a zip-lock bag and crush. Add melted butter and mix together. Press into greased 9-inch springform pan. Set aside.

Filling:

>3 pkg (8 oz) cream cheese, softened
>2/3 cup sugar
>7 egg yolks
>2 cups sour cream
>1 TBSP clear vanilla extract
>½ tsp salt
>12 oz white chocolate, melted
>raspberry extract
>pink gel coloring

Frosting:

>1 pkg (8 oz) cream cheese, softened
>1/3 cup butter, softened
>1 tsp clear vanilla extract
>1cup XXX sugar
>8 oz white chocolate, melted

Preheat oven to 350 deg. For cheesecake, beat cream cheese and sugar in a large mixing bowl until smooth. Add egg yolks one at a time, beating well after each. Beat in sour cream, vanilla, and salt. Blend in melted chocolate. Pour batter (reserve 1 cup) into prepared pan with crust. Add raspberry extract and pink gel coloring into 1cup reserve batter. Pour on top of batter and swirl with knife through batter (be careful not to hit crust with knife). Place springform pan into larger pan. Bake 45 – 50 minutes. Turn oven off and let cool in oven for 1 hour. DO NOT OPEN DOOR. Remove cheesecake from oven and cool completely. Refrigerate overnight.
For frosting, beat cream cheese, butter, XXX sugar, and vanilla until smooth. Gradually add white chocolate. Spread on top and sides of cool cheesecake. Decorate top with fresh raspberries.

Mayfield's Super Smoothies

<u>Sweet and Peachy</u>
> 2 ½ cups Mayfield Snow Cream
> ½ cup Mayfield Milk
> 1/3 cup sugar
> 1 cup fresh peaches, sliced

Mix sugar with peaches in a bowl until dissolved. In blender, combine all ingredients until smoothie reaches desired consistency. Garnish with a mint sprig and a peach slice. Add nutmeg and cinnamon to taste. Makes 4 servings.

Walter's note: I recommend making it just as it is above without the spices. It tastes like the best homemade peach ice cream you ever tasted.

<u>Very Berry</u>
> 2 ½ cups Mayfield Snow Cream
> 1/3 cup sugar
> ½ cup strawberries, sliced
> ½ cup blueberries
> ½ cup raspberries

Mix sugar with fruit in a bowl until sugar is dissolved. In blender, combine all ingredients until smoothie reaches desired consistency. Garnish top with berries. Makes 4 servings

<u>Strawberry Banana Smoothie</u>
> 2 ½ cups Mayfield Snow Cream
> ½ cup Mayfield milk
> 1/3 cup sugar
> 1 cup strawberries, sliced
> 1 banana, sliced

Mix sugar with fruit in a bowl until dissolved. In blender combine all ingredients until smoothie reaches desired consistency. Makes 4 servings.

<u>Chocolate Banana Smoothie</u>
> 2 ½ cups Mayfield Snow Cream
> 2 cups Mayfield chocolate milk
> 1 banana, sliced

In blender, combine all ingredients until smoothie reaches desired consistency. Makes 4 servings.

<u>Chocolate Strawberry Smoothie</u>
> 2 ½ cups Mayfield Snow Cream
> 2 cups Mayfield chocolate milk

1 cup strawberries, sliced
1/3 cup sugar

In blender, combine all ingredients until smoothie reaches desired consistency. Makes 4 servings.

Another Walter note: The Mayfields folks tell me that you can substitute Splenda for the sugar in all these.

Microwave Peanut Brittle
This is my favorite microwave candy recipe.
1 cup roasted, salted peanuts
1 cup sugar
½ cup white corn syrup
1 TBSP butter
1 tsp soda
1 tsp vanilla

Stir together sugar and syrup in a 1 1/2-quart casserole or 4 cup glass measure. Place in microwave oven and cook 4 minutes on high. Stir in peanuts and cook an additional 4 minutes. Add butter and blend well. Return to oven and cook approximately 2 to 3 minutes more on high or until nuts are golden brown. Add soda and vanilla and gently stir until light and foamy. Pour onto greased cookie sheet and let cool. When cool, break into pieces and store in airtight container.

Note: You may use raw peanuts. If so, stir nuts in with sugar and syrup and add 1/8 tsp salt.

Rosy Apple Tapioca
8 to 10 tart apples
½ cup sugar
4 TBSP minute tapioca
4 TBSP cinnamon red hots
½ cup water
whipped topping, optional

Peel and core apples and slice into 8 wedges each. Place in slow cooker. Mix sugar, tapioca, and candy. Sprinkle over apples. Pour water over all. Cook on high for 3 to 4 hours or until bubbly and apples are tender. You may serve hot or cold topped with whipped topping or ice cream.

Peach and Raspberry Cobbler
6 cups peaches (about 2-1//2 lbs.), peeled, pitted and sliced
½ cup brown sugar

2 TBSP fresh lemon juice
½ tsp cinnamon
1 cup raspberries
2 TBSP flour

Topping:
½ cup cornmeal mix
1 cup self-rising flour
1/4 cup sugar
6 TBSP cold butter, cut into pieces
2/3 cup plain yogurt

Preheat the oven to 375 deg. Spray a 9x13" baking dish with cooking oil spray, and set aside. Toss the peaches in a bowl with the brown sugar, lemon juice, cinnamon, and the 2 tablespoons flour. Gently stir in the raspberries, and spoon into the baking dish. Sift together the cornmeal, flour, and sugar. Cut in the butter, pulsing with the food processor or mixing with forks, until the mixture has a coarse, mealy texture. Add the yogurt and stir just until mixed. Spoon heaped tablespoons of the topping mixture over the peaches. They should be just about covered, although there may be some small spaces between the spoonfuls of batter; lightly moisten your fingertips and spread the topping if there are big spots where the fruit isn't covered. Bake 30 to 35 minutes, or until the fruit is bubbling and the top golden brown. Remove from the oven and cool on a rack.

Serve warm, with whipped cream, yogurt, or vanilla ice cream.

Special Lemon Mousse
Do you have your Girl Scout Cookies yet?
1 12 oz pkg cool whip
1 small pkg sugar free lemon Jell-O   (Regular will work)
½ cup lemon drop candies, broken fine
1 pkg Girl Scout Lemon Cooler Cookies   (Broken into crumbs)

Mix cool whip and Jell-O powder thoroughly. Spread in a 7x11" dish. Sprinkle candy crumbs over and then top with cookie crumbs. Allow to stand at least an hour in the refrigerator before serving.

Baked Fruit
Serena Brady   Morristown, Tn
1 large can pineapple chunks
1 large can pear halves
1 large can sliced peaches
maraschino cherries to taste
1/3 cup butter
1 cup brown sugar

Empty fruit into a 9x13" baking pan. You may drain if you wish. If you leave juice, you will have a heavy syrup to serve with the fruit. If you drain, the fruit will have a very rich taste and texture. Melt butter and brown sugar and drizzle over the fruit. Bake at 325 deg for 1 hour.

I should tell you that I changed a couple of things about this recipe. First, Serena did not say whether to drain or not and so I told you the consequences of each. Second, she suggested pineapple slices and peach halves. I used the cut up variety of both because I think this is great with pound cake for dessert and it looks prettier if you have different sized pieces.

Easy Apple Dumplings
 1 12 oz tube refrigerated buttermilk biscuits (not flaky)
 5 medium apples, peeled, cored, and halved (I use Golden Delicious)
 3/4 cup sugar
 3/4 cup water
 6 TBSP butter, melted
 1 tsp vanilla
 cinnamon

Flatten and stretch biscuits with hand. Wrap each biscuit around an apple half and place seam side down in a 7x11 or 9x13" dish. Combine sugar, water, and melted butter and pour over apples. Sprinkle with cinnamon. Bake, uncovered, at 350 deg for 35 to 40 minutes or until golden brown and apples are tender. Serve immediately with whipped cream or ice cream.

Buttermilk Bread Pudding
 7 to 7 ½ cups good French Bread cut into cubes
 1/4 cup butter
 4 cups buttermilk
 1 cup raisins (optional)
 4 eggs, beaten
 1 ½ cups brown sugar, firmly packed
 1 TBSP vanilla
 1/4 cup white sugar

Melt butter in a 9x13" pan and tilt pan to coat with butter. Toss bread and raisins together in large bowl. Mix all remaining ingredients together thoroughly. Spread bread and raisins in prepared pan. Pour milk mixture evenly over bread, pressing bread down to be sure that all is damp with the milk. Flatten top of pudding and sprinkle with white sugar. Bake in a 350 deg oven about 1 hour or until puffed and brown.

Kettle Corn
 3 TBSP popping corn

1 ½ TBSP oil
1 ½ TBSP sugar
1 spray vanilla
1 spray vinegar

Put oil and corn in a heavy pan with a lid. Mix so that corn is evenly coated. Spray with vinegar and vanilla. (If you do not have a spray, add about 1/8 tsp.) Turn on heat. Stir constantly. When about 10 to 12 kernels have popped. Stir in sugar. Cover and shake constantly to stir until all kernels have popped. This works great in the old fashioned corn poppers that have a handle to turn to stir. You can leave the lid off and just stir, but be warned, you will have a lot of popcorn in the floor.

Apple Cheesecake
Crust:
    1 cup graham cracker crumbs
    ½ cup finely chopped pecans
    3 TBSP white sugar
    ½ tsp ground cinnamon
    1/4 cup butter, melted
Filling:
    2 (8 ounce) packages cream cheese, softened
    ½ cup white sugar
    2 eggs
    ½ tsp vanilla extract
    4 cups apples - peeled, cored and thinly sliced
    1/3 cup white sugar
    ½ tsp ground cinnamon
    1/4 cup chopped pecans

Preheat oven to 350 deg. In a large bowl, stir together the graham cracker crumbs, ½ cup finely chopped pecans, 3 tablespoons sugar, ½ teaspoon cinnamon, and melted butter; press into the bottom of a 9 inch springform pan. Bake in preheated oven for 10 minutes. In a large bowl, combine cream cheese and ½ cup sugar. Mix at medium speed until smooth. Beat in eggs one at a time, mixing well after each addition. Blend in vanilla; pour filling into the baked crust. In a small bowl, stir together 1/3 cup sugar and ½ teaspoon cinnamon. Toss the cinnamon-sugar with the apples to coat. Spread apple mixture evenly over cream cheese layer and sprinkle with 1/4 cup chopped pecans. Bake in preheated oven for 60 to 70 minutes. With a knife, loosen cake from rim of pan. Let cool, then remove the rim of pan. Chill cake before serving.

Mayfield Holiday Recipes
With Scottie Mayfield
Recipes use Snow Cream, Snow Cream milk, Egg Nog, or Peppermint ice cream
Winter Wonderland French Toast
    6 slices of bread (any kind but slightly older French or white works best)

3 eggs
1 cup Mayfield Snow Cream milk
1 tsp. nutmeg
1 tsp. cinnamon
confectioners sugar
maple syrup

Beat together the egg, milk, and spices. Heat griddle or skillet to a medium high temperature and add just enough butter or vegetable oil to prevent sticking. Dip each slice of bread in the milk mixture, soaking both sides. Toast the bread on both sides until golden brown. Keep toast in a warm oven until ready to serve. Just before serving add a dusting of snow by sprinkling with confectioners sugar. Serve toast warm with maple syrup on the side. Makes three servings.

Holiday Eggnog Bread
2 eggs
1 cup sugar
1 cup Mayfield eggnog
½ cup melted butter or margarine
2 TBSP rum (or 2 tsp. Rum extract)
1 tsp. vanilla
2 ¼ cups all-purpose flour
2 tsp. baking powder
½ tsp. salt
½ tsp. nutmeg

Preheat oven to 350 degrees. Stir dry ingredients together. Beat remaining ingredients together and combine with dry ingredients. Pour mixture into a greased 9x5 loaf pan. Bake for 45 to 50 minutes.

Peppermint Chocolate Dessert
Crunch Mixture:
1 large box (12 oz.) crushed vanilla wafers
3 oz. can chopped pecans
3/4 cup butter, melted
½ gal. Mayfield Peppermint ice cream

Mix above ingredients and place half crumb mixture followed by layer of ice cream. Top with remaining crumb mixture. Freeze until ready to serve.

Fudge Sauce:
1 cup sugar
2 TBSP flour
1 TBSP butter
1 tsp vanilla

5 TBSP cocoa
1 cup Mayfield milk

Cook over medium-low heat until thickens. Pour on top of peppermint dessert before serving.

A wonderful holiday dessert that all ages will enjoy!

Chocolate Trifle

Maybe also from Diana Brock, but maybe not

    3 boxes instant chocolate pudding mix (4 serving size)
    5 cups milk
    2 pkgs brownie mix, prepared according to pkg instructions
    16 oz whipped topping
    6 Heath Candy bars, crushed

In a large bowl, combine pudding mix and milk; set aside to thicken. Crumble brownies and divide into thirds. Assemble ingredients in a clear bowl in the following order: 1/3 brownies, 1/3 pudding, 1/3 whipped topping, and 2 crushed candy bars. Repeat to use all ingredients. Chill before serving.

Rhubarb and Strawberry Mold with Yogurt Sauce

    2 envelopes unflavored gelatin
    ½ cup orange juice
    3 cups rhubarb, chopped
    1 ½ cups strawberries, sliced
    Splenda or other sugar substitute

Yogurt Sauce

    1 cup low fat yogurt
    1 tsp cinnamon
    Splenda or other sugar substitute

Soften gelatin on orange juice and let stand for 5 minutes. In a heavy saucepan over low to medium heat, cook rhubarb (stir it and liquid will be released. You will not need to add additional liquid) for 5 minutes or until tender. Stir in strawberries, and bring back just to a boil. Stir in gelatin and remove from heat and allow to cool for 5 minutes. Add sugar substitute for desired sweetness. Pour into a 6 cup mold, cover, and chill for several hours or overnight. Unmold and serve with yogurt sauce which you have made by stirring cinnamon into yogurt and adding sugar substitute to taste.

1/8 of this dessert is 64 calories and 11 grams of carbohydrate.

Brownie Mint Souffle with Mayfield Ice Cream

    1 (1 lb. 5.5 oz.) package White Lily Brownie mix
    1/ 2 cup water

1/ 2 cup oil
1 tsp peppermint extract
4 eggs, separated
Mayfield Vanilla Ice Cream
Mint Sprigs

Preheat oven to 375 degrees. Spray a 9 or 10-inch springform pan with nonstick cooking spray. Combine brownie mix, water, oil, extract, and egg yolks until well blended. In a small bowl, beat egg whites until soft peaks form. Gradually fold into brownie mixture. Pour batter into sprayed pan. Bake for 32-38 minutes or until center is almost set. Cool 30 minutes (center will sink slightly). Carefully remove sides of pan. Cut into wedges and serve with ice cream on the side garnished with mint sprigs.

Apple Brown Betty
 5 tart apples, peeled and cored (Granny Smith works nicely)
 1 ½ cups fresh crumbled bread
 ½ cup sugar
 1 tsp cinnamon
 1/3 cup apple juice
 4 TBSP butter

Lightly butter 6-cup baking dish.   Combine fresh bread crumbs, ½ cup sugar, and 1 teaspoon cinnamon. Layer half of the apples in dish. Cover with half of the crumbs. Pour over 1/3 cup apple juice. Dot with 2 tablespoons butter. Repeat with remaining apples and crumbs; dot with 2 tablespoons butter. Cover with foil. Bake in heated 375° deg oven for 25 minutes. Remove foil. Bake 30 minutes longer or until apples are tender. Makes 4 servings.

Slow Cooker Rice Pudding with Fruit
 ½ gallon milk
 1 cup uncooked rice
 1 cup sugar
 3 TBSP cold butter, cut into small pieces
 1/4 tsp salt, optional
 1 tsp vanilla extract
 ½ cup dried apricots or peaches, minced
 1/4 tsp ground cinnamon

Mix all together in a greased slow cooker. Cover and cook on low. Stir and check to see if the mixture is thick at 1 ½ hours. You may cook longer if you wish, stirring occasionally. The longer it cooks, the thicker it will be.

If you do not like apricots, you may substitute raisins or even just leave the fruit out altogether.

Slow Cooker temperatures vary widely among different brands. Only experimentation can tell you the correct amount of time for cooking in your slow cooker/Crock Pot.

Strawberry Trifle
 1 pkg yellow or white cake mix
 2 pints fresh strawberries, capped, sliced, and sprinkled with sugar
 1 box (5oz) vanilla pudding mix, prepared
 1 8 oz package whipped topping
 1/4 cup toasted slivered almonds

Bake cake in oblong 13 x 9 pan as directed on package. Cool. Cut cake crosswise in half. Reserve ½ for another dessert. Cut remaining cake into 8 pieces. Split each piece horizontally. Arrange half the pieces in a 2 quart glass serving bowl, cutting pieces to fit bowl. Mix half of the whipped topping into the mixed pudding. Pour ½ the strawberries with syrup over cake. Spread with ½ of pudding. Repeat with remaining pieces of cake, strawberries, and pudding. Spread remaining whipped topping on top and sprinkle with almonds. Refrigerate until ready to serve.

Strawberry Cheese Tarts
 1 lb cream cheese, softened
 ½ cup sour cream
 1/4 cup sugar
 1 tsp grated lemon peel
 12 packaged graham cracker tart shells (about 3½ inches in diameter)
 1 pint fresh strawberries, capped and halved
 ½ cup apple jelly

Combine cream cheese, sour cream, sugar, and lemon peel in small bowl; beat until smooth. Spread evenly into crumb crusts; refrigerate about 4 hours. About 30 minutes before serving, fit strawberry halves onto top of each tart. Heat apple jelly until just melted and brush over strawberries to glaze. Chill and serve.

Strawberry Mousse
 1 envelope unflavored gelatin
 1/4 cup cold water
 2 cups strawberries, hulled and sliced
 1/4 cup granulated sugar
 1 cup heavy cream, chilled
 3 TBSP powdered sugar
 whole strawberries, garnish

Sprinkle gelatin over cold water in saucepan; let stand 1 minute to soften. Stir over low heat until gelatin is dissolved, about 1 minute. Remove from heat. Place berries, granulated sugar, and gelatin mixture in food processor or blender. Whirl to puree.

Pour into bowl. Chill until mixture mounds when dropped from spoon. Beat cream and powdered sugar in chilled bowl until soft peaks form. Stir one-quarter of cream into strawberry puree to lighten mixture. Fold in remaining cream.

You may pour the mixture into a lightly greased gelatin mold, cover and allow to set. Or, you may spoon into 6 stemmed glasses or dessert bowls, dividing equally. Chill for 2 hours. Or, after lightening puree with cream, layer remaining whipped cream with strawberry puree in stemmed glasses. Garnish with strawberries.

Flamed Island Pineapple with Green Peppercorns in Caramel Sauce with Lime Sherbet

    Fresh pineapple slices cut about ½ inch thick
    sugar (about 1 cup)
    butter (about 1/4 cup)
    rum (about 1 oz)
    Lime sherbet

Make a caramel by heating the butter and sugar in a heavy pan until it starts to brown. Be careful, it will burn. Cook the pineapple slices in the caramel. Add green peppercorns and flame with the rum. To serve, place a slice of pineapple in a pasta plate and spoon some caramel onto it. Place a scoop of lime sherbet in the center.

Walter Note: Be brave and try this. It was, by far, the best dessert we had on the cruise and we had a lot of good desserts. I know the peppercorns seem strange, but give it a try.

Chocolate Nachos

    1/4 cup sugar
    1/4 teaspoon ground cinnamon
    8 6-inch flour tortillas
    1/4 cup butter (no substitutes), melted
    1 cup semisweet chocolate pieces
    2 teaspoons shortening

Combine sugar and cinnamon in a small bowl. Brush one side of each tortilla with melted butter; sprinkle with sugar mixture. Cut each tortilla into eight wedges. Arrange half of the wedges in a single layer on a baking pan. Bake in a 350 deg oven for 10 to 12 minutes or until edges are lightly browned (wedges will crisp upon standing). Meanwhile, melt chocolate pieces and shortening in a small saucepan. Remove wedges from oven. Spread in an even layer on a serving platter; cool slightly. Drizzle with half of the melted chocolate mixture. Arrange remaining wedges in a single layer on the same baking pan. Bake as directed above. Spread in an even layer on a second serving platter; cool slightly. Drizzle with remaining melted chocolate mixture. Serve warm or cool. Makes 64 wedges.

Apple Cheese Casserole
Carolyn Riggs   NHC Fort Sanders
    3 15 oz cans Luck's fried apples with juice
    apple pie spice or cinnamon and sugar
    2 stick butter
    2 cups sugar
    2 ½ cups self rising flour
    1 lb Velveeta style cheese (think Cheezy Does It)

Combine butter, sugar, flour, and cheese in saucepan and heat over low heat, stirring frequently until cheese is melted. This mixture will be thick and somewhat lumpy. Spread apples in a 9x13" pan and sprinkle with the spice you have chosen. Pour the melted cheese mixture over the apples and bake in a 350 deg oven for 20 to 30 minutes. Topping will be very brown, but the inside of cheese mixture must get done or it will be too gooey. (At least that is what Carolyn tells me. Personally, I find gooey sort of nice when it comes to cheese.) Serves 10 to 12.

Special Peach Cobbler (in honor of the Peach Bowl)
    1 stick butter
    2 29 oz cans sliced peaches in light syrup
    ½ cup self-rising corn meal mix
    ½ cup self-rising flour
    1 cup sugar
    1 cup milk

In a 9x13" pan, melt the butter. Pour in the undrained peaches. Mix together the remaining ingredients and pour over the peaches. Bake at 350 deg about 35 to 40 minutes or until mixture is brown and the juice appears thickened. Serve warm with ice cream.

Fourth of July Parfait
    1 ½ cups heavy cream
    ½ cup sugar, divided
    1/4 cup lemon juice
    1 tsp lemon extract
    1 tsp vanilla extract
    1 cup sliced strawberries
    1 cup fresh blueberries

In a large, chilled mixing bowl, using an electric mixer, beat cream, 1/3 cup sugar, lemon juice, and extracts until mixture mounds softly.   In a small bowl, add remaining sugar to berries. Mix gently. Spoon layers of mousse and fruit into dessert dishes. Serve immediately or chill for several hours before serving.

Ice Cream Sandwich Dessert
    1 ½ boxes of Mayfield Ice Cream Sandwiches
    1 jar of caramel sauce (Scotty says he likes Mrs. Butterworth's
    1 large container of Cool Whip
    1 bag whole or chopped pecans
    1 9x13" dish

Line the bottom of 9x13" dish with Mayfield Ice Cream Sandwiches. Pour jar of caramel syrup to cover them all. Ice over caramel sauce with cool whip, top with whole or chopped pecans. Refreeze and cut into squares when ready to serve.

Healthy White Chocolate Banana Pudding
    2 pkg Jell-O fat free, sugar free white chocolate pudding
    1 8 oz fat free whipped topping
    1 8 oz pkg fat free sour cream
    5 or 6 bananas, sliced
    1 box vanilla wafers
    4 cups skim milk

Mix pudding mix with skim milk and beat until thick. Fold in about 2/3 of whipped topping, sour cream, and sliced bananas. Line an attractive glass bowl with vanilla wafers. Pour in ½ of pudding mixture. Top with vanilla wafers. Add rest of pudding mixture. Top with remaining whipped topping. Chill before serving.

Fluff Stuff
    1 small pkg sugar free Jell-O (your choice of flavors)
    1/4 cup boiling water
    2 8 oz containers lite yogurt (in a flavor to match Jell-O)
    1 8 oz pkg fat free whipped topping

Dissolve gelatin in boiling water. (It will require some stirring, but that is all the water you need). Stir in yogurt. Fold in whipped topping. Put into a covered container and chill until set.

Coconut Sweetmeats from School and Home Cooking
Published by Allyn Bacon Co. In 1926. This was my mother's high school Home Ec. Book

    1/4 cupful powdered sugar
    1 1/4 cupfuls shredded coconut
    2 tablespoonfuls flour
    1/8 teaspoonful salt
    1 teaspoonful vanilla
    1 egg white

Mix the dry ingredients, then add the vanilla. Beat the egg white stiff. Add the other ingredients and mix thoroughly. Grease a baking sheet and dredge it with flour. Drop the coconut mixture by the teaspoonfuls on the baking sheet. Bake in a moderate oven (375 deg.) for 20 minutes or until slightly browned. Remove from the pan, and place on a cake cooler. When cold, store in a tin box.

These are recommended for an afternoon tea.

Holy Smoke
Shirley McCarroll   Harriman
        1 cup self-rising flour
        1 cup nuts, chopped
        1 stick butter, melted
        1 8 oz pkg cream cheese, softened
        1 cup powdered sugar
        1 cup whipped topping
        2 small pkg instant chocolate pudding
        3 cups milk
        8 oz carton whipped topping

Mix first 3 ingredients. Press into a 9x13" pan. Bake at 350 deg for 15 minutes or until done. Cool. Mix cream cheese, powdered sugar, and 1 cup whipped topping with mixer. Spread over cooled crust. Allow to chill. Mix pudding mix with milk according to package instructions. Spread over cooled cream cheese layer. Spread remaining whipped topping over top and sprinkle with grated chocolate or chopped nuts.

Easy Strawberry Cheesecake
        1 8 oz pkg cream cheese
        1 can sweetened condensed milk
        1/3 cup lemon juice
        1 tsp vanilla
        2 cups sliced fresh strawberries
        Prepared graham cracker pie crust
        1/4 cup warmed honey

In a medium bowl, beat the cream cheese until light and fluffy. Gradually blend in the sweetened condensed milk, then add the lemon juice and the vanilla. Pour the mixture into the prepared pie crust. Chill until mixture starts to set. Top with the strawberries. Drizzle the berries with the warmed honey. Serve immediately.

Strawberry Trifle
        1 pkg yellow or white cake mix
        1 pkg (16oz) frozen strawberries or 1 quart fresh berries, sliced and sweetened
        1 box (5oz) vanilla pudding mix, prepared
        1 8 oz pkg whipped topping

1/4 cup slivered almonds, toasted

Bake cake in oblong 13 x 9 x 2-inch pan as directed on package. Cool. Cut cake crosswise in half. Reserve ½ for another dessert. Cut remaining cake into 8 pieces. Split each piece horizontally. Arrange half the pieces in a 2 quart glass trifle bowl, cutting pieces to fit bowl. Pour ½ the strawberries with syrup over cake. Spread with 1 cup pudding. Repeat with remaining pieces, strawberries, and pudding. Spread Cool Whip on top and sprinkle with almonds. Refrigerate until ready to serve.

Mandarin Orange Ice Cream Sauce
2 cans Mandarin oranges
½ cup sugar
1/4 cup water
2 TBSP cornstarch
orange food coloring (optional)

Drain oranges, reserving the juice. Add sufficient water to the juice to make 1 ½ cup total. Stir in sugar. Add cornstarch to 1/4 cup water and stir into juice mixture. Place on medium heat and, stirring constantly, cook until mixture boils and thickens. Add food color to desired shade. Stir in oranges and allow to cool to room temperature before pouring over vanilla ice cream. This will achieve an orange and white sundae.

Anne's Best Fudge
2 sticks butter
4 ½ cups sugar
1 13 oz can evaporated milk
1 7 oz jar marshmallow cream
1 16 oz pkg chocolate chips

Combine butter, sugar, and milk in a heavy sauce pan. Cook (med heat) to soft ball stage (138 deg). Stir occasionally. Remove from heat. Add marshmallow cream and chips. Stir until completely blended. Beat until mixture is creamy and loses glaze. Turn into buttered 9x13" pan and allow to cool.

Simple Rice Pudding
½ lb white rice *(uncooked)*
1 ½ cups sugar
1/4 cup butter
1 pinch salt
½ gallon milk
1 tsp vanilla

Add all ingredients together in a large saucepan; bring to a boil. Turn heat to low and allow to barely simmer until thickened (about an hour and a half to 2 hours), stirring often. Pour into large bowl and sprinkle with nutmeg and sugar. Serve warm or chilled.

If you need raisins in your rice pudding, stir in about 3/4 cup raisins about 20 minutes before the pudding finishes cooking.

Blueberry Buckle
> 2 cups all purpose flour
> 2 ½ tsp baking powder
> ½ tsp salt
> ½ cup butter, softened
> 1 cup sugar
> 2 eggs
> 1 cup milk
> 2 cups fresh blueberries (or 12 oz pkg frozen)

Topping:
> ½ cup all purpose flour
> 1/4 cup butter, softened
> 1 cup flake coconut
> ½ cup light brown sugar
> 1 tsp cinnamon

Combine topping ingredients in medium bowl. Mix until moist and crumbly. Set aside. Mix flour, baking powder, and salt. In a large mixer bowl, cream the butter and sugar until fluffy. Add eggs, one at a time, beating after each. Add dry ingredients alternately with the milk. Fold in blueberries. Pour into a greased and floured 9x13" pan. Sprinkle topping evenly over batter. Bake in a 375 deg oven about 40 minutes or until cake tests done and the topping is evenly browned. Cool slightly before serving.

Slow Cooker New England Indian Pudding
> 4 cups milk
> 3/4 cup cornmeal
> ½ tsp salt
> 3 eggs
> 1/4 cup light brown sugar
> ½ cup molasses
> 2 TBSP butter
> ½ tsp cinnamon
> ½ tsp allspice
> ½ tsp ginger

Spray slow cooker crock with cooking oil spray. Preheat on high at least 10 minutes. Meanwhile, bring milk and salt to a boil. Stir in cornmeal, stirring constantly. Allow to come to a boil and cook, stirring for 5 minutes. Cover, reduce heat to low, and allow to continue to cook for another 10 minutes. In a large bowl, combine remaining ingredients. Gradually beat in hot cornmeal mixture and whisk until smooth. Pour into slow cooker and cover. Cook on high 2 to 3 hours or on low for 6 to 8 hours. Serve with a little whipped cream.

Hog Heaven Chocolate Freeze
    1 large box (12 oz) of vanilla wafers
    1 bag of whole or chopped pecans
    3/4 cup butter, melted
    1 jar of fudge sauce
    ½ gallon of Mayfield Hog Heaven Ice Cream
    1 9x13" dish

Crush the vanilla wafers and place them in a mixing bowl with the melted butter. Pour in pecans and mix all ingredients together. Line the bottom of the 9x13" dish with half of the crunch mixture. Spread the ½ gallon of Mayfield Hog Heaven Ice Cream to cover the crunch mixture. Then use the rest of the crunch mixture to cover the ice cream layer. Pour the jar of fudge sauce to cover the top layer of the crunch mixture. Refreeze and cut into squares when ready to serve.

Super Easy Peanut Butter Fudge
    24 oz (2 bags) Old Fashioned Creme Drops Candy
    1 ½ cups peanut butter (chunky or creamy)

In a microwave safe bowl, place the candy and the peanut butter and melt. It will take about 1 ½ to 1 3/4 minutes. Watch closely. Stir vigorously to mix completely. Turn into a 9x13" pan which has been sprayed with cooking oil spray. Allow to cool about 30 to 45 minutes and cut out into small pieces. Trust me, this works.

Easy Orange Parfaits
    1 4 serving size package cook-and-serve vanilla pudding mix
    1 3/4 cups orange juice
    1 8 ounce carton vanilla yogurt
    whipped topping
    orange peel curls or small wedges

Prepare pudding mix according to package directions, except use the 1 3/4 cups orange juice instead of milk. Transfer pudding to a bowl. Cover surface with plastic wrap. Chill thoroughly. Before serving, fold yogurt into pudding. Divide one-third of the pudding mixture among 6 glasses. Add a layer of whipped topping. Repeat pudding and whipped topping layers. Top with remaining pudding mixture. If desired, garnish with orange peel curls or wedges

White Chocolate Bread Pudding
    1 6 oz pkg white chocolate baking bar
    3 cups milk
    6 to 7 cups French bread, cut into cubes

2 eggs
½ cup sugar
1 tsp nutmeg
1 tsp vanilla

Break up chocolate and mix with milk. Heat in microwave until chocolate is melted. About 2 to 3 minutes depending on microwave. Stir in bread and allow to sit about 15 minutes. In a large bowl, beat eggs and add sugar, nutmeg, and vanilla. Stir in bread mixture. Turn into a 2 quart casserole which has been sprayed with cooking oil spray. Bake in a 350 deg oven about 45 to 50 minutes or until puffed and brown. Serve warm.

Caramel Apples
1 cup water
½ cup heavy cream
1 bag caramels, unwrapped
6 red delicious apples

In a heavy bottomed saucepan, combine water and caramel. Over low heat, stir mixture gently until caramel mixture is an amber color. Increase heat to medium low and cook, without stirring about two minutes. Remove from heat and carefully stir in heavy cream (mixture will bubble up and splatter a bit and then subside) Set aside to cool and thicken. Cover Styrofoam with waxed paper to catch caramel drippings (this will be stand for caramel apples). Insert popsicle stick into bottom center of apples. Dip top half of each apple into thickened caramel. Insert bottom of popsicle sticks into Styrofoam, allow apples to stand upright so caramel runs down sides of each apple. Refrigerate to harden.

Candy Corn Cookie Bark
12 Oreo chocolate cookies (the Halloween ones are nice if you can find them), chopped
1 ½ cups miniature pretzel twists, coarsely broken
1/3 cup raisins
3 pkg (6 oz each) white baking chocolate (or a 20 oz pkg white bark chocolate)
½ cup candy corn

Spread cookies, pretzels, and raisins into a 9x13" pan which has been lined with plastic wrap. Melt chocolate according to package direction in the microwave or on the stove. Spread evenly over the cookie mixture. Top with candy corn. Press to secure corn. Allow the chocolate to cool until firm. Break into pieces and store in a tight container. You may use more candy corn if you wish. It is also nice to pour about 2/3 of chocolate over the cookie mixture. Press on the candy corn and drizzle the remainder of the chocolate over the top.

Chapter 9
Miscellaneous

Fresh Tomato Tapenade
Tammy T. Algood   University of Tennessee Agricultural Extension Service and the
Tennessee Department of Agriculture Pick Tennessee Products Campaign
> 1 pound Roma tomatoes, quartered lengthwise and cored
> 4 tablespoons extra virgin olive oil
> 1 tablespoon herbes de Provence
> Salt and fresh ground black pepper to taste
> 2 large cloves garlic, chopped
> 1 pound fresh mozzarella, sliced into rounds
> Fresh basil leaves
> Extra virgin olive oil

Preheat oven to 200 degrees. Place tomatoes on parchment paper in a sheet pan in a single layer. Drizzle with 2 tablespoons of olive oi,l and sprinkle with herbes de Provence, salt, and pepper. Bake for 3-4 hours or until edges shrivel up and centers are still slightly moist. Transfer to a plate to cool. In a food processor, blend tomatoes with garlic and remaining 2 tablespoons olive oil until finely chopped (not pureed). Season again with salt and pepper. To serve, place mozzarella slice on a water cracker or crostini. Spread tomato tapenade on each round and drizzle with extra oil. Garnish with basil and serve. By the way, good Grainger County tomatoes work fine in this.

Grilled SPAM & Cheese Sandwich
SPAM Kid Chef of the Year
Jonathan Shankles, 1st Place
Won $150 + chance to win $1000 grand prize, plus $1000 to charity of choice.
> 6 tbsp butter, melted
> 1 tsp dry mustard powder
> 1 tsp Worcestershire sauce
> ½ tsp maple syrup
> ½ tsp garlic powder
> 3 to 4 drops hot sauce, or to taste
> 1 (12oz) can SPAM, cut into 1/4-inch thick slices
> 12 slices provolone or smoked mozzarella cheese,
> 12 slices firm bread

In a small bowl, combine butter, mustard, Worcestershire sauce, maple syrup, garlic powder, and hot sauce. Note: This recipe can be cooked in batches or in multiple

skillets at the same time. Heat large skillet(s) over medium high heat. Arrange SPAM slices in a single layer and heat until warmed through, 2 to 3 minutes per side. Brush one side of each bread slice lightly with butter mixture; place in warm skillet, buttered side down. Cook until lightly browned, about 3 minutes. Lightly butter tops of bread and flip slices over. Place one slice of cheese on each piece of bread and cook until cheese is soft, about 3 minutes. Place warmed SPAM slices evenly over 6 pieces of bread. Flip remaining cheese covered bread slices onto SPAM halves cheese side down. Place a weight, such as an empty skillet, over sandwiches to press down as they continue to cook for another 2 minutes per side. Cut in halves or quarters and serve warm.
Yield: 6 servings

Luau Grilled Pizza
Molly Shankle
> 1 ½ pounds homemade or frozen, thawed bread dough
> 2 to 3 tablespoons flour, for rolling out dough
> 1/4 cup olive or vegetable oil
> ½ teaspoon finely minced garlic
> 1 teaspoon dried Italian herb seasoning
> 1 (12 oz) can SPAM, cut into 3/8-inch slices
> 6 slices canned pineapple
> 3 tablespoons pizza or pasta sauce
> 3/4 cup sliced olives
> 2 cups finely shredded mozzarella cheese

Let bread dough rise in a large bowl until doubled in bulk. Preheat grill. Divide dough into 6 equal portions and place on a lightly floured surface; roll each portion into a 6 to 8-inch circle. In a small bowl, combine oil, garlic and Italian herb seasoning. Lightly brush SPAM, pineapple slices, and one side of each crust with oil mixture. Place dough, oil side down, on medium hot grill for 4 to 5 minutes, or until bottom side is lightly browned. Grill SPAM slices and pineapple slices about 2 minutes per side while dough cooks. Brush uncooked (top) of dough lightly with oil mixture and flip onto a large platter cooked side up. Remove SPAM and pineapple slices and cut into small pieces; set aside. Spread 1 to 1-1/2 teaspoons of pizza sauce onto each crust and sprinkle with SPAM pieces, pineapple pieces, olive slices, and cheese. Return pizzas to the grill for 4 to 5 minutes or until cheese is melted and bottom crust is browned. Serve warm.
Yield: 6 servings

Bohemian Macaroni and Cheese
> 2 (7.25 ounce) packages dry macaroni and cheese
> 1 green bell pepper, chopped
> 1 onion, chopped
> 1 large tomato, chopped
> 1 pound bacon - cooked and crumbled

Prepare both boxes of macaroni and cheese according to package directions.

Meanwhile, in a large bowl mix together the chopped bell green pepper, onion, tomato, and crumbled bacon. Mix in prepared macaroni and cheese to large bowl with vegetables and bacon. Pour into a 9x13 inch baking dish. Bake in a preheated 350 degree oven for 45 to 60 minutes, or until crispy on top. Serve warm.

Microwave Bread And Butter Pickles
Dorothy Atherton at Fairfield Glades sent us this recipe a few years ago and it is a perennial favorite. Anne thinks you need these whether or not you are going on a picnic.
>1 cup each, sugar and white vinegar
>½ cup water
>2 tsp salt
>1 tsp each, dried minced garlic and mustard seeds
>½ tsp each, celery seeds and turmeric
>1 medium onion, peeled and sliced thin
>2 3/4 to 3 lbs pickling cucumbers, sliced

Mix everything except onions and cucumbers in a large microwave safe bowl. Stir in the cucumbers and onions. Microwave 9 minutes on high, stopping to stir at 6 ½ and 4 minutes to go. Remove from microwave and allow to cool. Cover and refrigerate overnight before placing in jars. Be sure to distribute juice evenly if you use more than one jar. Store in refrigerator.

Note: I don't put these in jars. I guess you would if you wanted to give them away. However, I just keep them in a covered container in the refrigerator. They are so good, they don't last long.

Apricot/Cranberry Chutney
>½ cup diced dried apricots
>1 (12 ounce) package fresh cranberries
>½ cup raisins
>3/4 teaspoon ground cinnamon
>1/4 teaspoon ground ginger
>1/4 teaspoon ground allspice
>1 cup water
>3/4 cup white sugar
>½ cup cider vinegar

In a medium bowl, mix together the apricots, cranberries, raisins, cinnamon, ginger, and allspice. In a medium saucepan, boil water and sugar, stirring constantly, until sugar is dissolved. Add the dried fruit mixture and vinegar. Bring to a boil, reduce heat, and simmer for 10 minutes. Remove from heat, and allow to cool for 5 minutes. Serve immediately, or refrigerate in a covered container

Dressing for Turkey (or Chicken)
    4 cups each, cornbread crumbs and biscuit crumbs
    1 ½ cups chopped onion (approx)
    1 ½ cups chopped celery (approx)
    2 tsp salt
    1 tsp black pepper
    ½ to 1 tsp cayenne pepper (or to taste, the more pepper, the hotter)
    1 to 2 TBSP rubbed sage (or to taste, the more sage, the hotter)
    2 cups water
    4 cups (approx) turkey broth

Place the onions and celery in a saucepan with the water. Bring to a full boil. While waiting, mix all remaining ingredients except the broth. Pour the boiling water, onions, and celery over bread mixture and toss to mix. Add the turkey broth until the mixture is soft, but still holds its shape. Taste and adjust seasonings as necessary. Remember the finished dressing will be slightly hotter than the uncooked. Place in a 9x13" pan which has been sprayed with vegetable oil spray. Bake in a 350 deg oven about 1 hour or until browned and firm.

Now on the question of broth. I drain the drippings from the pan where I have roasted the turkey into the sauce pan with the giblets and neck and use that broth both for the dressing and the gravy. If there is not enough, I add a can of chicken stock.

Hot Cheese & Bologna Sandwich
    3 TBSP mayonnaise
    ½ cup chili sauce
    1 lb bologna, ground
    ½ cup Velveeta style cheese, cubed (I use Food Club Cheezy Does It)
    1/3 cup onion, chopped fine
    ½ cup stuffed olives, chopped
    8-10 hamburger rolls

Preheat oven 400 deg. In a small mixing bowl, blend the mayonnaise and chili sauce. Add the bologna, cheese, onions, and olives. Spread bologna mixture on each roll, dividing evenly. Wrap each roll in aluminum foil and bake for 10 minutes.

Ryan Hensley's Award Winning Lamb Skewers
This is from the award winning 4-H Club Grill Team
You will need bamboo skewers, soak the skewers in water the night before.
<u>Marinade</u>:
    4 cups of oil (preference on what kind)
    1 ½ TBSP table salt
    1 tsp ground black pepper
    ½ large onion diced or minced
    2 cloves garlic sliced or broken in half

Put all items in a large mixing bowl, stir together

To go on the bamboo skewers you will need.
  2 large green peppers
  2 large red peppers
  2 large onions
  2 lbs lamb (any cuts) cut into small pieces.

Any of these can vary as to how much you like.

Cut the peppers and onions into manageable sized pieces.
Put the peppers, onions, and lamb into the bowl with the marinade, mix it into the marinade. Let it sit it in the marinade a couple of minutes, Mix it again. Then load up the Skewers as you please, It should make at least 12 full skewers.

Teriyaki Marinade for Beef
  2/3 cup soy sauce
  ½ cup light brown sugar
  1/4 cup water
  2 TBSP rice vinegar
  1 clove garlic
  1 TBSP fresh ginger, finely chopped
  ½ cup orange juice

Mix all ingredients and heat to melt sugar. Pour over beef, cover, and allow to marinate in the refrigerator, covered, overnight.   Drain and reserve marinade. Grill or fry meat adding a small amount of marinade if needed to prevent burning. Be sure not to use any marinade which has not been heating to boiling after the meat has stood in it.

Easy Ham and Cheese Macaroni
  2 cups uncooked elbow macaroni
  1 pkg (10 oz) frozen chopped broccoli, thawed
  1 can condensed cream of mushroom soup
  ½ cup milk
  ½ lb Nice and Cheezy cheese, cubed
  ½ lb finely cubed ham
  salt and pepper to taste

In a large saucepan, cook macaroni in boiling water for 5 minutes. Add broccoli and return to a boil. Cook another 2 or 3 minutes. Drain. Stir all remaining ingredients into the macaroni, and continue to cook until cheese is melted. Add salt and pepper to taste. Serve hot.

Roast Leg of Lamb
  3 to 5 lb leg of lamb

2 garlic cloves, peeled and cut into slivers
6 or 8 mint leaves
salt and pepper

On the fat side of the lamb leg, cut 6 or 8 incisions, each about 2 inches wide and 2 inches deep. Into each of these, press about 1/4 tsp each salt and pepper. Also push a mint leaf and a sliver of garlic into each. Place the lamb on a rack in a roasting pan and place into a 400 deg oven. Allow to cook about 20 minutes. Reduce oven heat to 350 and cook about another hour or until the juices run clear if you stick a thin knife into the thickest part of the roast. The leg of lamb will need to have cooked about 18 minutes per pound for a medium well done roast.

Apple Deli Wrap
Washington Apple Commission
> Washington Apples such as Fuji, Cameo, Pink Lady, Gala, or Granny Smith
> 12" flour tortillas or wraps
> honey-mustard
> cheddar cheese, shredded
> deli meat (ham, turkey, or roast beef)
> romaine lettuce, julienned
> diced fresh tomatoes

Core Apples and cut into 1/8" slices. Set aside. (Dip them in a mixture of 3 parts lemon juice and 1 part water to prevent browning). For each sandwich: place one tortilla or wrap on flat surface. Spread with approx 1 TBSP honey-mustard. Place apple slices, 2 oz cheese, 1 oz deli meat and 1 oz lettuce and tomatoes over honey-mustard. If using larger tortilla or wrap, adjust ingredients to match. Wrap tortilla tightly around filling by folding two edges toward the middle overlapping the edge of the filling. Roll-up from one of the open sides. Cut sandwich in half diagonally. Serve immediately or wrap well in plastic wrap, and store in the refrigerator up to one day. Be sure not to overfill or it will be difficult to roll.

This is a basic sandwich which can be altered to suit your taste. Brie or other gourmet cheeses can be substituted for the shredded cheese. Thinly sliced red peppers add crunch with the apples. Kids can do these customizing them to their own tastes. The sandwich can be cut into smaller pieces for finger food or for appetizers.

Braised Sauerkraut
Another find by Mike Deaver
> 4 lbs kraut, drained, rinsed, and squeezed dry
> 1 onion, peeled and cut into 1/4" slices
> 1 carrot, peeled, cut in half lengthwise and sliced into thin semicircles
> 2 cloves garlic, peeled and crushed (or about 1 tsp)
> 1 ½ tsp caraway seeds
> 1 ½ tsp dried thyme

2 bay leaves
12 juniper berries (or 1/4 cup gin) (optional)
black pepper to taste
8 oz kielbasa cut into 1/4" thick slices
2 smoked pork hocks
2 cups dry white wine
4 cups chicken broth (2 cans)

Put the drained kraut into a 4 quart slow cooker. Add everything except the meat, wine and broth. Toss to mix. Scatter the kielbasa on top and bury the hocks in the kraut mixture. Pour in the wine and the broth. Cover and cook on low for 9 hours or until the broth is bubbly and the kraut has lost its crunch. Remove the hocks and remove any bones and return meat to pot. Discard bay leaves. Serve with boiled potatoes.

White Lily Yeast Roll Dough Pizza

Make your own toppings as creative as you like. Children love to top their own mini pizzas.
6 White Lily Frozen Roll Dough pieces
3 tablespoons chopped fresh basil
6 Roma tomatoes
1/4 cup olive oil
6 TBSP pesto
1 pound smoked provolone cheese

Remove six White Lily Frozen Dough pieces from the freezer. Allow White Lily Frozen Roll Dough to thaw at room temperature. Quick thaw the rolls by placing wrapped dough in the microwave for about 1 minute. Heat just until dough is soft, but not warm. Using a rolling pin, roll dough as thin as possible. Place on baking sheet that has been lightly sprayed with non-stick cooking spray. Allow to "rest" 10 minutes. Meanwhile chop basil and slice tomatoes into to 1/4-inch slices. Press dough and roll again if dough shrinks. Brush dough lightly with olive oil. Spread the pesto, then top with sliced cheese, then basil, and tomato slices. Fold sides up along edge to form an outside crust. Allow dough to stand in a warm place for about 10 minutes to rise.

Preheat oven to 400 deg. Bake 15 to 20 minutes or until lightly browned.
Makes 6 servings.

Orange and White (or Red and Green) Fudge

1 ½ lbs white candy coating
1 14 oz can sweetened condensed milk
pinch of salt
1 ½ tsp vanilla
2 cups orange slice (or red and green gum drops) candies, cut into small pieces

In a microwave safe bowl, place the candy coating, milk, and salt. Microwave about one minute and stir. Continue to heat in 30 second intervals, stirring after each until chocolate is completely melted. Stir in vanilla and candy. Turn into a 9" square pan which you have lined with aluminum foil. Chill about one hour or until completely firm. Use the foil to lift out the candy and cut into small squares.

You may do this using any color of gum drops for candy with a stained glass look. At Christmas, it is pretty to use only red and green gum drops. If you wish, you can melt the chocolate, milk, and salt together in a heavy sauce pan on medium heat. Watch it closely and stir often to prevent the chocolate from burning

Big Orange Fudge
Becky Stansberry
        8 tsp orange flavoring
        18 drops red food coloring
        24 drops yellow food coloring
        3 sticks butter, cubed
        10 ounces evaporated milk
        6 cups granulated sugar
        2 (12-oz) bags white chocolate morsels
        2 (7 oz) jars marshmallow creme

Combine orange flavoring with red & yellow food coloring in small glass. Set aside In large sauce pan, combine butter, evaporated milk, and sugar. Bring to a boil & cook for exactly 5 minutes while stirring constantly. Remove from heat and add white chocolate morsels and marshmallow creme. Mix well. Measure 2 cups of the mix and set aside. Add food coloring-flavoring mix to remainder and mix well. Pour orange mixture into 9x13 buttered glass dish. Spoon dollops of the white mixture on top of orange mixture. Dip through with a knife to marbleize. Cool. Refrigerate to harden. Cut into squares to serve. Store in container at room temperature.

Slow Cooker Candy
        1 box German Chocolate cooking chocolate
        12 oz semi-sweet chocolate chips
        48 oz almond bark (or 24 oz almond bark and 24 oz milk chocolate bark)
        1 16 oz jar dry roasted unsalted peanuts
        1 16 oz jar dry roasted salted peanuts

Chop all chocolates and place into a slow cooker. Pour peanuts over. Cover and turn onto low and allow to cook without interruptions for 3 hours. DO NOT OPEN THE LID. DO NOT STIR. DO NOT DO ANYTHING. After three hours, spread several cookie sheets with waxed paper. Turn off slow cooker, uncover, and stir contents for 4 or 5 minutes or until completely blended. Chocolate will not lose its shine. Don't worry about that. Using a soup spoon, dip candy and drop onto waxed paper. You may want to stir pot several times while dipping out the candy. Allow to cool and you are ready to eat. There is no need to refrigerate this candy.

Big Orange Funnel Cakes

    2 cups self rising flour
    2 eggs
    1 ½ cups milk
    1 TBSP orange extract
    orange food color
    oil for frying
    powdered sugar

Blend flour, eggs, milk, extract, and food color until smooth. To make a cake, place about ½ cup batter into a funnel. Allow to flow into the hot oil making a circular pattern. Fry about about 2 minutes or until brown on edges. Turn and allow to fry about an additional minute or until brown. Turn out onto a paper towel and sprinkle heavily with powdered sugar. To be sure that the oil is the right temperature, drop a scant spoonful of batter into oil. It should remain intact and cook brown on the bottom in a couple of minutes.

Frances Strange Fudge

    2 lbs confectioners sugar
    ½ cup cocoa
    ½ lb butter
    ½ lb process cheese (Velveeta or Cheezy Does It)
    1 tsp vanilla
    nuts (optional)

In a large bowl, mix confectioners sugar and cocoa. Melt butter and cheese and stir into the sugar mixture. It will require several minutes of stirring. When about half mixed, stir in vanilla. When the mixture resembles play dough, mix in nuts if using. Press into a buttered 9x13 pan and allow to sit about 1 hour before cutting.

At Christmas, we press this mixture into tree shaped aluminum foil baking pans or tree shaped plastic trays and allow to set. Then turn out and decorate with commercial icing to make Christmas trees. You can also press onto a buttered tray and cut out tree shapes or bell shapes with cookie cutters. Using the squeeze decorating frosting is easy and it is fun to let the kids help you make fudge Christmas gifts.

Index

207

209

To reorder <u>Secrets of Chef Walter</u> complete the following information and send with $9.95 plus $2.00 for shipping and handling to:

      Chef Walter Lambert
      3635 Taliluna Ave. B-1
      Knoxville, Tn 37919

Please send me_____ copies of
   At $9.95 each plus $2.00 shipping for a total of $11.95

I am enclosing $_____.

I would like the books signed for _____
If you are ordering several, attach a list of names for personalization.

To reorder <u>Secrets of Chef Walter</u> complete the following information and send with $9.95 plus $2.00 for shipping and handling to:

      Chef Walter Lambert
      3635 Taliluna Ave. B-1
      Knoxville, Tn 37919

Please send me_____ copies of
   At $9.95 each plus $2.00 shipping for a total of $11.95

I am enclosing $_____.

I would like the books signed for _____
If you are ordering several, attach a list of names for personalization.

Lemonade cake - 148
Buttermilk Bread pudding — 183
Choc. trifle - 186
Fudge - 193
Strawberry trifle - 192
Taca Soup - 30
Choc. Macaroon Cake - 145
Pineapple Lemon Pie - 160
Lemon Loaf Cake. 132
Italian Sausage & Beans - 92
Hot Fried Corn Bread. 38